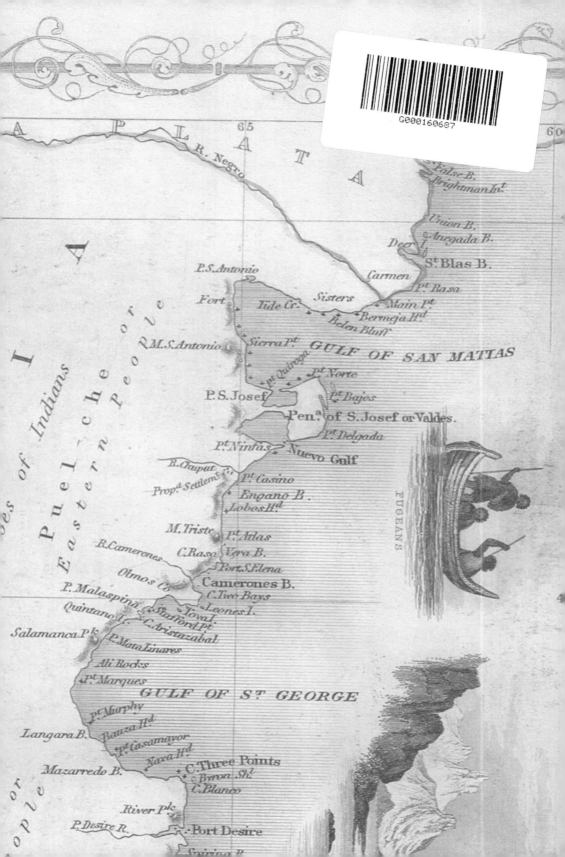

A P L A T A

A

I

A

R. Negro

P.S.Antonio

Fort

M.S.Antonio

Tide Cr.

Sierra Pt.

False B.

Brightman Int.

Union B.

Arregada B.

Deer I.

St. Blas B.

Carmen

Pt. Rasa

Sisters

Main Pt.

Bermeja Hd.

Belen Bluff

Pt. Quiroga

GULF OF SAN MATIAS

Pt. Norte

P.S. Josef

Pt. Bajos

Pen.ª of S. Josef or Valdes.

Pt. Delgada

Pt. Ninfas

Nuevo Gulf

R. Chupat

Prop.d Settlem.t

Pt. Casino

Engano B.

Lobos Hd.

M. Triste

Pt. Atlas

R. Camerones

C. Raso

Vera B.

Port. S. Elena

Olmos Co.

Camerones B.

P. Malaspina

C. Two Bays

Quintano I.

Leones I.

Stafford Pt.

Towil

Salamanca Pt.

C. Aristazabal

P. Mota Linares

Ali Rocks

Pt. Marques

GULF OF St. GEORGE

Pt. Murphy

Langara B.

Bauza Hd.

Pt. Casamayor

Mazarredo B.

Nava Hd.

C. Three Points

Byron Shl.

C. Blanco

River Plc.

P. Desire R.

Port Desire

Spring R.

I

ses of Indians

Puel-che

Eastern People

or

People

FUEGEANS

Dark Horses at the Patagonian Frontier

Dark Horses at the Patagonian Frontier

Riding the Pioneer Trail

JON BURROUGH

 AN OXFORDFOLIO PUBLICATION   for   **Signal**

An Oxfordfolio publication
(www.oxfordfolio.co.uk)
for

Signal Books
www.signalbooks.co.uk
Signal Books Limited
36 Minster Road
Oxford OX4 1LY

Design/typesetting Forewords, www.forewords.co.uk
Project editor James Harrison
All images © the author
Maps by Sebastian Ballard © 2016
Endpapers: Map from John Tallis's *Illustrated Atlas and a Modern
History of the World. Geographical, Political, Commercial and
Statistical*, produced in 1851 and engraved by John Rapkin.

ISBN: 978-1-909930-39-1
Printed in India by Imprint Press

*To Patagonia's pioneers, past and present, and
particularly to those dedicated few who have devoted
their lives to collecting and preserving their history
for those that follow*

CONTENTS

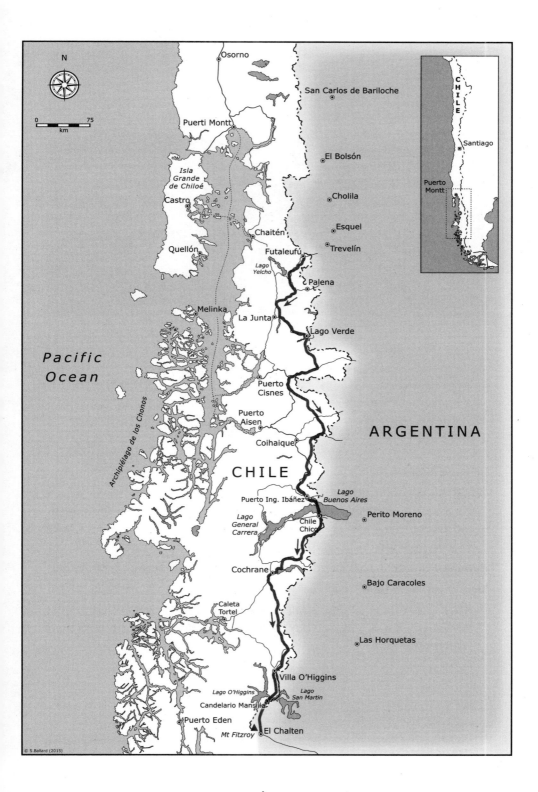

THE GAUCHO'S POEM

'MI HOSPITALIDAD'

Be Hospitable.

When the stranger arrives in your village, exhausted from travel, like a corpse on weathered saddle skins, wait for him away from the threshold of your cool and simple house and offer him your hand as a taste of your warmth.

Because you are master of your house, treat him as if he was your equal.

Do not ask who he is.

Perhaps a bad deed weighs on his conscience, heavier to bear in life than the spurs[1] he drags along your patio, piercing its swept earth with their crown of thorns.

---

[1] Guiraldes uses the word *nazarenas* to describe the large wheeled spurs preferred by the 19th century gaucho.

Perhaps too large a pride furrows his forehead underneath the *chambergo*[2] hat whose pretentious wing scorns the air which his passing creates.

Sit him down by the stove – the heart of fire in your peaceful home – and give him a strong bench on which to seat his weariness.

Move some hot embers close to his feet to dry the mud on his boots and so that the heat rises to his lips bringing with it the secrets of intimacy.

Let him speak and ease his words with your courtesy.

And when drowsiness clouds his eyes, give him your bed and watch over his rest stretched out on your sheepskins.

When he leaves he will take with him the gift of your brotherhood which enhances mankind.

Ricardo Guiraldes, 1886–1927.[3]

---

[2] *Chambergo* after the French soldier Schomberg and the 17th century Spanish royal body-guards, whose bell-shaped hats had one wing raised and pinned to one side—a hat style largely abandoned by the *gaucho* in favour of the black beret, but a name retained by the Chilean *huaso* as part of his traditional dress.

[3] Extracted from *El Libro Bravo* and translated by the author.

INTRODUCTION

A small man dressed in baggy trousers and black concertina boots stepped out of the trees. Everything about him said Patagonia. Cuervo, my big black *criollo* stallion spotted him first; even with only one good eye, Cuervo usually did. The man squinted up at us from a sun- and wind-dried and wrinkled face, dark clothes set off by a red cloth knotted round his neck. He was wearing the black beret, the trademark of the gaucho. Not for him the jaunty style favoured by the French onion seller; his beret was set squarely on the back centre of his head.

Cuervo had already carried me the best part of 500 miles down the Andean Cordillera. We had been tacking our way slowly down the wooded slopes to our next destination, the town of Cochrane in the south of Chile's Patagonia—a region called Aysén,[1] when the man appeared. It had been another gruelling eight days, but that night we had slept well and were relaxed as we pictured the pleasures ahead of warm showers and eating at a table.

Unusually for a gaucho, he was on foot, a condition in which most gauchos feel uncomfortable, and there was no sign of a horse.

He said something. The tone was friendly, but I did not understand a word. I could see from his expression that my young guide Hector was having similar difficulties, but he gave a sign for me to dismount, and for the next thirty minutes we sat on some logs and listened whilst our horses munched in the background.

His name was Juan Hueitra and he lived nearby. The name Hueitra was unusual and I found out later that it was an old Indian name meaning 'warrior'. At the time it was impossible to guess his origins, but as he spoke and my ear adjusted to his accent, some words became clearer. There was something intense in his eyes and he was clearly upset about something.

---

[1] There are several theories as to the origin of Aysén (otherwise Aisén). 'Aisén estuary' appeared on a map prepared by the Jesuit missionary Joseph Garcia following two journeys he and a group of Indians made in 1766/7, and may have followed either an Huilliche Indian word meaning 'an entry into the eastern interior', or a Mapuche word 'to scatter/separate oneself'—a reference to the scattering of islands off the Aisén coast, but Garcia did not repeat the name in his official report. When Fitzroy and Darwin reached the Aisén coast from the south in 1832/3, the area had been known by English sailors as 'Ice End'—the end of the Northern Ice Field—and this may have contracted in time to either spelling. Of the alternatives, historians have tended to prefer 'Aysén', and modern pronunciation is generally without emphasis, whatever the spelling.

It seemed he had been listening to a local radio programme about the origins of the very town we were about to visit, and whose fiftieth anniversary was imminent.

'Why did they call it Crocan?'

The locals continued to call Cochrane by its old name, El Pueblo Nuevo—New Town. Thereafter the closest most could come to pronouncing the new name was 'Crocan'.

'Who the hell is Crocan?' he asked. 'I've never met anyone of that name, and I've lived here all my life. Why didn't they call it Hueitra? We were one of the first ones here.'

It was a sentiment I had heard before—rarely expressed with any malice—but always with a sense that something was not right and needed to be corrected.

I knew a little about Admiral Thomas Cochrane,[2] but not why his name should come to be attached to a new town in Patagonia, not to mention the Chilean half of a large adjoining lake and a mountain nearly 10,000 feet high. I also knew that while Juan Hueitra's distant Indian ancestors might well have been amongst the first to reach Patagonia, it was less likely that they had done so in the Aysén area. Somehow, however, it seemed prudent to keep my incomplete knowledge to myself, but the encounter has remained with me, and I have often wondered what I would say the next time we met.

Juan Hueitra's ancestors would have been among the first adventurers to South America who walked across a dried up Bering Straits in, or about, 20000 BC and filtered south through North and Central America and down the Andes. Some remained in the highlands. Some stayed on the coast, to be joined later by Polynesian fishermen from across the Pacific. A few made it to the far south. They were all left undisturbed until the sixteenth century, when the Spaniards arrived, and Hernando de Magallanes gave the bottom quarter of the continent its name—Patagonia.

---

[2] Cochrane's unsuccessful attack on the garrison in Chiloë was as near as he came to 'visiting' Patagonia. His capture of Valdivia without ammunition, his taking of the Spanish flagship *Esmeralda* from under the guns of Peru's Callao and his one-ship pursuit of the entire Portuguese Navy across the Atlantic rank among some of the most extraordinary feats of naval history.

Political intrigue coupled with his own impetuosity and stubbornness came to a head in November 1822 when earthquakes all but destroyed Valparaiso and the house he had built there. The invitations he then received from both Brazil and Greece to help in their struggles for freedom finally made up his mind to abandon his intention to settle in Chile, and he was never to return.

Biographers are divided as to whether or the extent to which Cochrane profited from his South American adventures. The British suggest minimal, with the South Americans preferring maximum.

So inhospitable was this Patagonia that it remained unloved and under-valued by these new adventurers, whose attempts to populate it were inspired largely by a desire to ensure that no other European country should do so first. Initially, therefore, the original inhabitants—principally the Mapuche to the west of the Andes, the Tehuelche to the east, and the canoe Indian tribes on the Pacific and southern coast—were left alone again. It was probably the Tehuelche to whom Juan Hueitra owed at least part of his more recent origins. Inadvertently, however, the most signifi-cant contribution the Spaniards made was to introduce the one thing he had appeared to be lacking when we met. The Patagonian Indians were particularly quick to adopt and adapt the horse to their own use, and their subsequent development owed much to this acquisition.

When, some 250 years later, the countries of South America sought their independence from Spain and Portugal, many British soldiers and sailors, rendered redundant by the end of the Napoleonic Wars in Europe, jumped at the opportunity to join the rebels. Thomas, Lord Cochrane, the son of the bankrupt Scottish Earl of Dundonald, was one of them. Once independence had been achieved, many of these new arrivals stayed on, and as the nineteenth century progressed, so the flow of new immigrants from all countries of Europe increased, encouraged by the governments of the new republics.

At the time of independence, Patagonia was divided between Chile and Argentina, but since neither country had any better idea of what Patagonia represented than had the Spaniards before them, they were content to agree that each should retain whatever territory they had possessed at independence. There were too many other national priorities and diffi-culties to bother with an area to which there were no easy communica-tions, and which was apparently valueless and occupied only by Indians. Initially, therefore, the task of overcoming such ignorance was left to the initiatives and efforts of a handful of dedicated individuals. Increasingly, their reports revealed not only the existence of potential resources—animal, vegetable and mineral—but that the area was vast. There was now something worth arguing about, and the uncertainty of the agreed frontier formula began to raise real issues of contention. While there were reports of the traditional 'treasures' of gold and silver, it was the potential of a new 'white gold'—the wool on the backs of sheep—that suddenly made ownership of the land on which they would graze of special significance. Yet while there was now an issue of territory, there was still only a limited idea of exactly how much.

Unbeknown to either Santiago or Buenos Aires, a trickle of Chilean families, many of whom had been evicted from the lands they had settled in central Chile, crossed over the Andes and headed south. There was then no demarcation and few signs of either country seeking to establish any authority, and these settlers were merely following the route established over centuries by the Indians. They settled on whatever virgin land they encountered along the eastern fringe of the Andes. There they found similar settlers from Argentina, and for a while the two nationalities co-existed amicably, assuming common customs. Since communications to the eastern fringe were easier from the Atlantic side, it was not long before Argentine authority came to prevail, however loosely, and any opposition or resentment from those settlers of Chilean origin went unheard.

This was the situation found by the explorers and geographers sent to examine the frontier in the light of continuing national disagreement. These first settlers were subsequently those who suffered most when ultimately the frontier was resolved by international arbitration at the beginning of the twentieth century. They were 'squatters' at the bottom end of the legal rights ladder. Many were forced across the new frontier line to their country of origin or preference, but onto land much of which by then had been awarded to large companies. These 'returning' pioneers settled on whatever bits of vacant land were left, but now were constantly harassed by the concession holders or boundary police. Many of this group were of Indian or mixed race extraction, and they included two brothers, Hueitra.

History has tended to give credit for the opening up of Patagonia first to the explorers, whose journeys were either official or recorded or both, and secondly to the men who acquired the huge land concessions and created the infrastructures for development—notably the Braun and Menéndez families based in Punta Arenas. They had the vision and the courage of their convictions and they made their fortunes, but they also recognised that their success was possible only because of the many others who invested in their ventures.

For this second phase of pioneers—the men and women, employees of the Braun and Menéndez companies—their investment was physical—blood, toil, sweat and tears. They were the foremen, bookkeepers, shepherds, cooks, woodmen, boatmen, line riders, herdsmen and the *peones*—the unskilled labourers—and they came from all over the world. Some were itinerant, some seasonal, some with a return ticket to their country of origin, but they all had one thing in common—the security of a pay cheque. Since company employment needs were for single applicants, many out of this group were subsequently to leave and join with the 'returning' pioneers in raising their families.

Although Juan Hueitra would have had little understanding of many aspects of the life and times of a nineteenth-century British naval hero who became a national hero not only of Chile, but of Peru, Brazil and later Greece, he might have warmed to a man who was 'The Sea Wolf' to his

French enemies and *El Diablo* to the Spanish and Portuguese. Cochrane was a rebel and the cause to which he devoted his talents was the freedom of patriots.

Following some extraordinary feats of seamanship, ingenuity and daring against the French, which had earned him hero status in his own country, the then Captain Cochrane MP had been created a Knight of the Bath by his King, and when Britain and the United States declared war, he was promoted to Admiral and appointed to command the North American station. Then disaster struck.

He was incriminated—falsely—in stock exchange offences, convicted and sentenced not only to a year's imprisonment and a fine of £1,000, but also to be pilloried for one hour in central London. His name was struck off the Navy List, his banner of a Knight of the Bath was torn from his stall in Westminster Abbey and his armorial regalia was kicked down the Abbey steps. Although the pillory order was set aside, and he served his prison sentence and paid his fine, his career with the British Navy was ruined.

Thus when José Alvarez arrived in Britain from Chile some three years later, looking for recruits in his country's revolt against Spain, his offer to Cochrane of the post of Admiral of the Chilean Navy was tempting— far more so even than the offer he had previously received and rejected to head the Spanish Navy. Cochrane immediately accepted the Chilean offer and set about preparing for his family's emigration to Chile. His political enemies, however were not finished. A bill was introduced before Parliament, prohibiting British subjects from enlisting in the services of a foreign power. Fortunately for Cochrane, their efficiency did not match their venom, and by the time the bill was enacted he was eleven months into his new post and far away. Nonetheless, he was now an outlaw.

Cochrane's skill and daring in the services of Chile, Peru and Brazil was to earn him status as a national hero of each, and to secure the destruction of both the Spanish Pacific and Portuguese Atlantic fleets. His return home was to provide an outlaw with the unique satisfaction of demanding, and receiving, the full gun salute accorded as of right to the First Admiral of Brazil.

Much of the remainder of his life was spent in fighting for arrears of pay for his men and himself, but apart from the Brazilian title of Marquess of Maranhão, he returned little richer than he had left, and the estates he had been awarded in Chile and Brazil were subsequently appropriated.

The day before he was due to be buried in Westminster Abbey near the tomb of the Unknown Soldier, Queen Victoria issued orders for his banner of Knight of the Bath to be restored to its place, and after a frantic search his regalia were found in a junk shop and everything was reinstated just in time for the arrival of his coffin. He was not awarded a state funeral, and indeed no British Cabinet Minister attended, but twenty Brazilian soldiers under arms provided a guard of honour and knelt at his grave and the Brazilian Minister was one of the pall bearers.

His memorial, which bears the shields of each of the four countries whose independence he helped to achieve, reads:

> Here rests in his 85th year Thomas Cochrane Tenth Earl of Dundonald Baron Cochrane of Dundonald of Paisley and of Ochiltree in the Peerage of Scotland Marquess of Maranham [sic] in the Empire of Brazil GCB and Admiral of the Fleet who by the confidence which his genius his science and extraordinary daring inspired, by his heroic exertions in the cause of freedom and his splendid services alike to his own country Greece Brazil Chili and Peru achieved a name illustrious throughout the world for courage patriotism and chivalry Born Dec 14th 1775 Died Oct 31st 1860.

His obituary in *The Times*—not given to excesses even in 1860—described him as 'one of the great characters of a past generation ... No soldier or sailor of modern times ever displayed a more extraordinary capacity than the man who now lies dead ...'

Chile's own posthumous recognition of Cochrane has taken many forms, and continues to this day. The name of Lake Cochrane and Mount Cochrane came early in her modern history, and the subsequent selection of the same name for the new town nearby would seem to have been a matter of logic. Juan Hueitra's complaint was aimed at the lack of recognition afforded to the 'returning' pioneers of whom his parents had formed part.

My tale of Chilean Patagonia is woven along its Andean frontier with Argentina—the warp being the journeys I made on horseback in 2003/2004, and the weft combining the many colours of the frontier's history with tales of those pioneers I met or who preceded me, and to whose role history has paid such scant attention. The combined process of writing and weaving has proved to be more complex than I had first thought, and it has taken time to realise that my tale needed to be told in two books: the first, *Dark Horses at the Patagonian Frontier: Riding the Pioneer Trail*, and the second *Patagonian Odyssey: A History of Frontiers Won and Lost*. When searching for a title for the first book I recalled my meeting with Juan

Hueitra. What, I thought, could a retired English solicitor, an old pioneer and a disgraced admiral turned national hero possibly have in common? I then realised that perhaps I had been sitting on the answer: Cuervo, the only four-legged dark horse amongst us.

CHAPTER ONE

Boundaries, Borders and Frontiers

My journey down the Patagonian frontier was many years in the preparation—years which tested and defined the limits of those personal boundaries, borders and frontiers which shape each of our lives and against which we judge our successes and failures.

BOUNDARIES

Until my parents handed over responsibility for my upbringing to a boarding school at the tender age of eight, boundaries had been questioned frequently, justifications had been sought, and more often than not a patient answer had been given and even occasionally understood. This all changed with the new regime where boundaries were rules to be obeyed without question, and inevitably that brought me into confrontation with those who guarded them. Three 'points' a week resulted in 'punishment drill', four meant detention plus the drill, and five secured an appointment with the headmaster, who after a short lecture then administered a minimum of three strokes with a cane to my rear end. Inevitably I was assured that the pain I felt was nothing compared to that which he was feeling.

To bring a normality to these occasions, and perhaps even to make them more acceptable, there was always a certain ceremony attached. The head would ask if I knew the reason for my being summoned. Even though my attendances were often weekly, on each visit I had to be told why I had been selected, how many strokes I was to receive and even how I was to bend over—a simple toe touching exercise in which I had quickly become expert. Custom then dictated not only that I was expected to shake his hand afterwards, but that there were to be no tears as I took the long walk back to my classmates—running being forbidden. One day, however, my usual attendance was met with a startling proposal.

'Look, Burrough!' (Christian names were rarely used unless something of outstanding merit had been achieved. Climbing Mount Everest or riding the winner of the Cheltenham Gold Cup would normally suffice.)

'I really am fed up with seeing you. However, this time I am not going to beat you. I'm going to beat the chair. When you leave I want you to hold your backside in the usual way, and under no circumstances are you to tell the others.'

We both knew that others were certain to be listening outside. Still in a complete daze, I stood back and watched while he solemnly gave the chair four strokes which were clearly intended to hurt the chair. We then even shook hands before I left to do my piece of theatre. The following week, however, it was business as usual.

Punishment drill seems to have been the brainchild of an ex-Sergeant Major. Designed originally to discipline army recruits rather than boys aged between eight and thirteen, the drill required 'three pointers' to run for approximately an hour and a half round a large tree-lined area, holding a brick above their heads. Few of us had as yet developed into athletes and the furthest corners provided opportunities to sneak a rest and lower aching arms behind a tree. Inevitably, these were soon spotted by Sergeant-Major, whose parade ground roar would send the offender on his way. I remain unsure whether my arms are longer or shorter as a result, but the man I knew only as 'Sergeant Major' seemed to enjoy his job, as his recent obituary claimed—although the person it described was not one I would otherwise have recognised.

The struggle with boundaries continued on through the next stage of my formation. This time the responsibility for administering punishment passed to my immediate peers, and although the frequency, the ceremony and the pain were largely unchanged, at least one could register some form of protest by refusing to take the extended hand.

Lancing College stood high on the Southern Downs overlooking the Sussex coast. The chapel was a magnificent landmark for miles around, and a focus of the school's philosophy. This philosophy seemed to fit with many of my own experiences and recollections: metal bedside mugs of water which had frozen by the morning set an early stamp on the rigours of an average winter's day. Such rigours, not least showers at a similar temperature, no doubt encouraged stoicism in general and the development of adventurous personalities, of whom Lancing produced its fair share. These included Gino Watkins in the 1920s and Richard Mason in my time. Of Gino Watkins, whose preferred Pole was the North, Stanley Baldwin claimed, 'If he had lived he might have ranked, and in the opinion of men qualified to judge would have ranked, among the greatest of Polar explorers.' The kayak, in which he had shown skills equal to those of the Eskimos, was found empty in Fjord Greenland on 20 August 1932, months before he was due to sail for the Antarctic in *Discovery II* to lead an expedition from the Weddell Sea to the Ross Sea.[1] He was a mere 25 years old. Richard Mason, I recall, seemed to be Head of everything—a role model par excellence for any fourteen-year-old. On those rare occasions when he was called upon to administer the ultimate in the school's range of corporal punishments, it was said that Richard took himself off to the Chapel beforehand. Whatever took place there between him and his Maker no one knows, but I know of no reports of chairs being beaten. Richard Mason was subsequently engaged on a Royal Geographical Society expedition to map the headwaters of the Iriri River in Brazil's Amazonas, when he was killed by a tribe of Indians believed to be the Kran-Acorore. He was only 26, with a promising career in medicine ahead of him.

Those who passed through the British private education system during the 1950s and 1960s will have had similar experiences, others will write them off as part of a feudal past. I know not whether any adventurous spirit was awakened or destroyed by icy water or by the examples and tragically early demise of Gino Watkins and Richard Mason, but it is probable that I learned some self-discipline for later life, and learning to obey rules did give a useful insight when eventually my time came to enforce them. Of my contemporaries who also managed to survive, many went on to success in a wide range of occupations, but there were then fewer posts left in a disappearing Empire, and the traditional finishing school provided by conscripted military service was being phased out. This unique educational process left its scars on some; scars, which neither psychiatrist nor therapist could heal, and which often seemed to manifest themselves in exaggerated behaviour and superior attitudes, which others—not least those who had been through the same process—still find irritating. Since that time, and in a world which rarely if ever has changed so quickly, much needed to change and fortunately much has changed. Today, if my son had been subjected to a similar process, I would be expected to sue or inform the police or both.

On leaving secondary education, I had little idea about professional boundaries, but I was approaching a stage when I would have to learn about them too. In the meantime, I merely shared with many others a vague desire to save the world, or at least a piece of it, without the faintest idea of how or which part.

In order to play in that particular orchestra, I had first to acquire a

---

[1] Coincidentally, I was able later to identify with Gino Watkins through my uncle, Richard Walker's involvement as First Officer on the *Discovery II* expeditions between 1932 and 1936, when, after leading the rescue of the American flier Lincoln Ellsworth, he and a group of five other crew members were themselves stranded for weeks on the desolate shores of the South Shetlands. An account of this expedition is given by F. D. Ommanney in *South Latitude*, published by Longmans, Green & Co. in 1938.

relevant skill, and the then prevalent wisdom urged me to adopt a profession. First I tried teaching. Given the problems I had had with boundaries, it was a curious choice, but two years later I concluded that the profession seemed to stunt personal development and I needed to look elsewhere. Medicine seemed to be devoted to saving lives and was an obvious candidate, but having escaped the influence of even a modest scientific education and discovered that my knees weakened at the sight of blood or syringes, it had to be a non-starter. Engineering, too, looked promising, but I never recovered from the disappointment of being told that there was no perpetual motion, and if numbers were difficult, symbols were impossible. Many generations of my family had been called to the priesthood, but although occasionally I inclined an ear, I had heard no similar call and it seemed to me that even if I was going to save the world, it was also time that someone in the family should earn some money. I was left with the law, but should I try to become a bewigged barrister or someone called a solicitor?

I had thought the wigs looked smart, if mildly comical, but a heavy smell of tradition hung over my visits to the Temple and Inns of Court and brought back memories of previous uncomfortable boundaries. A number of eminent lawyers helped by advising that if I was unsure about wanting to be a barrister, I should not bother. So I signed Articles with a solicitor in the town of Guildford. There were long negotiations with my principal about pay—how much I should pay him!—but my father's new status as a parish priest helped to extract a compromise. For three years I would neither pay nor be paid, and for the remaining two years I would receive £3 per week (£42 in today's money).

My roommate and unofficial mentor was a former Police Inspector, Eric Loveridge. From him I learned that most defendants were indefensible, and he had a bottomless fund of enormously entertaining tales to prove his point. He explained that my job was to reconcile this fact of life with the fundamental English legal principle that we are innocent until proved guilty, and that solicitors had to earn their bread trying to maintain the balance.

Criminal law, being concerned with people who had broken boundaries, was bound to be fascinating. It often involved a forensic investigation, and ultimately the art of advocacy. Additionally at that time, there was a set of unwritten rules—a code—which even habitual criminals and hardened inspectors followed. The public were fed lines including 'It's a fair cop, Guv,' and tuned in avidly to *Dixon of Dock Green*—the everyday TV tale of an average urban police sergeant. In real life, however, the Sergeant Dixons did rule their stations, knew all the local criminals and their families and even administered justice with a smile and a cuff round the ear—often in front of parents longing to do the same. Few complained and solicitors ignored the Sergeant at their peril. Eventually, however, the growth in drug-related crime brought this world to an end and destroyed both the code and the Sergeant.

Unpaid or poorly paid young legal apprentices—'Articled Clerks'— were more than happy to give their all to building a defence in return for the modest travel expenses they could claim. Since those accused of crime seemed to have spent any money they might have acquired, the cost of defending them ultimately fell on the tax payer, and successive governments have wrestled unsatisfactorily with ways of reducing the Legal Aid bill. Today, even the overflow prisons are overflowing, most crimes of violence now involve drugs, terrorism is here to stay, the tradition of solicitor/client confidentiality has been broken, the number of lawyers prepared to provide a criminal law service reduces yearly, and all seem to be connected.

Having somehow persuaded the examiners that I knew enough to be admitted as a solicitor, the time came for me to earn a living, and following tradition, a country boy went to the big city—London—and the vast salary of £1,700 per annum (now equivalent to £23,800). For three years I investigated and prosecuted accident and personal injury claims, first on behalf of Trade Union members, and then—as poacher turned game-keeper—defending such claims for the insurance companies.

It was a time—albeit very short-lived—when supposedly I knew more law than at any other stage in my life. Theoretically, and since a lawyer is presumed to know the law and therefore should not charge for looking it up, I should have been at my most profitable. Instead, I was put to work in a branch of the law about which I knew very little—a curious process but one that seemed to be standard in virtually all occupational development.

There was a wide range of other skills to be acquired. Apart from the everyday practice of people skills and communication, these included the technique of persuasion, the arts of pleading, advocacy and cross-examination, the use of precedents and not least the art of knowing where to find the relevant law. As I struggled to acquire these, the instincts nurtured by family, school and training began to find their meaning in the parameters of legal professional conduct and practice. While boundaries were beginning to make a little more sense, I was to need rather more than instinct to deal with last minute instructions one morning to be at 'Court X at 10.30 today. All necessary detail in file', when on opening the file, I found it to be empty, my instructor unavailable and my client and a distant court waiting for me to take the lead. I recall that this was one of the few occasions when a frantic call for divine intervention was answered, and a crisis somehow averted.

Over the years, and as the traditional meaning of 'accident' as an act of fate has been replaced by the culture of blame, the infinite variety of problems presented by clients was exceeded only by their expectations, which ranged between... 'Someone must be to blame. It wasn't my fault. I want every penny you can get' and—rare even in those days, but now surely facing extinction—

'Yes, I know I've got burns because the thermostat on my water bed failed, but anyone can make a mistake, and if the hospital operation hadn't been successful, I wouldn't be alive today. So, no, I don't want to sue them.'

There were also many 'new' claims, where proof and sometimes motive were equally elusive.

'Grannie skittles ... ?'

'Oh, that's when a bus driver waits until an elderly passenger is on her feet and then slams on the brakes, sending her tumbling the length of the gangway...'

'Just for fun...?'

'Crash for cash' or its variation 'Flash for cash'—scams where drivers, often working in teams, deliberately cause accidents by braking, or by flashing lights to offer right of way, then claiming severe whiplash injuries from the resultant collision.

Client emotions inevitably became supercharged, and not least over boundary disputes. When later, during my travels down the Patagonian frontier, I puzzled over its prolonged and bitterly contested history, it was helpful to recall how boundary disputes at the level of the individual can cause even the most rational and intelligent to lose all sense of proportion when challenged over mere inches of their territory. No amount of advice as to the consequences in cost and neighbour relations would deter them, and in most instances it was reasonable to assume that the opponents were receiving similar advice.

Nowhere were professional boundaries more significant, or more finely defined, than in the practice of family law—a minefield of emotion and expectation on both sides, the more so when children are involved—when clients are at their most vulnerable and suggestable, and solicitors exceed their parameters at everyone's peril. For those solicitors who seek to add family mediation skills to their bow—as I did—the boundaries are even finer, and the absolute necessity of not giving the legal advice a solicitor has been trained to give, is the nearest he/she will come professionally to eating a doughnut without licking their lips.

In seeking a balance between the limits imposed and the results achieved, I was to find much professional satisfaction, but I was still grappling with boundaries when ultimately I decided to retire over thirty years later.

BORDERS

A first experience of a foreign border should always be unforgettable. Mine came in 1959, when I crossed the same Channel which had thwarted Napoleon and Hitler, and received the first stamp in my passport. Yet, apart from the frustration that very few people seemed to understand either my French or German accents, it all seemed utterly normal.

At a time when impoverished students hitchhiked everywhere, I quickly learned two lessons. The first—at a cost of two days thumbing at exhaust fumes—was that no vehicles stopped on the Autobahns. The second was that those drivers who were persuaded to stop—usually against their better judgement—needed to be entertained, ideally in their own language, but also expected to be allowed to practise their English and to be congratulated on their fluency. To pass the time, I worked out a delivery in both French and German, which, at a pinch, could be spun out over half an hour, and which flattered French/German food and drink by comparison with England's equivalent—a relatively easy task at that time. Having thus made a valuable contribution to the *entente cordiale* and its Anglo-German equivalent, I crossed France into a divided Germany and eventually entered Berlin.

Berlin, too, was then divided into four sectors, and I crossed into the Russian sector at a point then known as Checkpoint Charlie. The occasion was marked by barriers, brown helmets and uniforms of every shade of manure. A pointless interrogation took place whilst muzzles of weapons with minds of their own swung backwards and forwards across my navel. The faces of the soldiers showed a mixture of boredom, contempt and superiority at my transparent innocence and fear. My eyes darted from theirs, down to tobacco stained index fingers lying along the trigger guard, then to the black hole at the end of the barrel and back again. Suddenly I was waved through, but I had lost all desire to explore. I thumbled through my guidebook and selected the Opera House at random, but when I found it, the long gun barrel of a Russian tank sticking obscenely out of its drab, grey, pillared entrance threatened any attempt to go inside. A few days later, the international press announced the arrival of the Berlin Wall with a photograph of the very tank which I had been too frightened to take. I knew then that not only had I crossed a real border, but I would never make a living as a photographer.

Struggling back into West Germany, I headed south and for a while found myself again alongside the border between the divided Germanys, this time formed by mile upon mile of dense barbed wire. Only when I passed behind buildings did I feel free from the gaze of the tall observation towers, and it was with a huge sense of relief that my route eventually took me out of sight, and ultimately to the Alpine border of West Germany and Austria, where I was to spend some magical days literally learning the ropes of climbing.

There was to be only one isolated moment of indignity when an Austrian grandfather and grandson—one leaning easily on his Alpenstock, the other wearing shorts and gym shoes—loped nonchalantly past our roped foursome. Their passing comment, 'twelfth time up this year', was not intended to offend, and indeed was soon forgotten as our senses absorbed the breathtaking beauty of the surroundings. There can be few greater pleasures than falling asleep in a deep valley to the sound of distant cowbells and the yodelled serenade of parting guests; of being gently warmed awake by the early morning sun; of cooking breakfast over a wood fire, the body still tingling from a shower in a glacial stream; and finally of standing on top of our world, breathing a sharp freshness, looking down on a morning's achievement and over another distant world which belonged to someone else yet where no one and nothing moved. Our mountain border crossing was marked by no barbed wire, wall or conflict; only by a rare passport stamp which I was eager to own. Yet somehow this border left me with a sense of something new and different. The fact that I was in love with Francesca, otherwise improbably known as 'Frisky', whose father was our climbing instructor, may have had some influence, but that special sense returns each time I find myself near mountains.

Several years later, and as I sat at my office desk in London, I thought back to the Alps. Professionally, I had completed three years in the City and it was time for a break away from the regimen of law—away from Europe and things familiar—to explore new boundaries, cross fresh borders and probe new frontiers. Thus, I handed in my notice and found myself on the last of RMS *Arlanza*'s many voyages to Rio de Janeiro, and on the first leg of an intended world trip. I had a tape-recorder, five bottles of duty free whisky and £50. The limit imposed on travellers by Harold Wilson's government meant that I would have to stop frequently to earn sufficient for the next stage. After travelling extensively for some eight months around a vast Brazil—with the invaluable assistance of the Brazilian Airforce—I had acquired fluency in Portuguese as well as many hours of folk music to replay in moments of solitude. I had fallen into and out of love at least a dozen times, the promise implicit in my bottles of whisky had earned their face value many times over, and I even had two left. The ability to converse freely and exchange ideas in the local language had become a key feature of my travels, and I was very aware that the rest of the South American continent spoke Spanish. I decided there and then that this South American continent was enough world for me.

Once I had learnt enough Spanish—albeit with a Portuguese accent which caused a gratifying confusion as to my country of origin—I set off overland down the Atlantic side of Argentina to the Land of Fire, Tierra del Fuego, where the Argentine Navy helped me to fulfil an ambition of travelling round Cape Horn. I then returned to the mainland and crossed over from the Atlantic east to the Andes in the west. For some six weeks I travelled slowly north back up and along the Argentine side of Andean Patagonia. To my left, glimpses of endless trees, half hidden valleys, huge lakes, fast flowing rivers, blue veined glaciers and tier upon tier of snow-capped peaks were my daily companions.

Much later, I found out that Charles Darwin had stood virtually at the same spot at the head of the Rio Santa Cruz some 140 years previously, before he ran out of time and had to return to his ship, the *Beagle*. 'We viewed these grand mountains with regret for we were obliged to imagine their form and nature instead of standing, as we had hoped, on their crest, and looking down on the plain below.'

This was my first sight of a Patagonia without the pampas and steppes. I was fascinated and ate quantities of berries from the *Calafate* bush, which according to local legend would ensure my return. No one told me, however, that the effect could take up to 34 years to work through.

Throughout Central and South America, rivers and mountains are favoured border country, with the principal posts positioned at bridges or passes and the lesser posts in between. Human nature being what it is, the more isolated the post, the more bored and badly paid the officials are likely to be. For those on foot and following tracks as opposed to roads it is relatively easy to cross the line, whether intentionally or otherwise, but, apart from being potentially disastrous and even terminal, the consequences to the trespasser can also be wholly unexpected. Once, after walking over thirty miles under a cloudless sky to reach some converted cowsheds which marked the border between Brazil and Uruguay, it was to take me almost a day to persuade the official that I really did not have sufficient money to pay for a visa which we both knew, and ultimately he accepted, was not necessary.

Much later and much further north in Central America, when crossing the umpteenth border-bridge on my way south from Mexico, I noticed a man sitting under a large hat on the raised kerb and in the middle of the bridge. It seemed a curious place to choose, when there was shade, water and food at either end of the bridge, but several hours later I realised he had not moved. I also noticed from time to time that local women took him food and drink. Since I had time to kill, I asked the official in charge of the border post who the man was.

'He says he is a Mexican. But we cannot know for sure.'

'How long has he been there?'

'A few days.'

'And how long will he stay there?'

The official shrugged his shoulders, and I decided to go and talk to the man himself.

He was young—in his early twenties—and willing to talk. He explained that he was indeed from Mexico and had gone to Costa Rica to work. His car had been involved in an accident and had caught fire, and all his personal papers had been burnt. He had sent back news of what had happened to his family in Mexico, and they had been trying to obtain duplicate papers, but he had run out of money and in desperation had decided to try to make his way home by any means. He had managed to cross several border bridges, but finally had been caught in the back of a truck. The country he was trying to leave then refused to allow him to re-enter, while the country on the other side refused to let him in. He was told to sit in the middle of the bridge and had done so for several days while the locals brought him food. It seemed a plausible tale, and was simply told. I went back to the border official.

'He says he is Mexican and that his papers were burnt in a traffic accident in Costa Rica.'

'But how do I know he is a Mexican? Just because he says he is does not mean that he is.'

Frustrated, I decided to play my 'gringo' card. I felt uncomfortable, since I had invested much time and effort in denying any association with my fellow Anglo-Saxons north of the border.

'Look, *señor*, I am a journalist. From *The Times* in London. I believe our readers would be interested and many shocked to know how your country treats human beings. How you are prepared to allow a man to die in the middle of a bridge? To do nothing?'

'Are you really a journalist from London?' asked the official.

His back straightened, moustache quivered and his eyes lost their uninterested glaze. I nodded, sensing I had struck oil.

'Well Senor! My name is spelt ...'

Later I was to give details to the British Embassy and to be assured they would look into the situation and inform their Mexican counterparts. I never returned, and was to learn that such human tragedies are far from unusual.

That first 'world trip' ended with a journey down the Peruvian River Huallaga—a journey which was intended to take me via an unusual river route to Iquitos and thence across the Peru/Colombia border to Leticia, but which in fact brought me to the personal borders of real fear and awareness of my own mortality. With three Swiss friends, we built a raft using machetes and the traditional materials and techniques of the local rafters. A number of large balsa logs were joined together with bark strips and reinforced with several bamboo platforms. Oar blades, carved from a local hardwood, were lashed to long poles. These were the means of steering and, where required, propulsion. A wooden X frame was built across the platform to take the oars and allow the rowers to 'ride up' it as they rowed. Since we had no detailed maps, we tried to learn something of the difficult passes ahead from local rafters, but were unable to establish any consensus either as to names, location or grades of difficulty. Terms of employment of any guide included the cost of their return flights from our final destination, which our modest budget could not afford. Thus we set off guideless, and in terms of raft rowing, relatively clueless.

After several days we rounded a wide bend and faced a waterfall in the middle of which was a tall and very solid-looking rock. It took only a mini-second to calculate that our fifteen-trunk width was at least five trunks too wide to pass either side of the rock with safety. Being blessed with a more acute sense of survival than my colleagues, I was in the water swimming for the bank by the time the raft hit the rapids. Amazingly, it stuck half way over the first falls, giving time to transfer our belongings and the rest of us ashore. Our raft teetered on the brink but now refused to go over. Having resolved the initial problem of saving our skins and equipment, the next was how to try and tease our raft over the falls while hanging on to a rope to prevent it from reaching Iquitos without us. After much pulling from every angle, the raft slipped off its temporary perch and into the fierce current. For a moment it seemed that it would slide through, but first one then several logs caught the rock, and suddenly the raft reared up and flipped over the rock to crash back on the other side upside-down and then disappear downstream. The weight of the raft was substantial, and there had never been any realistic hope of our holding it, and we never saw it again.

Later and once we had had time to collect our thoughts, we estimated we were some days from the next river settlement. Our only option was to wait for another raft to pass, but we knew that few were making the trip.

The days we spent on that pebbled jungle shore were harsh. Our efforts in collecting the materials for the raft and building it had taken their toll. According to a study of my journal of tropical ailments, we were all suffering from salt deficiency, which left us lethargic, and our food supplies were limited. Loss of cigarettes shortened fuses further. We passed the time around a permanent fire, which we built to keep the mosquitoes and nocturnal animals away, and in occasional fishing expeditions.

Before starting out on our voyage, we had enjoyed a number of large fish which were brought stunned to the surface by small charges of dynamite, but on enquiring about the presence of *piranhas* in the Huallaga, we had been told that the river was too large and the current too strong for us to encounter them. Armed with that happy assurance, we had taken turns to cool off floating behind our raft. Now, with hunger becoming a problem and in the absence of dynamite, we turned to our First Aid kit, and with bits of chicken threaded onto bent needles we managed to hook a number of fish from the shore, which if not *piranhas*, certainly had the same dentist, and their execution was conducted from a respectful distance. They were the only river occupants interested in our chicken bait, but their flat pink flesh was full of tiny bones and had little nutritional value, leaving us with the largely perverse pleasure of eating them rather than the reverse.

Our camp was downstream of the fateful bend, and while we were wondering how any raft could possibly negotiate it, we noticed there was a small branch of the main river which cut the corner. It was down that branch that our rescuers came on our third day. Shouting and waving we were able to attract the 'crew's' attention, and in response to their signal we swam to the opposite bank, trailing our belongings in plastic bags and praying that no fish would mistake them for chicken entrails. It was an unimpressive raft based on a number of fuel drums lashed together with a few poles and powered by an outboard motor. Twenty minutes later we lost one of the drums, scraping over a ridge, and within minutes the flimsy raft frame began to come apart just as we drifted into a large bend.

What we did not realise immediately was that the bend generated a whirlpool, and as we circled helplessly towards the centre, more drums detached and the outboard broke off and sank. Once again we found ourselves in the river, scrambling our way to the rocks at the bend's apex, followed closely by the raft's crew of two.

There was a marked difference between our reaction and that of our former rescuers. We were alternately furious and deeply depressed. They were joking and smiling. We took stock of the damage to several of our precious cameras. They drew lots as to who was going to dive first to find the outboard. Their reaction, however, won the day, and soon we too

Raft trip on the River
Huallaga, Peru …

'… we set off guideless,
and in terms of raft
rowing, relatively
clueless.'

Lago Nahuel Huapi, Bariloche, Argentina.

Estancia Chacabuco, Rio Negro, Argentina, where the author
confused riding with diving.

Futaleufu, Chile. Nearing the start line.

Rio Futaleufu. The calm before the storm.

Catching Cuervo.

Toribio Baeza Miranda signing over
ownership of Cuervo and Rubia.

Isabel Castro and family after our
last supper.

No long goodbyes. Just turn and ride out.

First camp on Sr Mesa's land.

Cuervo on the 'village green' at
Puerto Ramirez.

Prudencia – now with the River Palena
between her and 'home'.

Some horses will go to extreme lengths to avoid
the *tabanos* – a sandbank in mid Rio Palena.

Valley Tranquilo – neither
poacher nor gamekeeper.

Cuervo after 'walking the
plank' at the first *pasarela*.

After La Mula. *Pasarelas* "are now mere interludes".

Sara Mario and friends. Note (now obsolete) implements and the prize bull's lookout behind.

Rio Correntoso. "No hay problema Hector".

Looking down of the Palena –"blue as a hare's armpit".

There were occasions when even a surefooted horse prefers discretion.

Occasionally we found ourselves beside the Rio Figueroa.

Last lunch before the long straight to Lago Verde.

Lily with some of "her babies".

were able to see the comical side, and Robert the cameraman was squirting water from his waterlogged favourite.

'Don't worry, *gringos*, there is another raft behind.'

Sure enough, within a few hours we saw another raft moving slowly downstream towards us. This was a proper raft, not as well made as ours had been, but with the same construction and with two oars. We had a grandstand seat as they crossed the ridge without problem and then showed us how to negotiate bends and whirlpools.

One of our many forms of ignorance was not knowing that on entering a bend, it was essential to do so sideways. We had always entered nose first, with the result that only one of our oarsmen was effective in paddling us out of the bend. The other was left back-paddling, and with monotonous consistency we had crashed into the rocks at the bend's apex, each time fearing we would lose our raft. The bark ties had held firm, but there was a limit to the pounding we could take and we felt that the logs were eventually bound to separate.

The approaching raft did not try to avoid the whirlpool. It entered casually and circled in it many times, the crew chatting and drawing on their cigarettes. Then, as the raft turned in the direction of the bend, the two oarsmen leapt into action, mounting the oar frame and pulling together. The raft eased out of the whirlpool current back into the mainstream of the river, and in one easy motion it rounded the bend and disappeared out of sight.

We looked at each other and smiled.

'*Putain!*' We all knew this meant that Robert was impressed. Robert was not easily impressed, being one of that rare breed who would rather dive into a river to discover its depth, than waste time with a measuring stick.

Our new rescuers had had time to shout that they would be waiting for us round the other side of the bend, and we left the crew of the first raft to recover their precious outboard and then to take their luck with the next passer-by.

We were to learn much more about Huallaga river craft during the next few days and to wonder how we might have fared without the free tuition. *Mal pasos*—difficult bits—came in all shapes and sizes, and usually involved bends. Some comprised a multi-tier approach, where the river descended a series of steps via an infinite variety of rock obstructions, shallows and eddies. The same stretch of river could contain infinite variations according to its depth and whether it was the dry or rainy season.

All these considerations came to a head, however, approximately half a day from our destination, when the river narrowed down a long straight 'canal', its sheer rock sides towering above us. We could sense that we were sliding down a steep watery slope, with our speed increasing every yard. The faces of our oarsmen showed a new intensity. A bend was coming, and it was clear that we needed to negotiate it without touching the sides—much as a thirsty drinker downs his first drink. Our speed and the force of the current were such that to do so would have been disastrous. The raft eased round to show us that the bend was going to be to the left, and both oarsmen gripped their oars and rode up the rowing frame poised to pull. Ultimately it was all about timing. At the precise moment, both pulled hard down on the oars, then climbed and pulled again, then again. By now the noise of the river drowned all other sound, but I am sure we were all shouting. Our direction changed but we kept to the centre of the river. Then we were through. Or so we thought.

Almost immediately the oarsmen changed direction to enter a second bend, this time to our right. The same procedure followed, and then suddenly there was quiet. I can remember hearing the sound of a bird calling. The oarsmen rested on their oars, each with a shy grin. So that was the passage everyone had talked about, each giving it a different name. That day I learned one more lesson—which, but for our oarsmen, might have been my last—that there are some 'borders' where a guide is a must, regardless of cost.

We were taken as far as the river port of Juanjuy. Our original objective had been to row our own raft via Juanjuy and on to Iquitos, but now we had no raft, and enquiries revealed that due to a shortage of raft building materials locally, few rafts were going on from there. This made our next decision easier. We would fly to Iquitos, and as it turned out, it was as well we did.

On arrival I headed for the British Consul, hoping he might have some helpful ideas about cheap accommodation before we made our way on to Leticia in Colombia.

'What did you say your name was?'

I told him.

'Where have you been? We have been looking for you for weeks. Your father has been killed in a car crash.'

He appeared to think he had done his job. Perhaps no one had suggested that there might be more sensitive ways to pass on bad news. In truth, though, nothing could have prepared me for the shock, the grief and the inevitable regrets.

I said my farewells to my Swiss friends and flew back to Lima and thence on to London.

On the flight home I caught the eye of a beautiful Peruvian girl, one of a group travelling to London. I was not in the mood for flirtation, but we exchanged details and agreed to meet up later. Some eight years later, I flew back to Lima to marry her. To my eternal regret she and my father never met, but by yet another of fate's strange quirks, it was he who had introduced us.[2]

FRONTIERS

'Frontier' is a fine modern word, and has long been a personal favourite, the more so since it has been extended to the 'very limits of knowledge'. J. F. Kennedy struck a common chord when he said, 'We stand today on the edge of a new frontier.' The word, then and now, has both the uncertainty and mystery of adventure with strong whiffs of optimism and hope. Its real significance is that we each have our own frontiers, something which Kennedy understood well.

The Wild West may have been tamed and the bullock cart wheels of the Great Trek may have stopped turning, but many of the frontiers crossed by the first pioneers are still there for each of us to savour—our first sight of the Pacific or the Amazon River, or our first experience of the jungle, where often only the indigenous can spot where others have been before. At those moments, the elements we associate with progress and change become irrelevant. The frontiers are virgin again and the often momentous process of crossing them is ours alone.

My own travels in South and Central America had taken me the length and breadth of the continent, and many personal frontiers had been crossed, but it was the Andes to which I have always felt a special affinity, one I can trace back to my happy association with the Alps. This massive range is quite literally the backbone of the southern continent, creating the magic circle of snows, glaciers and ultimately the purest of water which brings life to all it touches on its relentless and turbulent passage to the sea. Although the frontiers between Colombia, Ecuador, Peru, Bolivia and Chile lie across this backbone, only Chile and Argentina are divided by it.

Just as I found myself drawn to frontiers, so too was I attracted to those who had been there before—the pioneers and indigenous people. The general perception today is that both belong in the past. Most of the world has been surveyed and mapped. Each country has assumed control and defence of its borders, within which the recording of land ownership

---

[2] 'Generous, eager, thoughtful, kind,
He used his qualities of heart and mind
To serve his God through serving man:
His life was dedicated to a plan
Of love of God and love of man'.
The Bishop of Guildford's tribute to my father.

has been organised and extended. With ownership have come the laws of privacy, rights, fences, gates and locks. Anyone with access to a computer can home in on anywhere in the world overflown by a satellite. In theory, there should be nowhere left today for pioneers and Indians, yet as I was to discover, there are still many areas in the world where ownership plays a secondary role and people live very much as their pioneer ancestors did.

In South America, most members of indigenous communities—even the few nomadic tribes that remain—appear to have one level of acquisitiveness and exclusivity amongst themselves, but in the tradition of rural people the world over, they also share the same combination of independence and interdependence associated with those we call pioneers. Yet, collectively the Indians react far more strongly when their territory is threatened by outsiders. Then, even in their own idiom, something akin to a sense of proprietorship or sovereignty emerges, which they are prepared to defend with their lives.

That we know anything about Indians or pioneers is due largely to what we read or view, but there is a deep well of human sympathy for those who face nature and the elements with little more than their bare hands, and whose bearing and features so often reflect an unpretentious pride in what they are and do.

Aside from the romantic, and as the developed world increases its awareness of the damage its lifestyle continues to cause our planet, the knowledge and example of those closest to nature and the warnings they articulate have an ever widening and respectful audience. *The Heart of the World* by Alan Ereira gave an account of a visit by a BBC team to the mountain jungle of northern Colombia. The team were specifically invited by a group of Colombian Indians named the Kogi. Calling themselves the 'Mamas' (sometimes 'Mamos') or 'Elder Brothers of the Human Race', the Kogi had kept themselves apart for centuries, but had decided the time had come to teach the 'Younger Brother' about the balance between man and nature before it was too late. They chose to invite the BBC and told the team:

> Younger Brother thinks, 'Yes! Here I am! I know much about the universe.' But this knowing is learning to destroy everything, all humanity. The earth feels …

> The Mother is suffering. They have broken her teeth and taken out her eyes and ears. She vomits, she has diarrhoea, she is ill. If we cut off our arms, we can't work. If we cut off our tongue, we can't speak. If we cut off our legs, we can't walk. That is how it is with the Mother. The Mother is suffering. She has nothing.

Some years before the publication of *The Heart of the World* and during my time in Bogota, I had often noticed certain men—unusually tall for Colombians—standing alone on street corners. They wore long robes and their dark shoulder length hair, was capped by a white cone-shaped hat.[3] What set them apart from the smart suits shirts and ties, was their bearing and profile. Completely unfazed by the noise traffic and bustle around them, they exuded pride and self possession, and reminded me of photographs of North American indian chiefs. I learned they were members of the Arhuaco tribe, who lived in the mountains of the Sierra de Nevada, which tower to 15000 feet on the north/Caribbean coast. Visitors—particularly those carrying cameras—were not welcome, and on a later visit to that area, I was to confirm that dense jungle on the foothills of their homeland made access extremely difficult.

Very little was known then about the Arhuaco and even less of the Kogi, who live further up the same mountain. Following the Kogi's decision to contact the BBC and the documentary and book that followed, the outside world came to know more about the four distinctive tribes—each a survivor of the cultured Taironas who had been wiped out by the diseases and abuses of the Spanish. The Kogi and the Arhuaco share many beliefs and customs and occupy a land which is a microcosm of every ecological zone on planet Earth, capable of supporting virtually every variety of plants and animals. There seems to be a (silent) concensus that the Kogi have since become the spokesmen not merely for the four tribes but of indigenous communities from North America to the Amazon. High in the Kogi's list of concerns as to the damage caused to their environment and to the World, are the pollution of rivers and crops caused by large hydro-electric schemes and aerial spraying of crops—a concern echoed down the length of the Andes.[4]

Those with country roots may more readily identify with the harshness of conditions, simplicity of tools and homespun philosophy of the pioneer

---

[3] The hat and its colour symbolise the snowfields of the sacred peaks of the Sierra de Nevada.

[4] Twenty years on from the publication by Jonathan Cape of Alan Ereira's book and documentary, the Kogi asked him to return. They had seen little change in Younger Brother's behaviour and believed he would find it easier to understand their further and more urgent message by what he saw rather than what he heard. The result has been a further film produced under the Kogi's direction and entitled 'Aluna' – literally 'the mind', but also the name given by the Kogi to their sacred mountain. The film was made in 2011 and first screened the following year, and has been seen and approved by the Kogi themselves. It contains the following message '… Younger Brother is doing too much damage. He must see, and understand, and assume responsibility. Now we will have to work together. Otherwise, the world will die'. As Alan Ereira stresses 'The Mamas are very clear about how we should take notice of what they say. Listen carefully, think, make our own decisions. They don't want to tell us what to do' (quoted in The Guardian Professional.)

and the indigenous. They may even recall some of the smells with a sense of nostalgia. Few, however, could survive the conditions faced daily by those who occupy the high Andes or the Amazon jungle, where even the most sophisticated phytobotanist, biologist or homoeopathist recognises the depths of his or her own ignorance. At my own level, while my instincts reminded me that there was much to observe and both respect and fear, and while my country nose retained some of its fond memories, I could not communicate with the Indians save in Spanish or Portuguese, and often had to rely on an interpreter. In the jungle, views are few, travel had been a sweaty struggle and I never learned enough to identify those creatures, visible and invisible, which were likely to do most harm to my Anglo-Saxon body and blood. In the high lands—the *altiplano*—while non-indigenous lungs were always a considerable disadvantage, at least one knew the cause of one's discomfort and that acclimatisation was a matter of time.

Travel had not only re-introduced me to my mountain frontier, but also left me more deeply preoccupied in other matters. While I still nursed a perception that the world to which I belonged had something relevant to offer, it seemed that my own Younger Brothers had little interest in the priorities of their South American Elders, or in finding out what, if anything, the latter actually needed. Instead, the presumption reigned that the Elder Brother should aspire to have whatever the Younger Brother offered because it was inevitably better—the latest tractor, labour saving machinery or widget maker—and I had seen enough pieces of jungle cleared by heavy machinery, which, in two seasons had turned to a desert, dotted with idle and rusting equipment.

In my quest for guidance, I was steered to Fritz Schumacher, the author of *Small is Beautiful* and joint founder with George McRobie of the Intermediate Technology Development Group (ITDG) aka Appropriate Technology aka Practical Action. They each showed me much patience and understanding, and gave me many hours of their time, which I still treasure.

> In all kinds of production situations, it is necessary to find a technology that can meet production requirements whilst making fullest use of the immediately available resources—raw materials, credit, capital, labour, transport, markets—and which is acceptable or adaptable to the society that wishes to make use of it. Such a technology is called an 'appropriate technology' and it must be technically and socially appropriate.[5]

---

[5] Professor Harry Dickinson, 'The Development and Dissemination of Appropriate Technologies', Kumasi, Ghana, July 1972.

Along with many visitors to Peru, I had marvelled at the lines of irrigation channels carved into the steep slopes of the Andes even centuries before Christ. Today, they remain—often unused—not only as a testimony to the skills and organisation of those who built them, but at levels which are hundreds of feet above those achieved by modern methods. The 1,500 miles of paved stone highway which amazed the Spanish conquistadores on their arrival in the mid-sixteenth century and which linked Cusco, the Inca capital in Peru's southern Andes with Quito, the capital of Ecuador—the *Capaq Nan* or Opulent Way—had its parallel at sea level and the two were linked by scores of crossroads. The extraordinary Nasca Lines are drawn over miles of Peruvian desert with a precision which can only be appreciated from the air, and defy explanation even today. There are countless examples of gigantic stones, cut or carved with absolute precision to create buildings which have survived earthquakes and the ravages of centuries. Archaeologists continue to uncover lost civilisations, one on top of the other, each showing a remarkable level of sophistication. All these Andean marvels—achieved without their creators ever discovering either the wheel or the written word—demonstrated organisational, technical and building skills of the purest appropriate technology, capable of adaptation in many other countries today, including my own.

In South America, the publication of research results was beginning to expand beyond the continent, but progress in dissemination and application was limited. Similarly, although gaining ground in the UK and elsewhere in the world of the Younger Brother, few in South America were aware of ITDG's development philosophy.[6] Since etiquette, at government and non-government level, required that UK organisations could only respond to requests, it followed that so long as lack of awareness continued, such requests would be few. Breaking this impasse became my mission, and two Andean countries, Colombia and Peru, were selected.

While ITDG helped put flesh on the bare bones of my concerns, it was the UK organisations for volunteers in South America who helped me translate those concerns into a formal proposal to identify specific projects in Colombia and Peru with an appropriate technology need to which they—VSO, CIIR[7] and ultimately ITDG—could respond to requests for assistance.

My lack of qualifications now covered by official support and approval

---

[6] As a response to those who dismissed 'intermediate' as offering something 'second rate' or even 'second hand', ITDG substituted 'alternative' for 'intermediate'.

[7] At that time, VSO—Voluntary Service Overseas—had responsibility for Colombia. CIIR, the Catholic Institute for International Relations ('Catholic' having its universal as opposed to Roman connotation) had responsibility for the rest of South America.

(albeit without formal representation) I had a basis upon which to seek financial sponsorship, and over 500 begging letters and four years later, and with a few thousand pounds raised in my account, I handed in my notice again. My employers had known of my plans and had been very understanding. They were prepared to wait the eighteen-month absence anticipated, and while this gave comfort, at 33 I was unsure as to the extent to which I might be committing professional suicide as a lawyer.

The cheapest route to Colombia at that time was via the island of Trinidad, but with so many unknowns ahead it was inevitable that I should be feeling very anxious when we landed in Port of Spain, and was totally unprepared for my reception.

'Where's your ticket out, man?'

'But I don't need one.'

'You can't come in without a ticket out. You go on de next plane back to London.'

'But I checked with your people in London. They said it was OK. I am only going to be here a few days and then I fly on to Colombia.'

'You go on de next plane back to London.'

'But that's crazy!'

'Listen, whitey! You don' run this country now. You go back to London.'

I had never been on the receiving end of racism. It was an unpleasant but salutary experience, and my options were clear. I immediately made contact with my host and asked him to buy a ticket to Caracas as quickly as he could. Armed with the ticket I returned to immigration and handed it over.

'That should sort out the problem.'

'Where you get dat?'

I thought it was time to take the offensive. Behind the immigration desk was a large poster showing white beaches, sun, a smiling mouth full of white teeth and a welcoming caption.

'That's not really your business. You said I needed a ticket out. You have it.' I paused before changing tack.

'Do you know what that poster behind you says?'

My tormentor may have forgotten, but there was no way that he was going to turn round and look.

'What's it say, man?'

'It says 'Come to Sunny Trinidad. The land of sun and smiles.' Do you know I have been here several hours and all you have done is bellyache. You haven't smiled once. Do you know what happened in London today?'

'No. What happened in London today?' He was suspicious.

'Who won the sixth Test match?'

It had been a dreadful summer for English cricket. The West Indies touring side had slaughtered England in the first five Test matches, and finished matters off that same day with another thrashing in the sixth and final game. Every Trinidadian would have known this. Suddenly a big smile appeared on his face—one that stretched from ear to ear.

'How long you wanna stay, man?'

'Only a week.'

'You stay ninety days, man.'

The stamp in my passport was placed with slow and deliberate emphasis. Another new border had been crossed and I was one step nearer to my Andean frontiers.

This time, I was to travel extensively in Colombia and Peru, spending over six months in each. Just as my tape-recorder had been a key to Latin American culture, so Appropriate Technology took me to the pioneers. Ministers opened their doors to tell of their plans and priorities, university departments and institutes revealed their projects and experiments in appropriate technology with justifiable pride, and visits were made to numerous rural and urban initiatives to identify local needs. Indeed, such was the response that ultimately it was possible to put together a scheme for each of the two countries to form its own centre for appropriate technology, and for linking specific national engineering or technical resources within universities to a number of state and private-sector development projects. Invitations to ITDG/Practical Action and the British and Canadian volunteer programmes were to follow, and strong links now exist between Practical Action and the Schumacher College in the UK and Colombian organisations and universities. In 1985 the first international office of Practical Action outside Europe was founded in Lima, Peru where Practical Action Consulting Latin America is now based, and the office has grown rapidly to now number over 300 people and become one of the most active and productive in the world. A similar office was opened in Bolivia in 2007.

This optimistic summary reveals nothing of the defects, shortcomings, tears, frustrations, difficulties and convenient coincidences involved. Yet I met a number of truly remarkable pioneers, and while it would be impossible to name them all, I learned much from them, and one in particular.

Alvaro Villa was an engineer from near Medellín in Colombia—an area which was becoming increasingly dominated by the narco-barons, the drug lords. Alvaro had rare gifts which he applied through an organisation he founded, funded and named Futuro para la Niñez: Future for Your Children. He was a peerless 'enabler'. Knowing his fellow-countrymen well, he realised that for all their individuality and idiosyncrasies, they loved their children and were prepared to do almost anything for them. With their own practical intelligence, they established their own priorities. Alvaro would do his homework on a particular village and then visit. Conversations would ensue on the living conditions of the children, with Alvaro in the role of listener, playing questions back to the questioner. Everyone was encouraged to take part, and little by little, sometimes very quickly, first the needs—e.g. fresh water, better nutrition, health education and provision—then the priorities—water and nutrition—and finally the solutions—trout reservoirs—emerged. It was a fundamental principle of Futuro's philosophy that nothing was done for the people which they could not do for themselves.

Alvaro could not do this work on his own, and assistant 'enablers' were carefully selected and trained, and between 1961 and 1974 Futuro's philosophy had been applied in 250 communities. A large school was created in which all interested neighbours participated in improving the living conditions of their children, whether in the cultivation of vegetable gardens, construction of schools, aqueducts, bridges or fish ponds. It was an environment in which the list of appropriate technology needs was enormous: systems for the treatment of human excrement; production of organic compost; irrigation and extraction of underground water (pumps); a rice miller; cottage starch production and fish preservation; earth tile production and ovens; teaching aids based on local materials; fish breeding; organic material shredders—all were identified by the communities themselves.

Then the local *narcos* kidnapped Alvaro and demanded a ransom. For all his knowledge and expertise, he was not a wealthy man and received only modest expenses. His family was unable to pay, and soon afterwards his tortured body was found by the side of a lonely road. St. Matthew's 'A prophet is not without honour, save in his own country, and in his own house' has a traditional Spanish equivalent: *justicia, mas no por mi casa* ('Justice, but not for my own house'). I was in Bogotá when I heard the news and I wept at the loss and waste.

Peru proved to be the more difficult of the two countries, having recently had a new government which described itself as 'neither capitalist nor communist'.

Priority industries and natural resources had been nationalised and a land reform programme had appropriated the larger estates. The task of creating the cooperatives and communities and obtaining the people's 'conscious and active' participation in the process of social change was entrusted to a new organisation SINAMOS. On paper it all looked very promising and idealistic. In practice it was a jungle of sensitivity and suspicion, with SINAMOS at the centre. Indeed, with such vaulted and fundamental aspirations, this was inevitable. As a foreigner, I had to tiptoe my way through the broken glass.

With its immense but largely unrecognised technological tradition, Peru was a goldmine of appropriate technology, and I was to encounter countless fascinating examples of its application.

A young, highly qualified Peruvian engineer with a postgraduate degree from MIT was determined to provide a group of small farmers in the Andean highlands with a solution to their water shortage. Anticipating that they had little capital, he collected a number of designs for a windmill which could be built using a variety of materials, including some available locally, and he even organised lines of credit on favourable terms. He then set off for the *altiplano*. After some days of adventurous travel he arrived amongst the farmers, greeting them with enquiries about their stock. They smiled and he relaxed and set about explaining the function and advantage of the windmill and how it could resolve their problems. The farmers listened closely, particularly to the offer of almost free credit.

'How many would you like?' he asked.

The farmers all shook their heads. They were not interested, and the engineer came away, also shaking his head.

Another specialist was working nearby. He was an anthropologist, and when he heard of the visit and the farmers' rejection, he went to find out why. First, he asked the farmers how they and their families were.

'Don't you want to know how our cattle are doing — or the crops?'

The anthropologist shook his head. He genuinely wanted to know how the people were faring.

'People who come here always ask us about our cattle. They never ask how we are.'

A long conversation followed, and the anthropologist established, not to his surprise, that the farmers well knew the function of the windmill. They also understood that it could solve the problem of watering their cattle — and more. However, the engineer had shown them designs, all of which had a circular vane at the top of a tower. The sun was central to their culture and that of their ancestors. It warmed them and their crops, and they were unhappy at the idea of putting up a tower with a circle on top, in case the sun might be offended. The anthropologist understood.

He did not know, however — and it is at least possible that the engineer did — that a man called Savonius had invented a simple windmill design, which entailed splitting an oil drum in two and joining the two halves in the form of the letter S, with a metal pin. This 'contraption' was then raised on top of a tower, and functioned as efficiently as a circular vane. It is also at least possible, however, that the farmers might have found that alternative just as objectionable. After all, S stands for *sol* (the sun).

> The objectives of development very often reflect the ambitions of scientists and others, rather than the needs and ambitions of the people directly... the farmers.[8]

They—the farmers—and the Kogi too understood this and no doubt would have found a way of articulating that understanding.

My visit to Colombia and Peru, and the long preparation, execution and attempted implementation processes, took me to many more personal boundaries borders and frontiers, some of which were crossed more successfully than others. The trip brought me into contact with many saints and sinners, and the lessons to be learned were legion. The principles of appropriate technology make no less sense now than then, and their application is no less relevant whether in Europe or in South America. 'Technology' had seemed such a dry, soulless word until I was shown its human face and saw the same bright light of recognition in the faces of others.

Completion of my 'mission' meant a renewed return to the boundaries of my profession, and dreams of Patagonian frontiers were put on hold yet again. With partnership, marriage and a family of three, there were new priorities and responsibilities, and as the years ticked by, new concerns—clients, partners, schools, income, the mortgage, health—not necessarily in that order. My Patagonian dreams were essentially selfish, but in time I acquired four vital supporters, each of whom understood dreams. Why could I not take them with me? Economics and educational priorities suggested this was impossible, but my teenage son helped by observing, 'It's your dream, Dad!'

My partners at work ultimately split into two loose factions—those who wanted to make as much money as possible, and those who wanted to make as much money as possible and enjoy it. Some years later, however, when the direction of the partnership shifted to exclude the second faction

---

8   David D. Franklin, Patricia Juri and Edward Hoover, 'Una metodología de ingeniería de sistemas para trabajo interdisciplinario en la agricultura', Centro Internacional de Agricultura Tropical (CIAT), Lima, Peru, June 1974.

altogether, and it was clear that the returns from my area of expertise were not going to meet the expectations of the others, we parted company and two of my concerns were removed. One dream, and one Andean frontier, were beginning to appear with greater frequency.

At the southern end of the Andes, where I had eaten my *Calafate* berries and gazed west, the mountains along the Patagonian frontier between Chile and Argentina are lower and the pioneers still young, much of their history having been played out over the past 150 years. Unusually therefore, there are many pioneers living there today in circumstances little different from those experienced by their parents and grandparents, and whose memories and recollections are still fresh. I recalled some of those I had met in my travels and wanted to meet more, to share some of their experiences and to piece together their history. They had become part and parcel of my next chosen frontier, even though at this stage I had little idea just how complex that experience and history would prove to be.

CHAPTER TWO

Small Steps Towards a Patagonian Frontier

Over the years, I had kept a lazy eye on Chilean Patagonia and built up my knowledge of the area and its history. There were many surprises, one of the first being that it has proved impossible to travel the length of Chile by land—a distance of some 2,900 miles—of which virtually all the bottom half comprises Patagonia.[1] Even today, when there is no shortage of people who would regard such a walk or cycle ride as mere training for an objective of five or ten times that amount, no one has yet managed that particular walk.

The first problem facing land travellers remains the 'crazy geography', not only of the north-south Andean chain, which in principle forms the natural divide between Chile and Argentina, but also of parts of that chain lying across Chilean Patagonia itself. South of the island of Chiloë, the rather grandly named Pan-American Highway stops at a natural barrier formed by mountains, fjords and rivers and—surprisingly at this latitude—jungle. They each run the wrong way and combine to defy all efforts to link north and south by a land route. Although this same barrier formed the southern boundary of the Mapuche Indian territory, even they showed little interest in venturing beyond it. As centuries of subsequent visitors have found, the only way round into the main southern part of Chilean Patagonia is by sea to a port on the Pacific coast—Chaitén is the most popular—or by land east over the Andes into Argentina, then due south and then east back over the border, via Futaleufú or Palena.

Conversely, and from Chile's point of view, perversely, access to Argentine Patagonia is relatively straightforward, by road or, for those with time and patience to spare, by rail, or a combination of both. The main problems are high winds and distance.

In 1992 an American couple Douglas and Kris Tompkins, who had made a fortune from the fashion company Esprit, decided to buy a large area of land within the Chilean barrier described above, with the

---

[1] See Appendix 1.

objective of conserving its unique rainforest from exploitation. They are now believed to own a million acres, from the Pacific coast to the Andes, called the Parque Natural Pumalín. Such a large acquisition of frontier land was bound to cause resentment and awaken Chilean national sensitivity. The Tompkins' eco-credentials and intentions, however, are widely respected by the international Green movement, and the land is held by a non-profit making Fundación Educación, Ciencia y Ecología. Visitors are encouraged and no secret has been made of the intention to donate the land to the national park system once the infrastructure has been completed. Time will tell, but the Tompkins' funds and objectives have also since been applied to acquiring similarly large and sensitive areas in the Chacabuco Valley, off Punta Arenas in southern Chilean Patagonia, and in northern and southern Argentina.

While inspiring a huge diversity of rumour and feeling, it seems unlikely that even the Tompkins factor will produce a link between the Pan-American Highway and its Patagonian equivalent to the south—the Austral—and indeed the Tompkins couple have come out strongly against the idea. Currently, this remarkable 'road', otherwise 'Pinochet's folly', starts at Chaitén and winds down Chilean Patagonia as far as Lago O'Higgins, where it meets a second barrier.

Once again the problem is geographical, but this time in the form of Lago O'Higgins and the vast Southern Ice Field. Between them they cover the entire width of Chile—albeit never much more than 120 miles. The options for those going on south are to mount an expedition to cross the Ice Field or—once again—to go round it into Argentina, returning further south into the Chilean region of Magallanes and the famous Torres del Paine. At these latitudes, there is no easy outlet to or access from the Pacific.

The Southern Ice Field is some 215 miles long and although virtually all of it lies within Chile, there continue to be arguments as to where Argentine ice stops and Chilean ice begins, or even where/when water becomes ice or ice becomes water. Weather conditions are atrocious, and even in summer the season is very short and winds and mist make progress difficult. Since the first expedition by a Dr. Reichart in 1914, there have been many others. The extraordinary twentieth-century Patagonian explorer/mountaineer/priest Alberto De Agostini led at least four, but it was not until 1952 that the first complete lateral crossing was made by the Argentine Emiliano Huerta. Eric Shipton then attempted a north-south crossing starting in Chile in 1960-61, but after 52 days he emerged on the Argentine side. Thus, walking the entire length of Chile, north to south or vice versa, remains a challenge yet to be met.

As I made my way up the Argentine side of the cordillera in 1969, I did not know of either of these obstructions. Later still, I discovered that although the 1902 arbitration had fixed the border between Mounts Tronador and Fitzroy—and in so doing divided the major lakes including Lago San Martín/O'Higgins—Argentina and Chile had fallen out subsequently over a small area lying between the south of the lake and the Southern Ice Field. This area became known as the Laguna del Desierto. There was therefore an absence of official maps, and enquiries about possible crossings at this point were discouraged. The dispute had suddenly erupted into a nasty border war in 1964, and only after many more years of squabbling did the two countries agree to fresh arbitration, and in 1995 the Laguna del Desierto issue was resolved in favour of Argentina.[2]

Although being the first to travel or walk anywhere had never been part of my intention, theoretically this now meant that there was a clear route for me to take. I could avoid the first barrier by starting below it, and then travel as far south as the recently established 'town' of Villa O'Higgins, keeping close to the frontier, visiting as many national reserves or 'parks' and avoiding as much of the Austral road as was possible. If all went well, I could then cross Lago O'Higgins/San Martín, back into Argentina at Laguna del Desierto, continuing south along the frontier, and then re-cross into Chile's Torres del Paine National Park.

More than thirty years had passed since I had eaten *Calafate* berries, and although reasonably fit, it was becoming increasingly clear that to cover this terrain and distance, not only would I be riding a horse rather than walking, but the horse would need to be strong enough to carry my hundred kilos; significantly also, my equestrian career had been some way short of even modest.

I was born on a farm in Somerset, and for my first fifteen years animals with assorted names—Daisy, Buttercup, Wilberbabble, Chuffie and Peter, to name a few—were our friends and companions, and they were the cows, bullocks, pigs and dogs. Only the sheep had no names. For the rest, the names were perpetuated through many generations. Thus there was a Daisy VIII. There were also Queenie, Charlie, Jet and Foxy: the horses. The first two were huge, hairy-footed, gentle Suffolk Punch carthorses, whose working days were almost over and who were rarely ridden. Foxy belonged exclusively to my eldest sister, and Jet was a small black pony, whose name owed nothing to speed and everything to colour. He was short, fat and spoilt, but he gave me my introduction to riding, and, when a bad-tempered gallop was interrupted by a ditch neither of us had spotted, some jumping as well.

Otherwise I watched every Western shown. Soon there was no river

---

[2] It is these disputes which form the basis of *Patagonian Odyssey: A History of Frontiers Won and Lost* by the author.

that could not be crossed, no obstacle that could not be jumped. I could mount the wildest horse at a run, drop from any height into the saddle, turn on a 5p piece and out-gallop any arrow or bullet. It was also a time when my sister and I had nominated ourselves the national junior mixed double table tennis champions. Some twenty years later, the time came for these equestrian skills, honed to perfection in the back of cinemas, to be put to the test in Argentina. Inevitably there were to be highs and bruising lows. Don Roberto's observation that I rode like a sack of potatoes was one of the earliest lows. Months later came one of the few highs, when a long ride in search of Indian arrow heads ended with a steep winding descent. To my surprise my horse responded to the lightest touch. Fortunately he also knew every detail and obstacle on that route. A gate was opened and closed in one smooth movement and I experienced the supreme pleasure of being at one—one-handed—with my horse. The occasion was crowned by the words of the owner.

'I can see you have been riding a long time.'

Being a gaucho, he was not given to praise, nor would he have welcomed a hug from a complete stranger—and a *gringo* at that—so my ecstatic grin had to say it all.

Riding 'Western style' with one hand and two knees was my first experience of the pleasures of riding. Even the aches, pains and quivering thighs seemed to disappear more quickly. I had always thought of riding as a competition between horse and rider, made the more agonising by the English trot. However, it was clear that if I was proposing to ride the length of Chilean Patagonia, I needed some serious preparation.

I had learned my lesson about guides, but still had little idea as to their function. How could I find one who knew the way? I devised an imaginary advert.

> WANTED. Chilean guide. Must be patient, tolerant, sociable, with a good sense of humour, able and willing to cook, skilled with horses and their care, and with a tenacious desire to ride the length of Chilean Patagonia.

Did such a person exist? My preference was for an Indian who would know the origin and meaning of the many names his ancestors had left behind, have a unique understanding of Patagonian flora and fauna and who would teach me the skills of his tribe's 'horse whisperers', all in a Spanish I could understand. Further investigation revealed that such preferences were completely unrealistic, not least for the lack of Indians.

Identification of the Patagonian Indian tribes is confused by virtually every name having at least two alternatives. Essentially, the two principal mainland tribes were the Mapuche or Araucanos, concentrated on the Chilean side of the Andes but in the north-west corner of Patagonia, and the Tehuelche who roamed the length of the Argentine side and who divided into northern and southern groups. The Mapuche, who infiltrated east across the Andes and absorbed a number of northern Tehuelche tribes—a process known as 'araucanisation'—have survived in significant numbers and with influence in their traditional homelands, but the Tehuelche have been virtually eliminated. There were also a number of coastal tribes of 'Canoe Indians': the Chonos and Alcalufe on the Pacific coast and the Onas, Aush and Yamanas at the bottom in Tierra del Fuego. The Chonos had disappeared by the mid-1800s, the Onas Aush and Yamanas by the mid- to late-twentieth century, while of the Alcalufe, only a handful remain at isolated Puerto Eden.

Both the new republics started their relationships with their resident Indians with the best intentions. The Chilean *libertador*, Bernardo O'Higgins, declared publicly that all Indians were citizens with full rights, while in Argentina they were 'the first born children of America'. The concept was short-lived, and in reality the relationship was always fragile.

THE MAPUCHE

The most significant and numerous group of Indians in Chilean Patagonia, the Mapuche occupied the most northern part, below the River Bío Bío. Through 'araucanisation', their influence on the rest of Patagonia was eastwards. They did not penetrate due south. When the Spaniards arrived at the end of their long walk from Peru, the Mapuche called them *huincas*, foreign robbers, one of many words in Quechua, the language left by the previous and unsuccessful invaders, the Incas. Highly intelligent and fearsome warriors and defenders of their *mapu* (land), they held their northern boundary at the Bío Bío. From never having seen a horse, they quickly became expert horsemen and developed cavalry tactics to such good effect that under the leadership of Chief Lautaro they defeated and captured the conquistador Pedro de Valdivia in 1554, tried him according to Mapuche law and then executed him. After Lautaro's death, Mapuche resistance continued and for over 260 years they maintained their independence first from Imperial Spain, and then from Republican Chile. Today, the Mapuche survive in their traditional land. Oral records have ensured that much detail of their history has been preserved, and the Bío Bío still constitutes a divide between their culture and the rest of Chile.

THE TEHUELCHE

In Argentine Patagonia, the main Indian tribes divided into northern and southern Tehuelche. Each spoke their own language, and collectively they are often referred to as *Pampa*. The northern group, the Günün-a Künna, migrated back and forth across the country between the Rivers Limay and Negro, in the north, and the River Chubut (Chupat)—'meandering river'—in the south. Save for a small eastern section, the Günün-a Künna had all been araucanised by the end of the seventeenth century. The southern group, the Aonikenk, occupied the vast area south of the Chupat down to the Magellan Straits, living in small family groups and migrating in the summer from the lakes of the cordillera down the major rivers to the Atlantic coast for the winter. There are few preserved records of Tehuelche history prior to the nineteenth century, and few members survive today. From the 1840s, records owe much to the initiative of a small group of *huinca* explorers.

THE CHONOS

That anything is known about the Chilean Pacific Chonos is due largely to the Jesuits, Nicolás Mascardi and Diego de Rosales, Midshipman John Byron from HMS *Wager*[3] and the Franciscan, Francisco Menéndez, with over a hundred years separating their accounts.

The Chonos were the original inhabitants of the island of Chiloë, but appear to have been pushed south by other tribes to fish and travel the coasts and channels round the Guaitecas Islands, the Peninsula of Taitao

---

[3] Part of Admiral Anson's squadron of six ships, HMS *Wager* was wrecked on the leeward shore of the Gulf of Penas on 14 May 1740. Ultimately the survivors divided into two groups: ex-midshipman John Bulkeley was to lead 81 sailors, officers and marines south through the Straits of Magellan and up the Atlantic coast to Brazil with a small cutter and a long boat extended to accommodate them, while Captain Cheap and 19 officers and men (including a 16-year old midshipman the Hon. John Byron) were to head north up the Aysén coast to Chiloë in the ship's barge and a yawl. Of the first group, thirty reached Brazil, with a further four surviving their abandonment on the south Atlantic coast, and out of the second group only Cheap, Byron and three fellow officers reached Chiloë. A number of accounts of these extraordinary voyages were written by various crew members. First was a joint version by Bulkeley and John Cummins (the carpenter responsible for extending the longboat). Sequels followed by one of the officers, Campbell, and one of the abandoned four, Isaac Morris. It was not until 1768 that Byron's account *The Narrative of the Honourable John Byron* was published. The epic saga resurfaced in Peter Shankland's 1975 *Byron of the* Wager, and both Bulkeley and Byron's accounts were reproduced in 2004 as *The Loss of the* Wager. Of Cheap's group, the names of four marines who had to be abandoned to their fate on the north coast of the Gulf of Penas are preserved in the small islands Hereford, Crosslet, Hales and Smith; Cheap was given a canal. Two larger islands near the site of the wreck are named Wager and Byron.

and the dangerous Gulf of Penas. They used spears, wooden fish hooks and nets made of vegetable fibre. Only occasionally would they wear their *guanaco* skin cloaks, and otherwise dressed in little more than sealskin loincloths.

Eight to ten Chonos, often from the same family, paddled their *dalca* canoes from island to island. The *dalcas* were made from three planks of the local *cipres* tree, cut lengthwise and curved with the aid of fire and wooden pegs, and sealed with vegetable fibres. Their distinctive shape and the style of the paddles and anchor suggest a strong Polynesian influence. A sail was used in favourable conditions. The design and the Chonos' handling and navigational skills were legendary.

Midshipman John Byron described them as short, but broad and strong, with an olive complexion, long coarse jet black hair and fine white teeth. They chatted freely, but in a language no one but themselves could understand. They showed no interest in metal/iron, and could not understand its use. Great mimics (a talent they shared with the Fuegian tribes) they copied actions and sounds. Small mirrors puzzled them, and they kept searching behind them for the owners of the faces peering out at them. They erected temporary wigwams out of long poles and brushwood, or more permanent ones of bark and seal skins, on sites of circular heaps of discarded shells which acted as windbreaks. When Byron absent-mindedly threw some sea shells into the sea, the Chonos were very angry at the waste.

They knew nothing of seeds or cultivation and ate fish, shellfish, seal and sea birds. The women were the fishers, diving under the freezing waters for long periods, collecting sea urchins and mussels, while their children watched and learned. The men, meanwhile, sat around their fires, and the boys played with spears, bows and arrows.

When one of Byron's crew died, the Chonos showed a solemn and attentive interest in the body, even after burial, and Byron himself was to come across a Chonos burial chamber, set back from the shore along a rock corridor. A ceiling hole provided light and air, and a dozen bodies lay in two tiers, each in the foetal position.

Organised fishing expeditions brought all the Chonos men out in their canoes to a tidal creek, where at low tide, they built a wall of branches weighted with stones. When the tide rose and covered the wall, they paddled out to sea and threw their dogs overboard. These then barked and splashed their way towards the wall. The height of the wall was then increased, and they sat back to wait for the tide to recede. The creek became alive with fish, and the women then waded into the shallows, picking out the fish in their baskets.

Seal hunts were also well organised. Some Chonos landed and came at the seals from behind, clubbing them and forcing the rest into the sea where other Chonos were waiting in canoes. Those in the sea were killed with lances and arrows between the eyes. Others were caught in nets as they slid off the rocks.

At night, the Chonos went cormorant hunting, paddling their canoes under the cliffs where the birds were roosting. Torches of birch bark were lit and waved, and the dazzled birds fell into the canoes below. Others, higher up, were caught by climbing Indians and throttled quietly so as not to disturb their neighbours.

Byron was impressed by the Chonos 'killing machine', but less so with the men's refusal to share their food with him. It was left to their women surreptitiously to slip him morsels. Both knew the penalty for discovery was a violent beating, or worse, from a jealous partner or chief. Yet the Chonos killed far more than they could eat themselves. Even seals, captured alive, were killed, with no apparent custom for conserving food for travel.

Byron described a feast and a piece of the ceremony that followed. First, the men began to sway back and forth, groaning. The groans then turned to wails as they drove themselves into a frenzy, smearing their faces and limbs with coloured powders. Fiery brands were taken from the fire and put into mouths or against skin. Sharp mussel shells were used to cut and wound. Eventually, the men collapsed on top of each other, their bodies shining with blood and sweat. It was then the turn of the women to repeat the actions of the men, before they too fell in perspiring heaps. This went on for a week before life returned to normal.

These scenes mirrored much of what Lucas Bridges[4] was to witness among the Fuegian Onas and Yamanas over a hundred years later, although he spoke their languages and could understand and make sense of what he saw. To Byron and his crew, it was a madness, which emphasised the void between them. In a world in which they were ill-equipped to survive, they could only report what their wondering eyes saw.

Legend has it that Taitao/Taitau and his son Anahuac re-created this world, and that the Chonos, the 'Nation of the South', were moulded out of the local seaweed to live there. This land and the first Chono so created, were both called Acuau. In due course, a woman was created to complete Acuau's happiness. Taitao also planted a special conifer, the *cipres*, and gave the Chonos the knowledge of fire, and how to use tree resin to seal their *dalcas*, 'which rode like fish on the waves'. They carried the fire in their canoes, and the older women were responsible for maintaining that

---

[4] One of the truly great men of Patagonia, '*el Señor del Baker*' is referred to later in some detail.

fire day and night. When the winds and rain were strong, the Chonos took shelter until their oldest male, as their nominated chief, decided when to move on.

One such elder prophesised: 'Times of great confusion and darkness will come, when a black moon will cover the resplendent moon, bringing darkness to the earth. The north wind will bring plagues, sickness, and the channels will turn red. Then it will be near the end.' Thus, the Chonos always feared the north wind. 'And so it came to pass, and the Nation of the South was erased from the earth by the invasion of bearded men, who threw fire, and this fire was mortal.'

The first bearded men were the sailors from Europe. Pitting their skills against the elements, many of them perished. Their fearful and superstitious eyes saw cities, magically illuminated above the *mesetas* or plateaus of the islands. They told of golden balconies, of beautiful amazons and mermaids bathing in crystal waters, of guardians in towers watching over the four cardinal points. Sometimes the cities were palaces below the waters. One such city stood at the entrance to the Pangalito estuary, famous for its sea bass, salmon and bonito. Fishermen reported that seamen returned there from long voyages, their ship turning into a cloud of islands before advancing on the fishermen and driving them away. The king of the city was called Lin Lin.

The north wind has been, and the Chonos are gone. Some were the victims of target practice from passing ships. Those who survived the alcohol offered as payment for their services moved north and re-joined the same Huilliche tribe their ancestors had left, passing on their unique skills. Some moved south and joined the Alcalufe, who welcomed them and their *dalcas*. Only their names remain: Taitao, Acuau, the Archipelago of the Chonos and the island of Lin Lin examples in a long list.

Since the mid-1800s, when the Chonos are thought to have disappeared completely, rumours have brought treasure seekers to the Chono shell bank cemeteries on the islands of Traiguén and Acuau. In January 1996, a yacht with the latest sonar equipment was reported to have departed with two clay pots full of silver and gold coins, bearing the effigy of the Peruvian Inca Atahualpa.

'The Chonos lived in complete harmony with the nature around them.'

They had no interest in the metals for which bearded men would throw fire or die. It is comforting therefore to discover that no such coins were minted until the nineteenth century or later. Whoever hid them, it was not the Chonos.

For my part, attempts to establish routes and geographical reality were to remain painfully slow and frustrating, and I turned my attention to the equipment I believed was needed. The raft trip on the River Huallaga had taught me the value of local skills and materials, not least when on the spot repairs or alterations were required. Hence I felt that the Western-designed pack frames recommended by the experts could be crossed off my list. I would use whatever was used locally. Tent, sleeping bag, clothing and a good pair of hiking boots, neck pillow and thermal this and that, small tape-recorder and camera all seemed obvious choices. Advances in technology had brought out dry bags and the GPS. The former were invaluable, and the latter was useful in establishing where one was at any given time, but it was a constant disappointment that it could not tell anyone else. Mobile phones did not operate in the area, radio equipment was impossibly expensive, but internet was available in most Chilean towns and was to be my lifeline to family and home. Maps were going to be vital, but none of any value could be found in the UK.

One fear remained—that of failing or finding that physically or mentally I was not up to it. To make such possibilities even more difficult, I decided not only to tell everyone what I was proposing to do, but to attach a sponsorship element. I hoped thereby that if and when any inner voice urged me to give up, another could reply 'you cannot let all these people down' and my pride would do the rest. I chose ITDG, now renamed Practical Action, a local hospice for children and Oxfam. It then seemed that finally it was time to go.

I barely slept on the long flight to Buenos Aires. Never a good air passenger at the best of times, I walked the aisles or stood virtually the entire flight and was wide awake as the plane crossed the River Plate. There were still too many questions and too few answers.

I stopped in BA to try and collect as many Argentine maps as I could find of the frontier areas and particularly round Laguna del Desierto. The fact that there were very few took the best part of a week to find out. I then flew on to Santiago to stay with my nephew and his family, to study the Chilean maps, collect information and to try to make contacts in the south.

Having decided that my trek would start at the small Chilean frontier town of Futaleufú, I proposed to fly south to Puerto Montt, then cross the Andes into Argentina—following the traditional route of many pioneers, save that I would do so in a bus—to Bariloche, where I would try to bring my equestrian skills into the twenty-first century. It was a relatively short distance south to Esquel and Trevelin, where I proposed to cross back into Chile at Futaleufú. Even today, although there are many border points down the cordillera and an excellent network of buses, air traffic between the two neighbouring countries is limited to the capitals. Significantly, I learned also that neither country would allow a horse to cross from one side to the other without quarantine applying, and one glance at the procedures was enough to decide this was not a practical option.

In the Santiago-based Instituto Geográfico Militar, responsible for the country's maps, I picked out a route from a vast collection of maps, most of which had been revised within the previous twenty years. Essentially that route followed the valleys where these existed, and which tended to be coloured in a cheerful green. I selected six at scale 1:250,000, to cover the area between Futaleufú and Lago O'Higgins and which showed such detail as tracks and the names of isolated farms. Where the detail seemed to be insufficient or confusing, I had to refer to the larger 1:50,000 scale map, and a limited number at this scale were also selected. To have taken a full set of maps at this scale would have cost a fortune to buy and taken an extra horse to carry.

Initial efforts to establish contacts produced little, but following up a series of clues, I was fortunate to come across an expedition centre based in Coyhaique, the capital of Chile's Aysén region and founded by settlers in 1929. Emails then started to flow. The centre was able to recommend a guide, and we agreed to meet up at Futaleufú, where I would be advised on horse purchase and provided with basic saddlery and back up. Patagonia Adventure Expeditions was run by Ian Farmer and Jonathan Leidich, and had organised foot treks over the North Patagonian Ice Field, rafting down the River Baker and horse treks into the area south of the town of Cochrane. Highly experienced, they sought to provide modern comforts combined with traditional equipment, and to involve the local people. Each year new routes or ventures were introduced. They were familiar with much of the southern part of my route, but less so with the north. Finding them was a real breakthrough, and I felt I could now set off for my next destination, Bariloche.

San Carlos de Bariloche to give its full title, sits by the huge Nahuel Huapi lake and is backed through 240 degrees by snow-capped mountains. The remaining 120 degrees look east over the lake to the tufted spiky grass wilderness of the Argentine pampas. It is a breathtakingly beautiful area and one that has attracted Indian and European alike for centuries. The Tehuelche had it to themselves until the seventeenth century, when the Jesuit, Nicolás Mascardi arrived from Chiloë. It was to become a particular favourite of the Argentine explorers Perito Moreno and Ramon

Lista during the latter party of the nineteenth century, and their enthusiasm ultimately filtered through to a number of North Americans, among them Ralph Newbery (and later his brother George), Jarred August Jones (Juan Jones) and his friend John Crockett, who settled there creating the substantial *estancias* Traful, later La Primavera,[5] and Tequel Malal, from which they herded their cattle across the frontier into Chile.

The town of Bariloche was founded in 1902, but it was in the 1930s, after the National Park had been created, that German, Austrian and Swiss settlers arrived to put their stamp on the local architecture. Today, thousands of skiers are attracted in the winter, and horse riders, hikers and fly fishermen in the summer. I had visited several times, but never from Chile. I flew first to Puerto Montt and then travelled by bus north then east to the frontier. As we rose through the cordillera, my bus had to pick its way carefully through the fresh snow which had fallen on the higher passes, and then slalom down into a sun drenched Argentina. A deep blue sky reflected on the surface of the deeper blue waters of the lake, troubled by a gusting wind. Clumps of startlingly yellow broom curtsied and waved as we passed.

An old friend had a very large farm or *estancia* some way north of Bariloche, and I had been in correspondence with his manager, Eduardo, who promised a reintroduction to riding. It had been a long time since I had sat in the saddle, and as those over sixty know well, getting one's leg over does not get any easier.

I duly hired a car and met up with a gnarled walnut of a man called Julian. My horse was saddled and waiting and the plan was to start with a few hours jogging down memory lane. Julian was kind, patient and chatty and I soon relaxed. Too soon as it happened, because I was still listening to Julian when my horse went down a steep dip. I managed the downward motion by instinct and without difficulty, but seemed to be taken completely by surprise by the horse's sudden movement back up, and we parted company. I kept going in a dive which would not have looked out of place in a swimming pool, except that my arms remained stubbornly at my sides instead of stretching out in front of me. My last conscious thought was that my muscles were simply refusing to respond to the urgent messages my brain was sending. Some time later I came to and found myself propped up under a tree, focusing with difficulty

---

[5]   Both Ralph Newbery, Jarred Jones and Crockett contracted Texan cowboys to work for them—they were thought to ride faster—and many of these quickly set up on their own. Ralph Newbery and Perito Moreno were to become the closest of friends and together they created the National Reserve of Nahuel Huapi. George Newbery was less fortunate, losing his entire herd to a tempest. He sold up and joined the gold rush to Tierra del Fuego, where age, climate and conditions proved too much and he died there.

on a distant line of hills. Julian, whose parents relatives and friends were all centaurs, was leaning over me looking concerned and perplexed. Obviously he had never seen such a piece of riding incompetence.

I managed to drive back to Bariloche later that day and located a hospital with equipment for a brain scan. This revealed that whatever had been between my ears was still there and apparently in the same place, but a serious non-medical review was required.

The review process had started with a conversation Julian and I had had before I returned to Bariloche. It continued with his boss, Eduardo. I was very aware that but for a slice of good fortune, it might have been my own post mortem, but these were the experts and I needed their advice.

'How long are you proposing to ride in Chile, Jon?' asked Eduardo.

'I don't know exactly, but it looks like 55 days or so.'

Eduardo's face was inscrutable, but he did not waste words.

'You must be mad!' The words, machete sharp, cut right through me. It was a defining moment of my life, and I struggled to assemble a response.

'Why do you say that, Eduardo? What is a long ride for you two? What is the longest you or Julian have ridden?'

'Maybe eight days. We do that once or twice a year when we round up the stock at the far end of the estancia.'

The message was clear. Here I was, planning to ride 55 days plus, an incompetent horseman at best, old enough to be Eduardo's father and a poor physical specimen alongside either of them. Julian had said little, but his expression reflected similar thoughts and concern, which he was far too polite to voice.

For the next week I functioned on automatic pilot. I tried to address the more obvious deficiencies. I organised a concentrated session in the local gym to deal with those muscles which I felt, quite literally, had let me down. I booked myself time on a massage bench, and contacted another *estancia* to try to build up saddle hours and confidence gradually. Significantly, I also maintained email contact with Ian Farmer in Coyhaique, whose responses were both intelligent and sensitive.

'Don't worry, Jon. In Chile the horses and terrain are completely different. You are not rounding up cattle. You are going at your own pace. You can stop when you choose, and the guide we are getting for you is excellent. You can rely on him and the horses we will select for you.'

I wanted to believe what he said about Chilean horses and terrain, but I knew that I had been going at my pace and that I could not have asked for a better guide or instructor than Julian. The gym and massage sessions had made a difference, and my shattered confidence in my riding and physical condition had begun to pick up, albeit from rock bottom. I then had a call from Eduardo, who suggested a meeting. I was touched that he was prepared to take the trouble to visit me, but doubtful as to the outcome.

Within minutes of our meeting, a fundamental misunderstanding was resolved. Eduardo had thought that my intention was to ride 55 days virtually non-stop. His account of his experience was on that same basis. Even in the time of the original pioneers, 55 days 'on the trot' would have been undertaken only out of absolute desperation and lack of alternatives, and I was far from being a pioneer. I explained that my journey was always going to be in stages—possibly five—some shorter than others, with a maximum of some fourteen days for the final stage, and that in between horses and riders would rest up.

Eduardo's face changed and showed his relief. He knew that much thought, preparation and commitment had gone into the planning and he had no wish to be the cause of cancellation. He and Julian had also assumed an unspoken responsibility for me, but on this occasion no reference was made to my riding performance. Instead, Eduardo gave me a detailed article which he had copied on the care of horses and equipment. I needed his blessing, and without asking for it, I knew he had given it. It now remained for me to complete my preparations in the gym, build up my saddle hours and arrange my travel south via Esquel and Trevelin, then back across the frontier into Chile and to my meeting with Ian and my guide at Futaleufú—and the selection of our four legged transport.

CABALLOS AND CABALLEROS

If the tale of footprints in the sand, which may have given rise to the origin of the word Patagonia, was applied allegorically to the first explorer or pioneer's arrival there, then this would have shown his set of prints preceding the four of his laden horse, until their destination had been reached. Thereafter, the set of two would have been replaced by one set of four, and if God had chosen to intervene at this point, he would have had to carry horse and rider. As it is, the horse and rider—*caballo* and *caballero*, members, with the *cheval* and *chevalier*, *cavallo* and *cavaliere*, of the ancient European order of chivalry, attached to the horse and knight— have carried the history of Patagonia, and of both northern and southern continents, on their own.

There is evidence of a pre-historic South American horse, but none survived, and before the Spanish Conquest there were no horses, sheep or cattle on the continent. In Patagonia, there were guanacos, which were hunted for their meat and skins, but never domesticated. Their cousins to the north, the llamas—'sheep of the land'—were tamed, traded and used as beasts of burden, but neither llama nor guanaco achieved full camel status or were ever ridden.

Both the Argentine and Chilean *criollo*—meaning native American of Spanish/European extraction—developed from the horses which the Spanish brought over in the sixteenth century. Today's descendants can be found wherever there are cattle. The Argentine *criollo* developed in the pampas, and is normally referred to without the prefix. After the Spanish left, they ran wild and mixed with an assortment of lesser breeds. The Chilean *criollo* came on foot from Peru with Diego de Almagro and Pedro de Valdivia, a refining journey of several thousand miles down the length of the Atacama Desert.

Each breed has since passed through several centuries of development dictated by the priorities, needs and surrounding geography of the primary users. The Chilean *huaso* needed a horse with speed and endurance, and the ability to gallop sideways. The Argentine gaucho regarded endurance as the key, and also looked down his nose at mares. Also crucial to this process were the refinements and priorities of the army and the Indians—Mapuche and Tehuelche. In time, *huaso* plus Chilean *criollo* and gaucho plus *criollo* have become the inseparable symbols of their respective national pride and cultures.

The first impressions the Indians had of the invading Spaniards were of a super-race of centaurs. Man and horse appeared literally as one. The bloodied bits in the horses' mouths suggested that since they chewed iron, they would make short work of humans, but these fears did not last. Unlike their contemporaries in distant Peru, who never overcame their fear nor dared imitate their conquerors, the Patagonian Indians, particularly the Mapuche, stole the horses, stripped them of their saddles and bridles and quickly became expert bareback horsemen and developed novel and successful cavalry tactics. Apart from acquiring legendary riding skills, they trained and bred their horses to their requirements. Their training methods were in line with those of the gentle North American horse whisperer, contrasting not only with their reputation for brutality in battle, but with the traditionally harsh horse-breaking techniques of the Spaniards, still to be found among the Argentine gauchos.

The Indians had no problem eating their horses when they had passed their best 'ride by' date. They applied their own superstitions and potions to make them run faster, and they developed their own equipment, substituting wood and sheepskins for metal. The rate at which the Patagonian Indians absorbed the horse into their culture was astonishing. Even in the far south and as early as 1581, the Spaniard Samiento reported that the Indians—probably Tehuelche—whom he saw from the Straits of Magellan were on horseback. The date suggests that the horse had been absorbed throughout the length and width of Patagonia within less than forty years of its arrival.

Apart from being essential to *huaso*, gaucho, army and Indian, the *criollo* was the principal means of transport for everyone—from clergy to travelling salesman. Enormous distances had to be covered, over difficult and varied terrain and in all weathers. Different needs demanded different classes. At the top end, the Chilean *huaso* needed to show off horse and rider in public. The rider expressed himself through the horse—nervous, full of energy and with a shining coat—in the fine dress, saddlery and equipment and dignified form of riding, a Latin form of dressage. Important industries and skills in silver and iron work and in leather and wood grew up, and bloodstock owners established their socially important clubs. In the middle, smaller, even paced horses were developed for the women and clergy, and at the bottom, the strong patient workers—products of the eighteenth- and nineteenth-century threshing mares—suited the army, the *carabineros* and even, much later, retired English solicitors.

In fact, Patagonia lies to the south of *huaso* country—principally the central valley round Santiago—and the *huaso*, while deeply involved in and influenced by Chile's conflict with her Indians, whose blood many now share, largely avoided the damaging effects and aftermath of the international frontier dispute, and remained uniquely Chilean. Today, however, there are many on both sides of the border who identify with the *huaso* culture. Eduardo in Bariloche, an Argentine through and through, was a *huaso* fanatic, and had even built his own half-moon arena to practise for the competitions held throughout Chile, and *media lunas* are to be found in every *Aysenino* town. The gaucho has his roots in the Argentine pampas, but, although his nomadic instincts have taken him north to Paraguay, Uruguay and Brazil, where each country has been quick to adopt him as its own national institution, his profound influence has had politically negative consequences on Chilean Patagonia.

The Spanish soldiers of fortune had been either infantry (*peonia*) or cavalry (*caballeria*), and in Chile land holdings awarded for services gave the latter five times more than the former. Many became large landowners, who in their turn came to own virtually all the best land, and to form a rural aristocracy with considerable influence in central government. These were the rich *huasos*. Those they employed—essentially uneducated *campesino* riders with similar skills, qualities and faults to those attributed to the gaucho, but developed in more mountainous terrain—were accorded the virtues implicit in the Spanish title of *hidalgo*: honour, generosity and nobility. They were the poor *huasos*.

Distinctive dress, including flat, wide-brimmed, black or grey cloth hat (*chambergo*) or a straw hat (*chupalla*) and sleeveless short poncho (*chamanta*), together with saddles, bridles and spurs, gave rich and poor the opportunity to show off their *huaso* membership and region—the rich in silks and silver, the poor in cloth iron and wood. Such opportunities continue to be provided at festivals and at the three-day rodeos, *a la Chilena*, where, subject to strict rules, pairs of *huasos* compete in trying to pin a heifer between two flags on the wall of a half-moon enclosure: *correr en vaca*. A *huaso* code of behaviour broadly based on that of the traditional *hidalgo*, included the custom that only women sang to the guitar—a custom since abandoned—and that, on entering the house of someone he wished to honour, the *huaso* always removed his spurs.

The gaucho first took on a national significance during Rosas' successful campaign against the Indians. Rosas, a rancher with substantial landholdings, who had recently completed a successful first term as governor of Buenos Aires in what was then still a divided Argentina, had a strong rapport with his gaucho employees and they flocked to join his militia. There then followed a period of 'gauchesque' literature, led by José Hernández who wrote an epic poem in two parts entitled 'The Departure', then 'The Return', of a gaucho called Martín Fierro. Today most Argentine families own a leather-bound copy. In the language of that time, Martín Fierro and his fellow gauchos were

> Christians, shepherds, farmers and labourers: the most famous horsemen in the world: they are beings of noble and brave heart, of surprising intelligence: they are hospitable, temperate, and generous and habitués of such enormous rural areas, that they alone, have not been challenged by the incessant concurrence with immigration …

… and they were Argentine.

Martín Fierro—and indeed his horse—were the descendants of the sixteenth-century Spanish soldier-adventurer, mixed with Arab and native Indian. He adopted the Spanish guitar and the custom of song contests—*contra punto*—where one singer tries to out-improvise the other. Variations on the same theme can still be found in the impromptu lying contests, where the more improbable the lie the better, and in the card game *truco*, literally, trick. He wore a blanket skirt, *chiripa*, hitched up in front between the legs as a form of trousers, and carried a large double-edged knife, *facón*, with which grievances were settled, if necessary by killing, according to *buena ley*—good, i.e. gaucho, law. The gauchos of that time, identified completely with Martín Fierro, and adopted the poem and cultural code as their own.

Before long, the vast open pampas, over which the gaucho had roamed, were divided up and fenced into large *estancias*. Much of the reality and dress, and some of the rich vocabulary of Martín Fierro and his gauchos— which has always presented translation difficulties—disappeared. The *chiripa* was replaced by baggy trousers: *bombachas*. The *facón* shrank to dagger size, and rope-soled canvas shoes, *alpargatas*, were often preferred to the concertinaed leather boots. As the immigrants from East and West Europe flocked into the country and headed west, north and south, many adopted the traditions and lifestyle of the resident gaucho. Fifty years on from Martín Fierro, Ricardo Güiraldes, whose poem 'Mi hospitalidad' appears at the front of this book, also wrote his tribute to the tradition in *Don Segundo Sombra*, the tale of a young boy's apprenticeship to Don Segundo, from whom he learns the art of living according to the gaucho principles: 'patience in the face of adversity, endurance, the vocation and pursuit of freedom, self-discipline, prudence, loyalty.'

Inevitably, many gauchos fell short of such romantic ideals, and there were those, not least the rich *huasos*, who believed them to be uncouth, coarse, sly, tricky, violent and vengeful (and Argentine). Nonetheless, and in keeping with those the world over who make their living in solitary, isolated and often unbelievably harsh conditions, generous hospitality and discourse and sharing of scarce resources remain key elements of the gaucho code, from which my eventual guide and I were to benefit repeatedly.[6]

Just as the Indian absorbed the horse, so the culture of the *caballo* has absorbed much that was Indian. When the Spanish first arrived, the Mapuche numbered over a million and occupied an area of Patagonia extending across the Andes into Argentina. In their Mapundungun language, *mapu* meant the earth, their land, and *che* the people. There were also many subdivision tribes, whose names denoted their geographical relationship to the central territory of the Mapuche: the Puelche, the tribes to the east, and those to the south, the Huilliche. With the arrival of the

---

[6] The far from romantic reality of today's Aysén gaucho is described graphically in Nick Reding's *The Last Cowboys at the End of the World: The Story of the Gauchos of Patagonia*, published by Three Rivers, NY, in 2001.

conquistadors, who were never to advance beyond the River Bío Bío, an element of Spanish crept in to the Arribanos in the highlands, and the Abajinos, those below. Today, total Mapuche numbers—now including many of mixed blood—have barely reduced, but only an estimated 15 percent still occupy their original rural *mapu*, where language and traditional communities (*lof*), leaders temporal (*lonco/lonko*) and spiritual (*machi*) can be maintained. The rest are scattered through the cities and towns of Chile and Argentina, often struggling to make a living and encouraged by racial prejudice to hide their cultural identity.[7]

Although the sixteenth-century invasion of the Incas from Peru was unsuccessful in extending beyond the Bío Bío, a surprising number of Quechua words have survived in both Spanish and Mapuche vocabularies. They include *Aucca*, enemy, from which Araucania and 'araucanisation stem'; *Huinca* or *Winka* foreign robber, a word both the Mapuche and the Tehuelche applied to 'white' Spaniards; *Wakcha* or *huacha*, meaning orphan or someone who does not belong to a community; *Huasu*, an animal's back or something/body which is rough or rustic; and even *Chilli*—where the land ends.

Curiously, therefore, the national symbols of *huaso* and gaucho not only have their origin in the language of Indians, who have repeatedly sought to maintain their independence, but are both identified as orphans, rustics or those who do not belong to a community.

Curiosity and some confusion extend further over the origins of the word *Che*—perhaps the one word which, even today, most identifies Argentina, being Argentine and/or gaucho. Between 1869 and 1914 the

---

[7] It is possible that the largely peaceful process by which the Mapuche 'araucanised' the northern Tehuelche in Argentina over-extended their culture, since it brought about a rare concensus between Argentina and Chile that they had a common indian problem which required a common policy of extermination. It was as inevitable that they would defend their culture and mapu with their legendary courage,even against the combined forces and modern weaponry of two countries, as it was that they would lose, but they are still paying the price. In recent years, there have been many official declarations of support in both Argentina and Chile for their indigenous population, but a significant lack of implementation. Associations have been formed but too often they have been undermined both internally and externally, and the strength of traditional communities has been diluted. There have been many protests by Mapuche communities and families against the effect of hydroelectric projects, aerial spraying, land title allocation and forced eviction, and although publicity and support now extend beyond the continent, their opponents have tended to be large corporations or landowners with greater local political and legal clout. There are significant differences between the Mapuche and the Kogi – history, numbers, areas of influence, passivity, status (The Kogi's land was nominated a national reserve in 1977 and a UNESCO Biosphere Reserve), but they have many cultural similarities based on centuries of occupation,knowledge and understanding of the essences of their mapu/ aluna, and they face similar problems. They are still being denied recognition that the original people of the Andes have earned special rights.

majority of those immigrants to Buenos Aires who raised the population from 180,000 to over 1.5 million came from Italy and Spain, where *Che* was bread and butter to their vocabulary, a word for all seasons. Yet the same word is also as significantly Mapuche i.e. Indian if not Chilean, and the Mapuche have been in South America centuries before either Spaniard or Italian.

As our journey was to reveal, the majority of the original settlers in Patagonia were of Chilean origin, and those who did not originate from the island of Chiloë came from central Chile—*huaso* country. With a border at stake and Indian campaigns still fresh, Buenos Aires labelled the Chilean settlers as Indians, with the inference that they were therefore thieves or bandits, as indeed, some of them were or had become. After the border resolution in 1902, into which time the Welsh introduced a genuinely foreign element, some settlers crossed back into Chile, while others stayed in Argentina. Some Argentines crossed into Chile, often earning themselves the same label their government had applied to the Chileans. Some were trapped by border changes, others were forced to return to their country of origin. In time, Argentine mixed with Chilean, and both mixed with Indian, European, North African, Arab with Jew, Jew with Christian. Two factors united them—their struggle for survival, and the *caballos* upon which they all depended but ultimately sought to dominate to emphasise their superiority—and they donned the black beret as their common identity.

The creation or acceptance of national symbols belongs to the capitals, but in the case of both *huaso* and gaucho Patagonian reality, culture and history have been airbrushed out. The rich *huasos* and literary gauchos have each 'cleaned up' their orphans into the national *caballero* symbols of two proud nations.

On my short flight due south from Bariloche to Esquel, and as the white fist of Mount Tronador slipped out of sight, a history map of half-remembered names unfolded below. Lakes Mascardi, Steffen and Sunica; the small towns of Foyel, El Bolsón (formerly Valle Nuevo), Epuyén, Cholila, Trevelin (formerly Colonia 16 de Octubre); and finally Esquel itself—a Tehuelche name meaning both 'place of thistles' and 'bog'. Now there was a subtle change in the line of the cordillera to the west. No longer a fortress of rock with wide battlements, there were still distant peaks, but they stood out in isolation from a lower rock chain into which large green areas intruded, some split by the silver threads of rivers. I was witnessing one of the phenomena of the Andes, but from a viewpoint denied to the nineteenth-century boundary experts.

Far below me and over a hundred years previously, 30 April 1902 had been declared a local holiday in the small settlement of Colonia 16 de Octubre, and the settlers, the majority of whom were Welsh, were awaiting the arrival of a cavalcade of important visitors who were travelling on horseback south from Bariloche. The settlers emanated from a group of some 150 Welsh-speaking adventurers, who had arrived with such high hopes and expectations on a desolate Atlantic coast in 1865. Twenty titanic years of struggle later, thirty of them crossed the continent, to arrive at Colonia on 25 November 1885. Now well established, they were all dressed in their Sunday best—heads covered with caps, hats or bonnets, boots and shoes polished—and had made their way on horseback or in horse-drawn sulkies from their surrounding homes to the thatched village school, where the headmaster Owen Williams had prepared a show. The guest of honour was to be the Englishman, Colonel (later Sir) Thomas Hungerford Holdich, who, as one of the three Arbitrators, had come to inspect and ultimately resolve the disputed frontier. He was accompanied by the Chilean and Argentine boundary experts, Hans Steffen and Francisco Moreno, and members of each country's boundary commissions.

The visitors spent that night at the Estancia La Florida, where a large Argentine flag had been hung over a 'Welcome' sign. The owner, *comisario* and Justice of the Peace, Martin Underwood, one of the largest and most successful local landowners and, not coincidentally, a long-standing friend and admirer of 'Perito' Moreno, had prepared his fellow settlers well and ensured a maximum attendance. Meanwhile, inside the school, lines of tables and benches had been laid out and decked with an abundance of small Argentine and British flags, and the end wall was dominated by another large Argentine flag and a map. Similar examples of affinity to Chile were conspicuous by their absence. An 1895 national census had revealed that of 298 inhabitants, 56 per cent were Welsh, the rest mainly Chilean or 'araucanian' (*sic*), and the following year, Chubut's governor reported that 103 Chileans from '16th October' and 24 from adjoining areas had applied for consents, 'thereby recognising Argentine authority'.

In his long report to the frontier Arbitration Tribunal, Holdich wrote that he was 'deeply impressed with the strong national sentiment which pervaded the whole community ... their obvious loyalty to their adopted government [Argentina] and the general air of content and prosperity which prevailed amongst them.' He had also noted the large number of Chilean settlers in the region and that markets for local produce were in Chile. For Holdich and his colleagues, the most difficult and delicate problem they faced was that of communication. 'How was Chile to take effective possession of territory to which she had no roads and to which it seemed possible that no roads could readily be made?'

Both Moreno and Steffen were well aware of this problem, and during the run-up to the visit Chile had made desperate efforts to establish a road to the area from the Pacific. The conditions encountered were appalling, and Holdich's own conclusion that there was little probability that a road would be built proved to be accurate, and once the urgency of the Tribunal had passed, all work on the road was abandoned.

Ultimately, and while no less a triumph for Argentina than it was a bitter blow for Chile, it was no real surprise to those present that all the valleys—Foyel, El Bolsón, Cholila, Percey and 16 de Octubre—were awarded to Argentina. The Welsh had made their crucial choice.

To the west and across the new border, my destination Futaleufú, had not been founded officially until 1929, with the arrival of a group of surveyors to mark out the streets and plots, and the first *carabinero* or policeman. The latter's wages had to be paid in Argentine currency because the Chilean alternative had no local value. Three years later, and with the support of farmers and businesses in Esquel and Trevelin and Chilean pioneers and Futaleufú residents, work restarted on the road to the Pacific. All contributed in cash to the project, with the latter also providing labour, food and materials, but notwithstanding a visit to Santiago from the head of the Welsh community in Trevelin, it was the Chilean government who were to pull out of the project on the grounds that the Argentine presence was a threat to Chilean sovereignty in such an isolated area. It was to take a further fifty years before Futaleufú was finally linked by road to Chaitén, and another twenty or so before I arrived on my particular journey.

Before 1929, and apart from the Argentine Army—whose presence was justified officially in terms of national defence but in fact, also to promote territorial claims—there were few police and no passport control, with the consequence that the frontier between Nahuel Huapi and the valleys was to attract more than its fair share of lawlessness, bandits and official corruption along its entire length. Among the bandits or *pistoleros* was one group who had gained previous notoriety in Wyoming as the Wild Bunch and who have subsequently acquired an even greater fame among international readers and cinema goers. Attracted by the success tales of the Newberys, Jarred Jones, Crockett and their Texan cowboys, and escaping the Pinkerton Detective Agency, four members of the gang travelled via Punta Arenas to Patagonia where they re-formed as the Black Jack gang. They were Enrique Place (otherwise Henry Longbaugh (*sic*), James Ryan (otherwise Jorge Parker or Cassidy), Bob Evans, and a woman, Ellen Place (otherwise Della Rose or Laura Bovillon) and they were joined later by former members of the 'Wild Bunch', William Wilson, Harvey Logan (otherwise Andrew Duffy), a Chilean Juan Vidal and an Argentine, Manuel Gibbons. Each was an excellent shot and rider and spoke Spanish.[8] True to the Patagonian tradition, their names or aliases were as numerous as the subsequent versions of their exploits.

From 1903, James Ryan and Enrique and Ellen Place worked land—some 12,000 acres—they purchased in Cholila, building a house, driving cattle across into Chile and setting up a *boliche* (pub). In so doing, they earned the respect and friendship of their neighbours, including the Newberys and Jarred Jones, and even provided hospitality to the Chubut governor. Locally, neighbours helped out in return for Enrique's services as a horse trainer. Today's world knows the three as Butch Cassidy and the Sundance Kid and Ellen Place as Etta. The latter impressed the locals with her riding and marksmanship. It is reported that she handled men as well as she did horses, and could shoot a pistol out of another's hand or cut telegraph wires with one bullet.

There is general consensus that between 1905 and 1911 members of the gang were associated with a number of incidents in various parts of Patagonia, bringing a largely unwelcome notoriety to the area, whose problems many thought to have been eliminated by the Indian wars and resolution of the frontier. It was the kidnapping of Luis Ramos or Ramos Luis Otero by 'north American' bandits in March 1911 that brought matters to a head. By this time, it seems that Butch Cassidy, the Sundance Kid and Etta had already left the country for either Bolivia or the USA, and that the main perpetrators were Wilson, Evans, Vidal and Gibbons

One version of Otero's time in captivity—after he had been forced to write a letter to his mother asking her to pay £120,000 for his release—was that he and his companion were kept in a deep hole dug on land belonging to the Solis family of Lago Verde—where I was headed—the entrance being sealed with ropes and rawhide. A rat fell into the hole and Otero trapped it under his hat where it was kept for several days.

---

[8]   There are several recent sources related to Butch Cassidy. Bruce Chatwin draws on an account by Ascencio Abeijon (1973-75). A different but largely consistent version appeared five years later in Emilio Ferro's *La Patagonia inconclusa: relatos de un viejo poblador patagónico*. References here are to the Ferro version. Members of the Black Jack gang, probably Wilson and Evans, also killed Llwyd ap Iwan, one of the most respected members of the Welsh colony and a noted explorer, when attempting to rob his office on 29 December 1909. In Chatwin's account of the shoot-out on 1 December 1911, it is suggested that, Wilson, 'the crack shot', was in fact the Sundance Kid, that the man called Evans was an English member of the gang, and that Butch Cassidy ultimately escaped to return to the USA. Another version has Wilson committing suicide rather than face arrest. The jury is still out, and first hand witnesses are no longer alive. The time must soon be approaching for yet another version of the film.

By then famished with hunger, it was set to work chewing through the rope. Eventually one chewed rope end dropped down allowing them to escape. The fate of the rat is not recorded. Another version has Otero using a match dropped by one of his captors to set fire to the leather straps holding their wooden cage prison together.

Otero's family were well connected in the capital, and while Otero himself was fortunate to escape at least with his life, the incident tipped his already unbalanced mind over the edge and attracted the attention of the Argentine president Roque Sáenz Peña, who ordered the creation of the Frontier Police of Chubut to bring law and order to the region. The force, which came to be known as the 'Flying Police', had an Austrian major, Mateo Gebhart, in command and a Welsh settler, Milton Roberts, as his commissioner, and was made up of a mixed bag of nationalities who were required to be good marksmen and horsemen. Few other questions were asked, and their orders were simply 'to pursue the bad'.

Initially the Flying Police demanded documents, *papeletas*. Since few had any form of identity, an informal census was imposed on the inhabitants of the Argentine province of Chubut, and the queues to obtain documentation were to stretch some distance out of the provincial capital Comodoro Rivadavia, on the Atlantic coast. Those who protested or resisted, with or without *papeletas*, were given ten blows or *sablazos* with a sheathed sword. A Spanish travelling salesman who denied that he was either criminal or fugitive and protested that he would complain to his Consul, was given a further twenty *sablazos* for good measure and told to make his complaint. Another man, who was patrolling a telegraph line, took fright when he saw the police approach and tried to escape. He was caught and handed over his papers but was so terrified that he was unable to explain himself. While the blows rained down, Gebhart checked the documents before ordering his men to stop. 'We can't take the blows back, but they will stand to your credit next time.'

If the Flying Police came across anyone with a criminal record, he was a dead man, and his corpse was dragged to the nearest river or precipice. José Pozzi, a noted robber, was shot four times but refused to reveal his accomplices.

'Then you die.'

The fact that Pozzi's response, 'See if I care', was recorded, suggests that at least one otherwise impotent witness was impressed.

Of those fortunate to survive, over fifty 'bandits or rustlers' were handed to the gendarmerie. It was not until 1 December 1911 that a patrol caught up with members of the Black Jack gang in Rio Pico. Eight days later and having crawled to within 25 yards of the gang's camp, they were spotted and the gang opened fire. Two of the police were wounded by

Evans, who in turn was shot whilst trying to escape. Wilson, who had an injury to his left hand, tried to escape into the nearby woods, but he too was chased down and shot. The rest of the gang escaped and mysteriously disappeared.

In that lawless time and region, women were scarce. Etta impressed all with her 'amazon' qualities, her riding and marksmanship, and one neighbour described her as dressing like a man, cutting her hair very short and using a wig. There appears to be no record that she ever knew or met Helen Greenhill Beckar, otherwise 'La Inglesa', born in Yorkshire in 1875, who came to Patagonia with her parents when she was fifteen. Elena, as she came to be known, quickly learned to survive in a lawless and predominately macho land. Tall and slender, she dressed as a *huaso* in black baggy trousers (*bombachas*), knee length boots, Chilean spurs, short jacket and poncho, and wore a wide brimmed hat to hide her golden hair and a bandanna to cover her nose and mouth. Apart from the rifle under her saddle, she also carried a pistol in her blouse. She too acquired a notoriety as a marksman, rider and companion of men, but none of them had the kudos of a Butch Cassidy or Sundance Kid, and tales of 'La Inglesa' and her no less extraordinary life have attracted less attention.

Her parents set up a cattle business in a small Chilean village, and while still living in Chile Elena married Manuel de la Cruz Astete, a trader in Argentine Patagonia and twenty years older than her, and they moved across the border. Her first child Armando was born in 1898 and was joined two years later by Cesar Eulogio. It seems that Manuel soon became involved in minor rustling and was arrested for stealing a steer during a roundup in Chile, but in 1904 the body of a man in his fifties was found and reported to the police. The man was Manuel and he had been beaten to death. Eight months later, Elena Greenhill, a widow aged thirty, married Martin Coria, 34, the son of a cattleman from Patagones. No arrests were made relating to Manuel's death, but it seems to have been regional common knowledge that Coria—probably encouraged by Elena—was responsible.

The police did become involved, however, in enquiries over allegations that Coria had forced another widow, Mercedes Sifuentes de Jara to sign an authority over her cattle, which he had then sold, pocketing the proceeds. The local Inspector visited the Coria house to arrest Elena in her husband's absence, but was disarmed with one rifle shot, and the patrol ran off, leaving two of their members behind as prisoners. These two were then put to work for several days, cleaning out the Coria house. Soon afterwards, Elena was taking *mate* with a neighbour while Coria chatted to three of his men in an adjoining room. Suddenly there was a shout.

'No one move.'

A police patrol under the command of the same Inspector and accompanied by two cattlemen, who had been assaulted by Coria's men, and the brother of the widow Mercedes, had surrounded the house. They then opened fire, and a shootout continued until the police ran out of ammunition, whereupon Coria sent out a *peon* (labourer) with a message. Since the peon happened to be a deaf mute, it is unclear how the message was to be communicated, but the Inspector was persuaded to enter the house and was to remain there—effectively as a prisoner—until morning.

Coria then immediately lodged a complaint with the police, maintaining that he had been the victim of an unprovoked attack—that after an order 'Not to move', the police had opened fire and he and his men had been obliged to return fire to defend the children: two of his own and three of the visiting neighbour. It was a clear abuse of authority.

Given that the authorities extracted from the widow Mercedes had been obtained at gun point, Coria showed a rare bravado and cheek by adding that, when asked to show them to the Inspector, he had done so, and that the Inspector had then spent the rest of the night drinking in his house. The neighbour was later to back him by agreeing that the Corias had been obliged to shoot.

Similar incidents involving allegations of rustling and armed intimidation were to continue, until Coria fell ill and travelled to Buenos Aires for treatment. At the beginning of October 1914, came news of his death at the age of 43 and after nine years of marriage. Elena could not live without either animals or men, and a few months later she joined up with Martin Taborda, sending Armando (18) and Cesar Eulogio (16) away to Buenos Aires. Ignoring the ill feeling she and Coria had generated throughout the province with both the police they had kidnapped and humiliated, and the cattlemen (large and small) they had assaulted and robbed, she and Taborda set off for Chubut to buy land.

Elena Greenhill, aged 42, widow of Coria, was on her knees washing clothes at Laguna Fria when Sub-Inspector Felix Valenciano and agent Norberto Ruiz, both dressed as civilians, spotted her and shot her in the back, once in the lung and once in the back of her neck. Taborda was also shot but escaped, only to be captured after a long chase.

Valenciano and Ruiz were accused of murder and sent to prison for a year, but released shortly afterwards. They were, after all, brave policemen doing their duty. Before long, Valenciano was to chance his luck further by killing three shepherds, but the case against him was dismissed, and the two continued to ply their shady trade with the police forces of several provinces.

Elena left her children a large flock of sheep and authority to recover all moneys owed, which surprisingly—given the environment and the character of her murderers—was to include the 11,000 *pesos* she was carrying with her to purchase land. In her defence, it is said that she merely joined in the prevailing practice of mixing cattle or moving fences to include stock or land belonging to others, and it seems unlikely that she would have been interested in the fascinating tales she left behind her.

The Flying Police brought some order to the region and established their authority, but in time they grew beyond regional and national control. Abuses of every form were committed against innocent settlers, who complained bitterly. Ultimately there was no alternative but to dissolve them. Major Gebhart, who had started out a *peon* on the Estancia Laguna Romero in the far south, was later appointed administrator of the Estancia Lago Posadas and ultimately died in Buenos Aires in 1914, just as his country of birth was entering the First World War.

Even after arbitration, politics at the frontier have proved to be a difficult horse to handle, particularly for those dressed in the uniform of authority. Border issues have continued to arise out of uniformed excesses and abuses, and those who have suffered most have been the settlers. At that time and for those drawn by their Chilean origin or affinity, the nearest crossing to Futaleufú was far from straightforward.

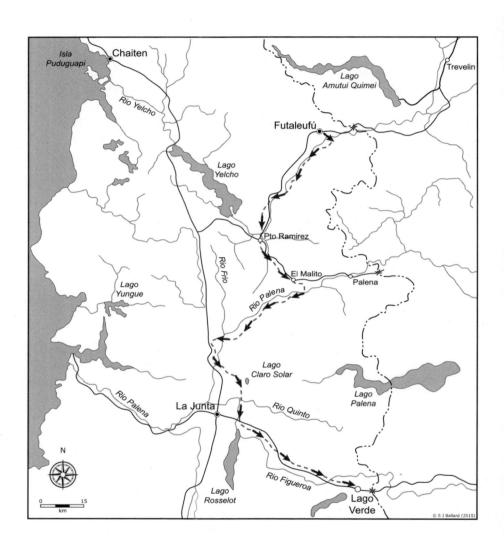

© S J Ballard (2015)

CHAPTER THREE

A Particular Journey: Futaleufú to Lago Verde

*I*n Trevelin, I reached the bus station just as the last of the few buses to the frontier was about to leave, and we were soon rattling our way down a red earth track away from a clean and modern town and past a succession of lush green fields, winding streams and willow clumps. Half of the dense cloud of dust we created plumed out behind while the remainder filled the inside of the bus. Through the red haze I caught glimpses of fat, contented cattle watching our progress, clearly unfazed by dust-making dervishes. Our destination was 'the green wall', originally some thirty miles but three days ride from Trevelin. Known as El Limite, the thickly wooded pass is barely wide enough to contain the mighty Rio Futaleufú (formerly Rio Grande), let alone the frontier. Eventually we were stopped at a barrier long enough to justify the existence of several bored Argentine frontier guards, before piling into a waiting pick-up truck and driving to a similar Chilean barrier. The experience left a feeling that, apart from the drivers everyone would have preferred us not to have bothered to come. I was also half expecting to meet the Moraga family.[1]

Legend has it that the Moragas were the first Chileans to enter El Limite, and that they built their house strategically at the meeting of the river and the mountains, and refused to share with anyone. When the parents died, their seven sons took over and put into effect a plan for dealing with would-be settlers. Visitors were invited to spend the night and regaled with glowing details of the land ahead, but by the next day they had disappeared, some of their bodies being found later floating downstream. Such a fate awaited two brothers called Ceballos, who came from Trelew to El Limite between 1919 and 1920, looking for land to settle. After months without news, other members of the Ceballos family came looking for their missing brothers, and having learned that they had been seen entering the Moragas' house, they knocked on the door and asked for lodgings. The next day, the bodies of two of the Moraga brothers were

---

[1]   Some versions call them 'Pichun'.

found in the river. The Ceballos were later arrested by the Argentine gendarmerie and taken to Puerto Montt for trial, but the pass was now open.

The first arrivals left an account of inhabitants dressed in skins to protect them from the rain, looking like savages as they struggled to clear spaces between the trees for their plants and animals. 'I lived five years in the woods. When we could make a clearing it was as if someone had taken my hat off and I could see the sky.'[2]

I was to find a small frontier town set out in the classic Spanish grid form of streets and squares. As is the custom in Patagonia, the houses were made of wood, mostly with corrugated iron roofs, each with its garden/vegetable plot at the side. There were earth streets, a central tree shaded square with the inevitable bust of General O'Higgins, a bank, a small school, general shops, lodging houses, two 'hotels', several small chapels and a police—*carabinero*—station. There was also a free email centre, where preference was given to local schoolchildren, and a local radio station. Horses vied with pick-up trucks and the occasional lorry, each throwing up clouds of dust, but everyone put their rubbish in the street bins and took an obvious pride in their community. They were also extremely friendly, anxious to be questioned but respecting any preference for privacy.

Mountains towered on every side and thick woods crowded the slopes to the snow line. The Rio Futaleufú, with a deserved reputation for kayaking and rafting, was a constant background presence, with rashes of yellow broom completing the visual palette.

A crash course in Mapuche taught me that Futaleufú meant 'Big River', and that names in general are formed of two parts. When applied to people, the first part gives the lineage, the family tree. The second imparts individuality, the surname. Thus, the Mapuche Chief Quilipan's name was created out of his father's feat of killing three pumas, and Chief Calfucura's name incorporated *Calfu* (blue) with *cura* (stone), the *curras* of the pampas. It is also possible that the *cura* may have reflected the magic meteorite stone which Calfucura carried with him, which could determine the truth and, when struck, could produce thunder, lightning and rain to order—a 19th century Margaret Thatcher handbag.

In Futaleufú, I met Hector my guide to be, and Jonathan, who was to select our horses. I bought two: Cuervo (Crow) and Rubia (Blondie) from Toribio Baeza Miranda for £175 each, and we signed up in the house which Toribio had built himself to a design by Hansel and Gretel. Independently, Hector bought a mare which we called Prudencia, but he kept details of

---

2   These included the Sepulveda brothers, Calixto Vega, Juan de la Rosa Baeza and Eulogio Espinoza.

the price to himself. We located the horses through the local radio station, which broadcast our requirements over a twenty-mile radius, the response being almost immediate. I also received help from the local police chief, Major Aldo Barrientos Vera, who gave me a letter addressed to all *carabineros* in the region, requesting their help in the event that we should need it.

My first introduction to a jet black Cuervo was to watch him crash through the corral railings followed by his harem of five mares, one of whom was Rubia. Somehow he appeared to have worked out that our arrival meant an end to a life of leisure. It was a short-lived freedom for the mares, but longer for him. Once lassoed, it took three hours to shoe him while he kicked hell out of even the wooden parallel bars between which he eventually had to be secured. After watching this, I suggested that perhaps Hector might like to ride him, but after two days as pack horse he had calmed down and thereafter became my sure footed, inquisitive but tame mount, companion and even friend.

Rubia was a beautiful but dumb blonde, whose descents of rocky cliff paths were to be full of drama, muttered equine abuse and extravagant gymnastics. She would be our preferred packhorse, but ultimately showed a remarkable passivity when facing the *tábanos*—horseflies—which were later to drive the other two to distraction.

Prudencia was named after a relative of my wife, who was always called to mind when a cautious approach was indicated. Since initially she was to be my mount, the intention was to send a reassuring message to my family, but on the second night she chewed through her halter and went home, and was only narrowly prevented from doing the same 24 hours later. Her schooling report might have suggested that she needed time to address her 'neurotic disposition'.

Each of our horses had two front white feet and a star on the forehead. I was assured that these were all good signs, and that four white feet was a sign of inferiority. In the Patagonian tradition, and provided one has no pretension to be a gaucho, there was little prejudice against mares—and we had two. Cuervo, Rubia and Prudencia were each Argentine *criollo*, but with Chilean accents. Cuervo and Prudencia probably had a threshing mare somewhere in their ancestry, and Rubia had been made to measure for a pint-sized Hector.

Jonathan's tasks included an introduction to the mysteries of packing, saddling and general handling of horses, preparation of dry bags, folding and storing large maps, camping, fire making and woodcraft. He was also a superb cook. His last supper would have graced any four star restaurant, and was so good that our hostess Isabel Castro's mouth remained open throughout the meal, while her husband's mild deafness suddenly became acute, possibly out of male pique. Jonathan also showed a deft human touch just as Hector and I were about to set off. He took me aside and said, 'There will be no long goodbyes. Just turn and ride out.'

He had sensed my anxiety and rightly anticipated a reluctance to do what had to be done. We had discussed the problem of maintaining contact via local radio stations and by leaving messages with truck drivers, and we knew there would be long periods when we would be out of contact. We had also discussed and agreed procedures in case of mishap and injury. He had even offered to lend me his dog for company, although I suspected the dog might have views of his own. And so finally we set off, to a chorus of Chilean yodels—but without the dog. Our next meeting was planned for Lago Verde, eight to ten days ride away, and accessible by a ten-hour truck drive from Jonathan's base in Coyhaique.

We had half a day left and almost immediately forded a succession of small rivers which were busier than any I had encountered in my 'training'. The horses took them with such ease that my confidence jumped to just below nonchalant and it was to stay there for the rest of the day. We continued down a slender valley which in parts barely contained the Rio Futaleufú. Some of the wider sections were cleared of trees, but their blackened stumps stood out against a lush green, occupied by lazy Hereford cattle and elegant, inquisitive horses. Other areas remained thickly wooded, with assorted species of giant beech, pine and oak, and paths rutted by the wooden wheels of ox-drawn log carts. Plumes of smoke trailed from the chimneys of occupied huts, and there was the distant sound of axe on wood.

In theory, where a river chokes a valley completely, there are three options: to turn back, to cross or to try to find a 'shoulder' out. In the case of the Futaleufú the first two were non-starters, and within two hours of our departure we were to have our first experience of the Patagonian rope trick at a place appropriately called Las Dificultades, where two local fence leaners suggested that we would be well advised to go on foot.

As I looked up a near vertical wall of rock however, my heart sank.

'We can't go up that, even on foot.'

Hector heard my thoughts and remembered the advice given.

'We'll go up on foot and lead the horses.'

The horses did not appear to disagree, and we dismounted. There was a path of sorts, formed of dynamited rock, which zigzagged upwards, just wide enough for a well fed horse—of which we had three—and with a sheer drop one side down to the river. After leaving the town which bears its name, the river gathers speed, width and ferocity. Indian names have been forgotten and stretches and bends have been re-stamped by modern kayakers. The Gates of Hell led into Hell Canyon. Zeta was followed by the Throne; both being Grade 5 plus in kayak terms. The Wild Mile crashed into the Terminator, then Khyber Pass and Himalayas. The Entrance was followed by The Pillow, Mundaca, Shark, More or Less and finally the brutal House of Stone. All this pent up energy, crammed into a length of approximately thirty miles, provided thrills and occasionally fatal spills during the summer months for those skilled kayakers with a return ticket to Santiago, North America or Europe. For the remainder of the year, the river resumed its traditional role of isolating Futaleufú from the rest of Patagonia. I wondered what names the Mapuche or Tehuelche might have chosen for the bends. Their neighbours on the coast, the Chonos, had their *dalcas* and legendary skills, but I doubted they would have seen the need to try them on such a river. Nor did they practise suicide until the white man arrived and opened his Pandora's Box of alcohol and disease.

Led by Hector on foot, the horses did not hesitate and surged upwards. The long climb was followed by an equally tortuous level section, where we crept round the mountain wall along a narrow ledge and into the next valley. Yet another wall spider creep, and we then started our descent. The mares slithered and farted their way down. Cuervo placed each foot carefully and securely and went at his own pace. I used hands, feet, back and backside, and was a long way behind when finally we reached the woods.

Our first night was spent in that valley, close to the river. Señor Mesa farmed some 900 acres, which, he explained with a series of sharp karate chops, meant across and up both sides of the valley.

He had been savaging tree stumps with an axe when we met, and he managed to explain that this was not only therapeutic but ecologically sound, without using either word. He had spent his early life in Argentina as a gaucho, and watched intently as we unloaded the horses, put up our tents and set our fire. He recognised and appreciated our traditional saddlery, particularly our pack horse system, but declined an invitation to share in a busted carton of wine.

'Ulcers,' he explained.

Instead of the wooden cross-tree frame which some pack-saddlers prefer, our dry bags were compressed between a pair of large circular frames made of wire. The frames resembled over-sized toasters, save that the wire was bound with leather. Each pair of toasters was then linked to the other with rawhide straps. After ensuring that the weight of each pair was approximately equal, they were slung across the horse, so that one hung down on each side. Several sheepskins protected the horse's back, and two leather tubes packed with tough grass kept the toasters from rubbing on the flanks. It was a simple, time-proven system.

Señor Mesa was back stump savaging when the sun rose and we were sipping our coffee. He explained that further progress up the valley was impossible, and that we would have to take the 'third option' of crossing the river. Noting my concern, he added that we could do so by way of a small suspension bridge—a *pasarela*. We could then continue on down the other side of the river to the next settlement at Puerto Ramirez.

No hay problema—no problem—is a familiar phrase throughout Latin America, but despite knowing that its use has little regard for reality, it rarely failed to bring comfort. In fact, we knew of the bridge's existence, but not where it was. Our travel policy was evolving. Our maps were our guide, and the local people our confirmation. Hector was the horse expert and could read paths where I could see none, but he also seemed to know someone who was known or related to virtually everyone we met. The fact that he did not know this part of Chile was never to prove an obvious disadvantage. Importantly, he was also a good cook and wanted to do the trip almost as much as I did.

The ride from Señor Mesa to Puerto Ramirez took us two days, and taught me to hate roads or tracks bearing any form of traffic. Roads, walked or ridden, gravel or (occasionally) tarmac, always seemed straighter and longer, and progress had to be assessed against the next bend or brow. I preferred to be surprised and also to ride on soft grass. Cuervo shared my dislike of traffic, and showed his feelings by rearing and bucking whenever a vehicle appeared. Either reaction tested my ability to stay on board. Hector therefore developed a plan of shielding us with the other horses, although we were not always close enough to make this successful.

'Grip tight with the knees and hold the reins short,' was the advice.

However, the knees were not yet always up to it. I could manage a maximum of two hours in the saddle before suggesting a short break. Thighs, knees, back and neck all complained, and a sore coccyx caused trouble until a new use and location were found for circular toe blister plasters.

Our second night brought a first experience of the dreaded *tábanos*, the large horseflies. January was their favourite month, and they attacked in swarms from dawn to dusk. Their main targets were the horses, whose manes and tails could only swish so far. The neck, chest and legs suffered most, and there was a limit to the number of times a horse could stamp its foot or direct a twitch or tremor to the appropriate spot. For the rider, too, there was a limit to the number of *tábanos* that could be pinched, slapped or crushed, and my hands were soon stained with Cuervo's blood. On higher ground they suddenly disappeared, but they were to be a constant irritant, and when they could not find a horse, a human was an acceptable alternative. Hector told me that they had been known to drive horses mad, and it was therefore less surprising to find the next morning that Prudencia had bitten through her halter and gone home. Hector eventually managed to obtain a lift back to Futaleufú to find her, and later that day he galloped her back down the road bareback. He had been rather shamefaced when he left, but reappeared with a broad grin, and it had cost us only half a day.

The Rio Futaleufú was never far away and we crossed and re-crossed by bridge several times, before it turned off into Lago Yelcho, famous for its trout, leaving us to crunch our way into the six-hut settlement which is Puerto Ramirez. The equivalent of a large village green was our next camping site, with a new and gentler river nearby. The days had been very hot and our water consumption ran into gallons. This, in turn, increased the number of 'pit stops', but despite never mastering that smooth mount so favoured in the TV Westerns, I was acquiring a certain proficiency both in mounting and sliding off with the help of a large log or boulder, and Cuervo was picking up the routine.

Eighty-five years previously, Alfredo Cid was one of the first to travel from Futaleufú to Chaiten via Puerto Ramirez, which then had no name. When he and his colleagues tried to cross Lago Yelcho in a makeshift boat, they foundered in mid lake but managed to reach an island where they were to spend 41 days marooned while they tried to build another boat. Just as they reached a point when cannibalism was becoming a serious option, a young couple, fleeing from an authoritarian father, passed by in another boat with a pig and some poultry. Spotting Alfredo Cid and his colleagues, they stopped to help. The pig's prospects immediately slumped to zero, and ultimately due to his sacrifice they all reached Chaitén safely. The total journey took Cid and his friends two months.

Hector and I had a long way to go to Lago Verde, and for a while we switched direction east back towards the frontier. The Rio Palena, much wider than the Futaleufú, blocked our route south. The only way across it was by ferry. Once across the river, we proposed to double back to the west until we met a southbound valley. The next morning however, Prudencia made her second—and final—break for home, this time without the excuse of the *tábanos*. Fortunately Cuervo was already saddled up, and Hector enjoyed his second gallop in as many days to bring her back. He explained that homesickness can affect horses for over a year, and their memory is such that they can retrace their route exactly, even at night. But he assured me: 'She'll give up once we cross the Palena.'

Our next objective was the ferry, marked by a small dot on our map and bearing the name El Malito. First we had to complete a long climb and longer descent through narrow valleys. Fences prevented us from leaving the unmade road, and the heat, dust and monotonous crunch of horse-shoe on stone detracted from the rugged beauty of the mountain ranges on either side. It was a relief to break out into open country, where the motor horn 'clonking' of the golden ibis (*bandurrias*) and even the strident calls and dive-bombing habits of the plovers were a welcome diversion. I recalled that to the English poacher, plovers and jays are a nightmare, with their constant alarm cry, which gamekeepers recognise immediately as evidence of an intruder.

A seven hour slog took us the fifteen miles to El Malito, where we enjoyed a shared kitchen and supper with the young owner of a two-room hut beside the river, before falling into our tents. No fire preparations in the morning meant an earlier start, and it was not long before we reached the chain ferry crossing the Rio Palena. In contrast to the Futaleufú with its white turbulence, the Palena was a slumbering blue giant. There was no mistaking its volume and power, which sped us across to the other side, but the horses embarked and disembarked with no sign of concern. Although Prudencia gave no indication that she might now regard her route home as closed, the ferryman promised to hold her if she should try.

To the east and up river, lay the frontier settlement of Palena, otherwise Alto Palena, which, with no easy connection to our route south, we had decided to miss. Under the 1902 Arbitration, Lago Palena had been cut in half, leaving Chile with the upper valleys, which in turn were to form part of a huge land concession transferred to the Anglo-Chilean Pastoral Company. Even more isolated from Chile than Futaleufú, its first settlers were in fact mostly Argentine, with close connections across the new border. Following Arbitration, the local settlers were to be subjected to over sixty years of harassment, with heightened tension and uncertainty. The Chilean president was forced to issue a public denial of the maps of his own respected Instituto Geográfico Militar, and the Argentine gen-darmerie repeatedly defied presidential directions. Only in 1966, when a British resolution under the original Arbitration process backed the Chilean claim, was the matter put to bed and peace finally brought to the area—a peace which, with our other priorities, neither Hector nor I had any wish to disturb.

Stretching back to the distant west, away from Alto Palena, was the Tranquilo valley, and for the rest of that day we meandered down a piece of Patagonian paradise. Lush green grass, grazed to parkland perfection by roaming cattle, was broken by standings of blue and pink lupins. The valley sides leant back to increase the sense of openness, and instead of blackened stumps, the trees were lime coloured willows and poplars. Down one side ran the metallic blue ribbon of the river, and in the distance the white peaks of the Cordón Blanco touched the sky. The ibises and plovers were now joined by several varieties of hawks, which hovered, swooped or simply sat on fence posts. None were deterred by the presence of three horses or their cargo. Neither poacher nor gamekeeper, we simply did not exist.

It took us some time to find a small *pasarela* over a subsidiary to the Palena, where we had been told we needed to cross. Initially the horses were against the idea, even when we tried to lead them. Unlike the solid constructions we had crossed previously, this was decidedly rustic, and looking at the rusted wire supports, we shared the horses' concern, but there was no alternative. The combined rivers had narrowed at this point, and instead of a bloated surge there were now breakers, waves and boulders. Hector and I tied up the horses and edged our way over. The boards were buckled and the bridge dipped and swayed alarmingly. If Cuervo could be persuaded to cross, Rubia must follow, and surely Prudencia would not wish to be left behind.

Cuervo was nervous, but allowed me to lead him on to the bridge. Just as I felt he had decided to cross, he put a foot on a plank end which reared up. He snorted and backed away, but the bridge was too narrow for him to turn. It dipped and swayed and I wondered which side we would go over.

'Hold the reins shorter!' Hector shouted.

I also remembered to tshhh, tshhh, tshhh in his ear. His eyes and ears told me what he was thinking, but gradually the swaying and dipping stopped, and he calmed enough to put another foot forward, this time across a plank which stayed put. We inched up the slope, across the middle and then down to the other side. Rubia followed with her customary flurry of legs and theatrics and, as we had hoped, Prudencia preferred our company to her own.

We spent the next hour wandering along faint woodland trails, unsure which one to follow. I was beginning to despair that we would never find our next destination, when we heard voices. Many of the aches and pains went on hold as we emerged onto a large clearing, at the back of which stood a wooden building with a large Chilean flag fluttering overhead. We had reached La Mula, the site of a small isolated school for local farm children.

Our original plan had been to cut south from La Mula and on down the Rio Tranquilo, a route which looked as green and promising on our maps as the valley we had just ridden. Local enquiries, however, revealed that such a route was impossible. The river was too high, no one lived there and no one had been all the way down for many years. Neither Hector nor I were planning to blaze trails. We had only one machete with which to cut a path, often through impenetrable clumps of bamboo, and neither of us was keen on running the risk of losing our sense of direction by constantly having to double back. The only viable alternative was to try to reach the bottom end of the Tranquilo river by riding round the obstacle, but this meant travelling first west, then south and finally east, a diversion likely to cost us two extra days.

We made good progress the next day, meandering through woodlands and crossing our constant companion the Palena by a series of *pasarelas* before struggling up the first of a series of valley break-outs. Cuervo picked his way over tree roots, through bogs, up and over shining rock ladders and down fissured slopes. He did not slip but slid deliberately. Every step was measured and the *pasarelas* were now mere interludes. From the high ground, the Palena looked so still and peaceful, occasional clearings so manicured, and the wisps of rising mist so like smoke, that it was hard to believe we were miles from anywhere.

The saddle sores had gone, but as daylight began to fade the pain in both hips became more difficult to ignore, and as we came out of the umpteenth descent and saw a woman trying to herd a cow and several rebellious calves, I knew it was time to stop.

The cow and several of the calves suddenly broke away and fled. Hector wheeled Prudencia and set off after them, while I tried to help direct the remainder into a corral. Cuervo knew what he was doing, and despite my involvement we completed our task, as Hector brought back the others and closed the gate on them all. The woman, showing an awareness of us for the first time, then invited us to camp in the shade of the corral, and after we had completed our chores, pitched our tents and washed our feet in an adjoining stream, the invitation was extended to cooking supper in her kitchen. Our relief was huge. No fires that night or the next morning, but our supplies were low, and according to the woman, we were at least ten hours' ride, or one long day at our pace, from the nearest store.

'I am Sara. I have some eggs, but I was keeping them for Christmas, when the children come home.'

She then promptly forgot her plans, offering us ten—rather more than half of what she had—and waving our protests aside. She explained that a daughter, aged ten, was boarding in Palena and a son, aged seven, was boarding at the La Mula school.

'I used to take my daughter to school each day,' she said, 'but it got too much.'

Palena lay well beyond the chain ferry, and it had taken us a day and a half to reach her farm.

The wooden hut where Sara lived was small but warm. The main room was dominated by the inevitable wood-burning stove; the furniture limited to a table and several chairs, and the walls undecorated, save for a clock and a calendar. A small annexe by the entrance served as a pantry and store. Another door led off the kitchen to a sink, and then to two small bedrooms. Outside, a flock of geese played in the stream, which supplied water to the sink via a plastic pipe, and a queue of chickens, ducks, calves and foals waited their turn for food or bottle. The windows and entrance door faced south to steep wooded slopes and snow-topped peaks. To the north lay the remains of several ancient, handmade, wooden, wheeled implements, the vegetable patch, corrals and, far below and beyond, the Rio Palena.

A hawk which had been watching the geese slid off his pine perch and swooped at them. The gander was the first to flee to the safety of the barn, the others following in a gaggle of noisy protest, as a brown and white piebald horse came over the hill. The rider dismounted, tied and unsaddled his horse, and after a while inside the barn came over towards us. He showed no surprise at seeing us, but took our extended hands in turn and walked into the annexe, where he left his hat and boots before waving us into the kitchen. The kettle was on the stove and within minutes, he was extending his *mate* with his right hand. This was Mario—not Sara's husband, as we first assumed—but her brother. His piebald mount was one of seven he had reared, and of which he was justly proud. Our report on the hawk and the geese was dismissed as old news.

That evening and thanks to Hector's cooking skills, all four of us enjoyed a three course feast combining our soup, the remains of our rice and Sara's free-range eggs. Conversation continued in candle light, over countless sips of *mate* and long into the night.

Mate, pronounced 'mattay', is both the herbal tea and the gourd in which it is served. The tea is sucked through a silver 'straw' with a bulb-ended colander. The routine, to which sharing is the key, varies from district to district, as do the shape and decoration of the gourds. The host prepares the herb in the gourd and then pours in boiling water. The temperature has to be right. The silver straw is placed in the gourd and the herbal tea sucked through it. Temperature and taste are tested first by the host, and the gourd refilled and handed with the right hand to one of the guests, who receives it without comment, also with the right hand. Having sucked his fill, the guest hands it back to the host, without commenting on its quality and without moving or stirring the colander in the herb. The process is continued until all the guests have had their turn, or a recipient says *gracias*. This is the signal that they have had enough, and no more is offered.

To a stranger, the herb is bitter and an acquired taste, but with recognised stimulant and diuretic qualities. Its use and the protocol attached are an important element of companionship, conversation and acceptance of visitors throughout Patagonia, and no one mentions hygiene.

Mario and Sara's grandfather had settled the land, and while he was alive this included all the land we had crossed back to La Mula. It had been he who had donated the land to the school, and a cousin who had given us permission to camp there. Another cousin had been the ferryman who had taken us across the Palena. Some years back, the grandfather had been drowned with the two grandchildren he was trying to save as they crossed the Palena in winter. This last piece of information was given without any change of emphasis or tone and so naturally that I struggled to keep my reactions to myself. To encourage the flow of the conversation, my national instincts came up with a question about the weather, and I asked Mario about the winters.

'They're pretty bad. Last year, we lost 48 sheep in the snow.'

Again, the tone and simplicity of the statement gave nothing away, but the preciseness of the head count hinted at the extent of the disaster and invited the question: 'What happened to the rest?'

'That was all we had, apart from the cattle and horses.'

'What about them?'

'They were OK, but we had two prize bulls. They went up into the foothills, up near the snow line to avoid the snow. We didn't see them again and thought they had gone too, but last year one of them appeared and stood up there.'

He pointed out of the window to the wooded slopes to the south of the house.

'He was there all day, just looking down at us. Then he disappeared, and we have never seen him since. I don't suppose we ever will.'

Along its length and across its width, Andean Patagonia has many physical and climatic similarities. These have produced similar work conditions and practices for those involved in the rearing of cattle. Away from the fenced flatlands, cattle are left to follow their own instincts through the narrow mountain passes to the higher ground, where, as the snow melts, fresh pastures roll back. Hungry cattle will go anywhere for food and develop an extraordinary agility, which combined with their natural strength, takes them across icy rivers, up and down near vertical paths no wider than themselves, through dense woods, round fallen trees and thick undergrowth, and over the highest rocky passes. Left to themselves through summer and into early autumn, they reproduce unseen. Their calves are born not knowing man, and bulls go savage. They will go to any length to avoid leaving their birthplace. These are the animals which the herders/cowboys—Chilean (*huaso*) and Argentine (gaucho) –have to collect, select, brand and drive to market, riding horses trained for the terrain where they work.

It was now our turn, and I gave an account of our travels, and in particular the last day's ride. Mario agreed that they were tough.

'But it's worse getting out to the west. You are the only visitors we have had come through here, apart from a couple from Holland. They stopped here a few years back on their way east, but they were on foot. It's not easy to find the trail, but I'll come with you tomorrow to make sure you start off right.'

I thanked him and accepted his offer, but I was curious as to how he managed to drive his cattle and sheep into and out of the valley, and indeed how they made a living. Mario explained.

'Once a year, a buyer does the rounds, selecting cattle and agreeing a price. We then drive them across the river to a place the cattle trucks can reach.'

'So, once a year you get paid?'

Mario nodded.

Mario and Sara were still pioneers, even though their original land holding had shrunk. They both felt an obligation to their grandparents to keep going, but Mario had no children, and neither was optimistic that Sara's children would wish to carry on.

'It's not an easy life, but it's a good one. We have all we need and we'll carry on as long as we can.'

The key was in the word 'need', and its meaning lay all around us. Apart from the felled trees, the valley was much as it has always been. Apart from the clock, which I noticed was working, their only mechanical need was for a power saw. All other needs were simple necessities, with nature providing the rest. Thus in Patagonia, simple objects and nature fill the vocabulary. 'Smooth as a worms gallop', 'blue as a hare's armpit' and 'light as a plover's broth' all speak of a life experience in and around nature.

The next day, Mario waited patiently whilst we broke camp and packed Prudencia. Hector had not been happy with her and felt that Rubia had earned a change. We had slept well and breakfasted in the kitchen, once more avoiding our fire chore. Sara's farewell was warm, and her parting gift was a further ten eggs, which she had boiled overnight. Mario and his piebald horse led the way, and for half an hour, we followed until we reached the valley wall. He stopped and pointed to a faint track, which we would have had difficulty finding on our own.

'Up there,' he said. 'You'd do better to lead them,' pointing to the horses.

And with that, he turned and rode away. I was sorry to see him go.

That morning we struggled up a succession of near vertical climbs and descents, over bare rock, ruts, tree roots and fallen trees, through bogs and over streams. Much of the time we were hemmed in on all sides by trees and clumps of bamboo, and only had glimpses of the Palena below. We saw little of the wildlife we heard; the occasional flash of feather, pug marks and tracks in the mud, and once the crashing sound of an escaping pig or deer, which spooked Cuervo.

He was an inquisitive horse. Every space had to be investigated, usually without breaking pace. He rarely needed encouragement to climb, his whole body surged with effort. Such was my confidence in him that it was now rarely necessary to dismount, and when we did so, Hector and I were in unison.

We were now headed for Lago Yungue, where there was reported to be a large new house, owned by some Belgians, and a radio. We were anxious to report our change of route and the extra time this would entail. We finally emerged onto a large open space, where piles of brushwood breathed puffs of smoke into a light wind, and lines of neatly stacked logs pointed our way. Ahead lay the lake, but its 'hare's armpit' tranquillity was misleading. Instead of an hour of lakeside pleasure, we stumbled and tripped over rounded stones and boulders which littered the edge, before reaching the meadows surrounding the house.

The Belgians had chosen a perfect spot for their three-storey timbered holiday home. The upper floors overlooked the lake on one side, and a large curve in the river on the other. We picked our way past a number of inquisitive colts, down a gentle slope to the sandy shores of the Palena, now even wider than before. While we had been struggling out of the valley, the river had curved north, seeking an outlet to the sea. Frustrated by the Andean spine, but continuously fed by lesser rivers, it had turned back south again and was now to surge past us for a further two days, until we turned east. Swollen to several times its original size, the Palena finally breaks out at La Junta, where it takes the melted snows of the entire area due west and into the Pacific

Hector found that the radio was not functioning, and after a lunch on the beach, we continued along the river until we came upon a small hut. Unsure of our way, Hector checked with a man standing at the door. It was as well he did. The man had been clearing fallen trees which blocked the trail ahead, but without waiting to be asked, he strode ahead for the next hour to guide us to the alternative crossing he had prepared over the Rio Correntoso. There was no *pasarela* where we arrived, and while relatively narrow, the river was aptly named. The man, whom I later baptised Moses, pointed out the line of a ridge below the surface, and Hector elected to ride Rubia across first. He urged her into the water, but she refused to go any further and he had to turn back. Moses then offered to try. This time Rubia was bullied, battered and beaten across, skidding and sliding off the ridge. Prudencia was then pulled across, leaving Cuervo, Hector and me on the bank—each with a river to cross.

'Are you happy to ride Cuervo over?'

To my surprise I was. I had every confidence in Cuervo and just a little in myself.

No hay problema, Hector.

Cuervo almost ambled into the water with the minimum of urging, and I felt him brace himself against the current and spray. Only once did a foot slip, and he shrugged that off. Safe on the other side, I felt exhilarated, and looked back at Hector, smiling and nodding on the far bank. He then joined us later having found a bridge of fallen trees to clamber over. Moses quietly disappeared, brushing our thanks aside, and I began to realise and marvel that he was typical of virtually everyone we had met.

Moses had told us that the climbs ahead were not too bad, and in one sense, he was right. At least they were dry. Yet again I was amazed at the horses' surefootedness and determination. We went up and up almost vertically, with few bends and twists. It was relentless and exhausting, but suddenly we were among the bamboos at a new level. Below, we had a brief glimpse of the road which was our target for the day, but the view of the mountains beyond took what was left of my breath away, and I slid off to savour it fully.

Our inevitable descent mirrored our way up. I had noticed that Cuervo would occasionally grunt, as if to tell me that the effort had just hurt. Sometimes he would appear to be clearing his throat, which I learned was the prelude to a sneeze. We began to grunt and clear our throats together. As my thinking hours in the saddle increased, I began to identify with some of those features which I imagined to be the daily bread and butter of the gaucho: how he uses his riding time to compose lyrics and songs; how the words and music reflect the surroundings and the rhythm of man and horse; the syncopation of shoes clicking on stone; the wind, rain and sun, the mountains, waters and sky; what lies ahead and what lies behind; the melancholy of being alone, and the delight of company. I was still deep in thought when Cuervo and I charged out of the last slope and on to the grass verge of the road, and beyond it—once again—our constant companion, the Palena.

Hector appeared to be in trouble. The strain of hauling on the tether to our *pilchero*—packhorse—was affecting his right shoulder. I suggested that he might try alternating hands, but he felt this would not give him the same control over the two horses. The offer of some cream from my medicine pack, and my volunteering to do the camp chores, proved more acceptable, but were immediately regretted by me. We had gone flat out for over six hours and had made good progress over a challenging section, but as I stumbled over the boulders to wash my feet and fill the water containers, I was hit by a wave of tiredness and stiffness, such that I teetered dangerously and all but fell in the Palena—next stop, the Pacific. Reminding myself that it had taken Sara eight hours to reach La Junta, which was still three hours further south, somehow I completed the unloading, put up my tent and collected wood for the fire, while Hector led the horses off to nearby grazing. Hot soup, rice and pasta just about met our needs and we both toppled into our tents.

Previous nights had been plagued by sleeping bag zips which jammed, a mattress which was several inches too thin and a pair of mosquitoes which found their way in but not out. That night, zips worked, a poncho provided the missing padding and I slept so soundly that by the time Hector broke surface the pots and pans were washed, the water supply replenished and the fire burning. His shoulder had improved and we both felt ready for the next target, Lago Claro Solar—Lake Sunlight.

In general, but with some difficulty, we had met our targets, but had not managed much more than fifteen miles per day. Our starts were always later than we intended. The tasks of firing up for breakfast, washing up and packing tents, dry bags and the *pilchero* always seemed to take longer than expected. Hector insisted on securing our bags and saddling all the horses, and I accepted that this was his area of responsibility, but delegation did not come easy to him. That morning was no exception, and we were not away until 11am, despite rising four hours earlier. The rest of the morning was a gravel crunch south. Mountains lined our left, and we were looking for a break which would mark our change of direction east. What diversions there were included flicking or pinching *tábanos* off Cuervo's neck and flanks, and a visit to a cottage cheese 'factory'. This was a collection of three small but new huts. Had Hector not spotted a woman in white overalls, we would have missed the pleasure of acquiring five kilos of delicious fresh cheese.

Our map indicated a trail off to Lago Claro Solar, but when we reached the fork, we found a sign indicating not only that a new gravel/stone road was under construction, but that it should have been completed six months previously.

Acercando a la Gente—Bringing the People Closer—boasted the sign.

At least the backdrop was magnificent. The road led up towards a distant range of spiked white peaks, which formed a continuous wall to the Mirta valley as it curled to our right. This was the Cordillera de Castillo (Castle), with Cerro El Condor looking up at adjoining Cerro Barros Arana.

Many peaks in Patagonia are called Castle, Fortress or Cathedral. Some have the name of the discoverer or of a contemporary public figure, but because the opening up of Chilean Patagonia was a gradual, often stuttering process, there was often a lack of awareness of the names that had been applied already elsewhere. During the build up to the frontier Arbitration, the Chilean team of experts were led by Barros Arana, whose preference for historical theory and libraries often blinded him to the more practical approach of his Argentine opposite, Perito Moreno, to whom the description of Cerro Barros Arana—albeit in mountaineering terms—of 'fairly difficult in parts' would have been a considerable understatement.

Apart from the stones, we had to contend with a fierce sun, and it was not long before we were looking for shade, water and a short siesta. The valley was substantially cleared and well stocked. The farms appeared to have been long established, and the new road had brought the 'benefits' of gates, cattle grids and improved access to markets. There was an air of wellbeing. Even the occasional roadside graves looked like neatly painted wooden kennels.

We entered narrow but dense woodlands of towering *coigüe* (beech), oak and *tineo*, the latter with a canopy of white flowers. Felled examples of each cluttered the sides of the road: huge haphazard hulks, destined to rot where they lay. Tunnels of large corrugated metal tubes had been placed at intervals under the stone surface to carry away the streams and surface water, and to attract Cuervo's insatiable curiosity. I was unable to take my eyes off the procession of wooden marker posts, which gave a running report on the distance covered, and distracted from the depressing monotony of endless straights ahead. When one eventually announced '5 kms' I was still trying to work out 'to where', when the road ran out and was replaced by a swathe of bare red earth leading up a steep hill.

'That's it, Hector! You go on and find a site. I'll walk the rest.'

I wasted a prayer that the lake lay over the hill.

It was not the best camping site we had chosen. We could not reach the lake because of a dense band of trees, so there was no fresh water, but it was flat, dry and there was good feed for the horses. Our cheese and Sara's eggs were almost gone, but Hector turned out a standard soup and pasta. Despite our tiredness, we agreed to try to extend our next day's target by forfeiting breakfast, but just as I was preparing to fall into my tent, there was a shout from Hector.

'We've got to move.'

He ran towards me, ducking and weaving. Moments later, a large brown-yellow insect went by my ear humming loudly to itself.

'What is it?'

The problem was that I did not know the Spanish for a hornet. What I did understand was that he had disturbed a nest of them, and that since Hector was clearly worried or frightened or both, the situation called out for my urgent attention. I then remembered that I was very tired and about to go to bed.

'Why don't we build up the fire? The horses are a long way off and they aren't going to be troubled. Once we're in our tents, the "bees"'—I could not remember the word he had used—can't get in.'

'But they're not bees!'

'Yes, Hector, I know they're not bees. I can't remember what they are called, but we have them at home.'

A long discussion followed over the respective virtues and vices of Chilean and English hornets, and while the Chilean variety seemed to be much bigger and better, eventually we decided we would stay put, build up the fire and fill both tents with smoke. Our sleep that night was to be disturbed only by breathing difficulties.

While I had wondered why Hector seemed to sleep so soundly, I had not spotted that each night all the sheepskins went into his tent. That made two for each of two saddles, plus one for the *pilchero*, plus two pairs of *pierneras*—goat skin leggings—plus poncho and sleeping bag. Fortunately for the tent, he was a mere five foot four. He was a good guide and companion, mature beyond his 23 years, and with a good sense of humour. He wanted to ride the length of the Tenth and Eleventh Regions—from Chaitén in the north to Villa O'Higgins in the south, which almost exactly matched my own dream. His family was from Chaitén, where he and his father had worked with horses before Hector moved off to Coyhaique. There he had worked his way up to manage a supermarket, until Ian's organisation had poached him to work as a guide on trekking and rafting trips to the Northern Ice Field and the River Baker. I had met his teenage wife and rosy cheeked son in Futaleufú, and knew their plan was to save and buy a small plot of land in Coyhaique. He was a skilled and gentle horseman, and in the tradition of Patagonian men an excellent cook. He fitted my proposed advert for a guide almost exactly and while I did not begrudge him his sheepskin mattress, I wished that I had had the idea first.

Next morning, exercising an iron discipline, we were away by 9am without breakfast and followed the wooden pegs through woods and clearings until they, too, ran out and we emerged onto open slopes and had our first view of the lake. The presence of a number of cattle indicated a small settlement, and Hector was attracted by the sound of a voice coming from a barn; in response to his shout, a small girl emerged. We had interrupted her private conversation with some lambs. She did not know the path to El Macal, our next objective on the map, but she thought her mother might and pointed to a nearby hut. In no time we were invited to breakfast by the mother, who looked no more than ten years older than her five-year-old daughter. Having told us that her husband had gone off to La Junta for the day, she quickly added that her parents lived in a hut on the slope opposite, and if we followed her pointed finger, we could see their house. Hector was nonetheless an immediate attraction, and he rather enjoyed playing games with the daughter on the floor. I sat in the doorway throwing crusts to the chickens and ducks squabbling under the floorboards, and marvelling at the instant hospitality given, the sharing without question of modest and limited resources and the absence of suspicion or surprise.

We had made a good start, and while two days to Lago Verde seemed realistic, we were unsure whether to take the Rio Quinto, which looked the most direct option on our map, or the Rio Figueroa, which involved another road. The woman did not know the answer, but nor did she know why the lake was called 'Sunlight'.

The next group we were to meet had just finished a roundup, and despite the fact that it was not yet midday were well into a celebration. A raised hand and barely coherent comment, which seemed to indicate that we should turn right at the tall burnt tree, was followed by an invitation to dismount and join the party. Since the sun had as far to reach the yardarm as we had to go, I was pleased that Cuervo immediately made up his mind that he knew where the burnt tree was, and left us with the simpler task of waving our thanks over our shoulders.

There proved to be a number of burnt trees, but half an hour later and having passed the third, we turned right at the fourth. The trail was very faint, but eventually the inevitable hut appeared and Hector set off to enquire. He was gone a long time.

'He says the Rio Quinto is impassable. He tried to go through only yesterday and had to give up and come back. Apparently the river is too high and there are parts where we will have to cut a new trail. We can try it, but we'll lose a lot of time if we can't get through.'

It was a message we had heard before.

Jonathan or Ian were to bring supplies up from Coyhaique to Lago Verde that weekend, and we guessed that since they would have to travel up and down the road adjoining the Rio Figueroa, we would meet them if we took that route. We duly set off for the road, and some eight miles of long open valleys and several streams later, we spotted plumes of dust which gave its position away.

Once on the road and in the absence of any grass verge, we were fortunate to meet no traffic. Again, the straights were long and the hills were steep, but now dense woodland crowded in on both sides, blocking any views. Gradually, however, the mountain walls shrank and lost their snow, the woodland barrier receded, and we caught glimpses of isolated trees which, despite appearing to be rooted in rock, still managed to grow to great heights until the day when they could hold no longer. After days of persistent sun, the weather was beginning to break, and in preparation Hector donned his poncho and *pierneras*. I hoped my poncho would be enough, but when came the rains, they were torrential.

Another brief enquiry revealed that there was a large *galpón* (barn) ahead, but not how far. We ground on mile on mile, and just as I was beginning to curse everyone and everything except Cuervo, and the rain had penetrated to my skin, the unmistakeable shape of the *galpón* loomed out of the mist, and we turned in through an open gate.

Hernán Recabal came out of an adjoining hut and opened the double gates to the barn, and within minutes we were all inside. Bales of hay were offered, and the horses launched into them as if they had not eaten for days. Ducking hanging haunches of meat, we stripped off saddles, bridles, sheepskins and dry bags and laid these out on the wooden mangers. I assumed, at best, that we might be allowed to sleep on the hay, and therefore welcomed Hernán's invitation to dry out in his kitchen. He was a small man in his forties, rather frail and reticent. Few words were exchanged, but these included a quote for the price of the hay.

Once inside, we were invited to hang our clothes and shoes around the stove. Out came the *mate* and for a while Hernán sucked alone. He then offered it to Hector and then to me, and I knew the first phase of Patagonian hospitality had been completed, and that we had been accepted. What I had interpreted as reticence was in fact due to Hernán's state of health. He was a sick man. As evening turned to night, our clothes steamed dry, and the rain clattered on the metal roof, Hernán explained that both he and his brother had inherited the illness from which their mother had died, and which was now slowly shrinking his brain.

He had been to the United States seeking treatment, but had been told that only palliative care was available, and he had returned with a cocktail of medicines. His father, now in his nineties, had settled an extensive area of land, but now lived in Coyhaique and was unlikely to return. There was a photograph of him on the wall astride his favourite horse at the age of eighty-eight. He looked entirely at ease, albeit a little frail. Hernán had come up from Coyhaique to administer the farm, and because he was also the local district Mayor, visitors were frequent. The barn, the only one of its size for miles, was a symbol of his status.

While Hector prepared supper, Hernán and I sat in a corner talking. I was questioned about the youth in England, the drug problem, education and politics. He was concerned to explore the merits of sending his children abroad, either to pursue a specific course or simply to learn from the experience. I never found out how many children he had, but the problems he described in Coyhaique sounded familiar. He recognised the values of relative isolation in Patagonia, and had many plans for development of the farm and for tourism in the area. The belief that tourism held the key to future prosperity was widely held, and that afternoon we had passed an American-owned hotel and kayak centre which showed what was possible. Despite a certain diffidence Hernán was very astute and he had the capital, but with his health he knew that time was not on his side.

Hector produced another culinary triumph—one befitting a Mayor's parlour—and as we sat down to enjoy our supper, it was Hector's turn to lead the conversation. Despite the age difference, he and Hernán shared a remarkable number of common contacts and friends, and they exchanged reminiscences long into the night. Eventually Hernán broke off to explain that he had to perform his 'medical chores', and showed me to a room which was clearly his bedroom. Clothing and various articles were removed to reveal a mattress, approximately a foot longer than the bed it lay on. Hector was offered a bunk in the room adjoining.

During the night I had to make one of those nocturnal trips which were becoming an irritating feature of life. It was pitch dark and I was unfamiliar with the geography. I felt my way in the direction of where I recalled the door to have been, falling over a chair and then a pair of shoes, and wasting valuable minutes feeling round the frame to locate the catch, which was on the wrong side. Eventually I stumbled out onto an open veranda and to the wooden railings. I was not going to be able to go any further. The rain had stopped and there was a full moon, and as I scanned the southern sky I hoped that the chickens roosting under the hut would not be disturbed. The next morning, Hernán observed that I could have used the receptacle under his bed.

Lago Verde was some 18 to 25 miles away, and we were going to need more than one day. Hernán suggested that we should aim for another large *galpón* which lay in between, where 'Lily' would give us a big welcome. The weather was overcast as we turned the horses out to grass and collected up our bags. The hay offered for sale the previous evening became a gift, and Hector collected what was left to add to Rubia's load. As we prepared to leave, several visitors arrived, tethering their horses at the gate, and went into the main hut to share a *mate* with Hernán. I seized the opportunity to clamber on to Cuervo unobserved, using my customary platform—in this case a log. Unfortunately the log slipped under me and I fell heavily on my butt. I waited for the laughter and comment, but none came. Instead Hernán came over looking concerned, and Hector explained that I had slipped. Now I had to try again with an audience of professionals, and without the log. Praying to the gods of equestrians, somehow I managed the complete manoeuvre broadly in keeping with someone who professed to have ridden nearly 150 miles, and exchanging farewells, we rode out of the gate.

As we passed the tethered horses, one of them moved aggressively towards us. Cuervo bristled.

'Watch him, Jon,' warned Hector. 'He's a *cojudo*.

I did not understand. *Cojudo* was slang in Peru for someone who had done something idiotic, or alternatively was a full time idiot. Peruvians regard it as strong but fairly inoffensive. In Chile, however, a country richer in slang than most, and with many words considered by others to be crude or offensive or both, *cojudo* was much stronger and could cause offence.

Hector explained.

'In Patagonia, a *cojudo* is a male stud horse. Untamed, we call them *potros*. Some people ride them out of preference, but as they are very aggressive, they take some handling.'

I made a note to add *potros* and *cojudos* to Patagonian roads and *tábanos* on my unwanted list.

Without realising it, the day before we had ridden off Map One. Opening Map Two was therefore a big event. It showed what appeared to be a long straight track with a mountain range to our right: the Cordón Media Luna (Half Moon). Not for the first time, however, the situation on the ground was very different. The road now wound constantly and the hills were long and steep. Occasionally we found ourselves beside the River Figueroa, which otherwise clung to the mountain range and rivalled the ferocity of the Futaleufú. Away from the river, the main valley was narrow and heavily wooded. Piles of fencing poles alternated with stacks of split logs, denoting changes in the trees which otherwise were difficult to spot, but in general there was little sign of life. When, therefore, a large hut, painted bright blue and set back from the road on high ground, suddenly appeared, it was something of a shock.

There had been little traffic, and we had just remounted after a short stop, when a distant dust cloud warned of an approaching truck, and we moved to put our defence system into operation.

'It's Ian,' shouted Hector, recognising a green pick-up.

The truck skidded to a halt, and two men emerged. The driver was Ian Farmer. We had not met, but his messages had provided information and constant practical encouragement at times when they were most needed, and I was very aware that for this alone, I owed him a great debt. His companion had to be his father, of whom I had learned a little from Hector. While there were a few surprises about age and appearance, it was as if we had met many months before, and after the initial handshakes and pleasantries, the discussion turned to practical matters. Ian had been to

Lago Verde and had left some supplies there. He had gone on to the Rio Quinto valley to see if there was any sign of us, and there being none, he had investigated potential routes south, made some useful contacts and then decided that his best option was to return to Coyhaique and await news. His first visit to Lago Verde had left very favourable impressions, which we were subsequently to confirm.

It was a real pleasure to exchange experiences in one's own language, but we were all conscious that each had a long way to go. Ian's parting comments were that the Lago Verde valley was close by and that our way forward was flat, but we were soon to find out the different impressions that travel by truck and on horseback can leave. The curves and hills returned, and before long the rain cascaded down. By the time we reached the head of the valley, we were both soaked to the skin again. We passed one *galpón* but it stood alone and there was no one to be seen. Then we came upon one which was roofless, but with a long hut nearby, and as we stopped to enquire, the door opened and out came 'Lily'.

Lilia Sandoval Caro—to give her full name – was a character. Short, brunette and in her early forties, she stopped talking only to smile. Lily was full of plans and projects: a first storey to the rear; bungalows, each with views of the River Figueroa below; a conversion of the unfinished *galpón*. The tourists would flock in. She showed me into a back room, piled high with new mattresses, linen and electrical equipment, and explained that these had been taken from her former business in anticipation of her plans. Solar panels powered the lights and radio, and a new TV and several washing machines gathered dust in a corner of the front room, awaiting only the arrival of mains power. I was invited to test one of the new mattresses on the floor that night, while Hector was offered a bunk in an adjoining shed. We were both delighted.

It was eight o'clock when her husband came in. He had been herding calves in from a distant part of the farm. One had escaped and gone off towards Lago Verde, but he did not seem unduly concerned. Lily had prepared us for his arrival.

'He's a good man. Short on words, but a good man.'

Short, wiry, with a mat of black hair, pinched cheeks, dark skinned and with the inevitable Patagonian moustache, he was indeed a man of few words, being content to sit in his corner by the stove drying out. He smiled easily, but it was a while before the *mate* was offered. I felt we did not have any obvious place in his world.

'I thought the good Lord told us to rest on the seventh day,' I offered, since it was a Sunday.

'The good Lord was not a farmer,' he replied.

We all laughed. It was the only thing he said that evening, but it broke the ice. Lily was more than happy to let Hector do the cooking, and we were grateful for her home produce to supplement our remaining supplies.

'I'm always hungry,' she said. 'I can't stop eating and I keep putting on weight. I'm getting really fat. Do you think I'm fat?'

She was moving in that direction, but Hector and I both shook our heads.

'And I'm always in pain.'

I had noticed that she often sat down and seemed to be out of breath. She explained that she had recently had a hip replacement, and although she did not believe it had been well done, it was also apparent that in Patagonia patients did not complain about their medical treatment. Like Hernán, health stood between her and her plans, but with her optimism, energy and good humour she deserved to succeed.

Lily's new mattress and Hector's customary sheepskins gave us both a good night's rest. Lily's husband crept past me at first light, and Lily followed to feed 'her babies'—white turkeys by the dozen, chickens of all shapes and sizes and a formidable collection of geese and ducks. On my way to the grazing horses, I passed the topless *galpón*. It was an impressive size, with a large loft. The main timber uprights were sunk in the ground, but cross beams and rafters were all neatly jointed, the one completed side being a nailed shiplap. Only the most rudimentary tools could be seen.

With so much wood on hand, timber was the logical material for construction. Stone, however, was also available in unlimited quantities, and I had asked Hernán whether he thought that the preference for wood with its limited life revealed some subconscious acceptance that 'home' in Patagonia was for today rather than tomorrow. His answer had been that stone was cold.

We left Lily with the promise that I would send her a postcard from somewhere exotic. The rain had stopped, and we resumed our zigzagging under a hot sun. The only person we passed was Lily's husband, returning with his truant calf, but while we offered our warmest thanks, his response was minimal. During the last section of the river and the Cordón Media Luna, the *tábanos* returned and ruined our lunchtime siesta, but as we entered the open expanse of the Lago Verde valley, they disappeared. The green lake appeared briefly, followed by a tantalising glimpse of the distant reflection of sun on metal roofs. The fence line on either side of the earth track, widened so that we could ride on a broad grass verge. Little did I know that this long straight ride to Lago Verde would not only last an eternity, but would be our last. Ten minutes short of the town, I dismounted and watched in horror as I peed blood.

CHAPTER FOUR

An Unwelcome Interlude

*T*here are defining moments in our lives when the minute hand on our clock races round uncontrollably before stopping altogether. So it was for me that day in Lago Verde. Slowly I became aware that I was standing, shoulders drooped, gazing across Cuervo's saddle into the middle distance, but I had no idea how long I had been there. I glanced across at Hector. His face showed concern. He knew something was wrong, but said nothing, and I had yet to collect my thoughts, let alone share them. My mind was still in turmoil—that nightmare time when thoughts will not stop spinning. After a long pause I climbed cautiously back into the saddle.

'It's OK, Hector. Let's find somewhere with a hot shower, bed and anything other than rice to eat.'

Whatever the cause for my concern, we were ten days from Futaleufú and rather more from Coyhaique. We needed to find grazing for the horses who had earned a good break, to locate the supplies left by Ian and report to him. A visit to the *carabineros* led us to the owner of a field and an offer of grazing for as long as we wished, and also established a secure place for our equipment and saddles. Our food supplies were where Ian had left them, and the local school housed an internet connection. At this point I felt able to confide in Hector. This was not due to any lack of confidence in him. We had spent nearly two weeks together, and he had impressed me in so many different ways and situations, but I had needed time to recognise that a problem shared was a problem halved, and that solutions required his help and support. His response and understanding were immediate and positive, and we were quickly able to discuss and share out the remaining priorities.

I was anxious to contact Ian and my nephew in Santiago, but to leave my family out until I knew more about my problem and prognosis, and it was Hector who organised my access to the internet. There was no doctor in Lago Verde, but there was a medical post, which was closed for the day.

Looking back, it is difficult to record all the detail: the stages of fright and panic; when they came and went; how each was dealt with, or avoided. Some moments, however, are still vivid. I was frightened and very ignorant. I knew nothing of the causes of whatever was wrong, and could only guess what labels others might attach.

Our next task was to find somewhere to eat and sleep, and enquiries led us to a simple wooden hut on the outskirts of Lago Verde. The wooden plaque nailed to the gate read 'Doña Dora'. *Doña* and *Don* are traditional Spanish titles of respect, Sir and Madam being near, but not exact equivalents. The use of these titles is waning, and when Doña Dora's generation has passed on, they may well have been consigned to officialdom.

The kitchen door opened to reveal a diminutive woman in her eighties. A young girl peered out from behind her skirt. Hector introduced us. Inevitably, he knew someone known to her, but it was also clear that this was a lady he respected. Her full name, Doña Dora Figueroa de Solis, was a Lago Verde history compendium, and fittingly she used *usted*, the formal you, in conversation rather than the more familiar *tu*, and there was a subtle indication that a similar response was expected. She had a presence, despite her immediate friendliness. A face wrinkled by years and tragedy inspired respect, even without the Doña and the *usted*, but a grandmother's face and touch, and a playful flicker in eyes and mouth, drew the children and young people of Lago Verde to her door. To them, she was *Abuela*—Granny—and she always had a tale to tell.

For my part, it did not take long for me to warm to Doña Dora, and over *mate* I soon added her to my growing list of confidants to my predicament. Her response was immediate, practical, measured and reassuring.

'There is no qualified doctor in Lago Verde, but we have a medical post and the auxiliary who runs it is very good. Very professional. If he doesn't know the answer, he will tell you.'

Later, showered and sated by a magnificent supper, we talked until I could sit or think no longer, and mumbling my apologies I clambered up a narrow ladder to my attic bed and fell asleep fully dressed.

The process of diagnosis started the next day with the medical auxiliary and some basic tests.

'I can't see anything wrong, but clearly something is. I think it would be better if you stopped and went to see a specialist in Coyhaique.'

Surprisingly, this was helpful. Many questions would have to wait for answers, but at least I could close on our current journey and concentrate on the practicalities that followed such a decision. Hector would assume responsibility for horses, tack, kit, and food supply, and even while I focused on how I might get myself to Coyhaique, a possible solution presented itself.

At breakfast that morning we had been joined by another guest, who had not only referred to Doña Dora as *Tia*—Auntie—but, inevitably, knew

Hector, and I had left the three of them in deep conversation to attend my appointment. On my return, I passed what I had earlier taken to be an abandoned or derelict vehicle parked on blocks on the grass outside. The bonnet was now up and someone was bent over, working on the engine. I stopped to see if I could help, and the mechanic straightened up to reveal himself as our fellow guest—Juan Carlos Campos, owner of the only bus service between Lago Verde and Coyhaique—and this was the bus.

Juan Carlos had recently established a passenger and freight service to Lago Verde, to supplement a more popular and profitable route he ran between coastal Chaitén and capital Coyhaique, where many of the passengers were foreign tourists on a limited budget. After a long and uncomfortable drive of several days down the Austral, the bus would pull up outside a small guesthouse owned by Juan Carlos and his partner in uptown Coyhaique, and it was then logical that most passengers would elect to stay there. Not only did Juan Carlos possess the practical skills essential to survival in Aysén—as driver, mechanic, carpenter and builder he had rebuilt his buses many times over, often with cannibalised parts from different makes and was currently extending and modernising his guest house over two storeys—but he was also genuinely interested in mankind, a good listener, conversationalist and fount of information about Aysén and the adjoining Argentine provinces. Little wonder, therefore, that any concerns I might have had as to the age and condition of his bus were soon forgotten, and, together with a mass of local freight but no other passengers, we were on our way to Coyhaique by lunchtime. The Hospedaje Daniela became, and has remained, my home away from home.

It took several days to match my physical geography to the appropriate expert, and thus arrange an examination and tests. The specialist was thorough and professional. He was the only expert in his field in all Patagonia, but communication was not his forte.

'You have cancer. It is malignant, but the prognosis for this particular cancer is optimistic. I recommend that you return to your country for treatment as soon as possible.'

We were both staring at a small screen which showed the tumour clearly. I could not take my eyes off that grey piece of malice, and felt a wave of anger and self-pity.

'Sh**! Sh**! Sh**!'

The word kept repeating itself long after all the asterisks had dropped off. My eyes moistened, but no tears came. Instead I remembered the clumsy message giving me news of my father's death. Then there had been tears and emptiness—many tears over many years. This time, however, I sensed a light—a light with warmth—which seemed to shine through my despair. For no obvious reason, I recalled a cadet soldier ritual, and my mind played over it.

'Halt! Who goes there?'

Long pause … while trying to remember the password.

'Moriarty.'

'Pass Moriarty, and be recognised.'

Moriarty so easily converted to Mortality.

So started the steep learning curve to understanding which those ignorant of cancer must follow when their turn comes. I was better prepared for the diagnosis when it finally came in my own language.

'Yes, you have cancer. It is malignant, but you are fortunate in that it is localised, and can be removed by surgery. The prognosis is optimistic.'

Then, following surgery, and in answer to my questions: 'I can see no reason why you should not return to complete your journey.'

Somehow I was not surprised. Somehow I knew I would go back, and I believed I would be allowed to finish. On this occasion, I had had much time to contemplate my own mortality. That grey piece of malice—the cause of my fears and uncertainty—had been removed, and while annual check-ups and tests were to follow, I had not been sentenced. I was being released on licence. Somehow I had survived a special experience, shared by many others, and had emerged as they had done, grateful, wiser but ultimately still ignorant, but at no stage had I been allowed to feel alone. In Patagonia, from Lago Verde to Coyhaique, each day brought support with a new face. Then my family took over, from Santiago to Lima and then back to Oxford. I was not allowed to doubt that I should return. If the first part of my journey had been to fulfil a personal dream, its completion had now become a family and friends affair.[1]

---

[1] Some twelve years later, 'grey malice' has made an unwelcome re-appearance, and the terms of my licence have come up for renewal. Two books are almost complete, however, and once again, I believe I will be allowed to finish.

CHAPTER FIVE

Doña Dora's Tale

A winter had passed, but brought little change as we drove up from Coyhaique. Between the turn off at La Junta and Lago Verde, the gap where Hector and I had joined the road, was where we remembered it. The same pair of black mongrels ran out to bark. Smoke curled from Hernán Recabal's chimney. A few more stacks of wood were waiting for collection, and the Rio Figueroa was its turbulent emerald self. *La Loca* Lily waved from her doorway, as we stopped to give her husband a lift. He had finished his barn, but Hector and I were strangers to him. Forty-five miles, which had taken us nearly three days to ride, clattered by in a mere hour and a half. The long final straight, which had preluded so much disappointment and angst, was now our avenue to a new adventure. It was easy to believe that the distant metal roofs were glinting a greeting again.

We parked on the grass outside Doña Dora's house, and unlatched the wooden gate. The same chickens and ducks dashed for cover, as Doña Dora opened the door. A brief look of bemusement was replaced by a warm smile of recognition.

'We said we would be back.'

'I knew you would. Come on in. Your old room is free.'

We had hardly been away, and were expected. Lago Verde reopened her welcoming arms and we felt at home again.

Hector's immediate task was to find three suitable horses within budget, and Ian already had made initial contacts.

'It would be best if I went on my own,' said Hector.

He added that the price would go up fifty per cent if the owners saw a *gringo*. Since I could offer little in any event, I decided to visit the graveyard.

The graves had the best view in town. I had thought it was a universal custom for the occupants to face east-west, but there were as many facing north-south. There were many small crosses, few memorials and the barest of detail on those there were. Dried flowers and empty Coca-Cola bottles were *de rigueur*. 'Emily Phillips Rosa' caught my eye, and later Doña Dora told me that the Phillips family had lived in Futaleufú and may have come from the Welsh settlement.

The sun beat down as I gazed south over the town to the circle of mountains beyond. The inner fold divided to reveal a triangular wedge of the vivid green lake which gave the town its name. Beyond, roll upon roll of snow-capped ranges stretched to the eye's limit. This was the direction of our first stage to La Tapera of two to three days. Despite the heat, I shivered as I felt a confusing mix of excitement and anxiety, and as I left through the archway entrance, I wondered how many of those I was leaving behind me, had ridden that way.

'Keep an eye on us.'

Lago Verde was a neat town; isolated but content to be so. That isolation had condemned it to the slow lane to development, but had also enabled it to miss out on selection for the Chilean concession policy—under which leases over large tracts of land were offered for purchase (usually) by Companies, subject to colonisation conditions. Unusually, therefore, individual settlers—among whom the large Solis family were prominent—found vacant land to settle and build up their community. In the town, plot sizes and houses were similar; single-storey, corrugated iron on wood and a generous area for animal, fowl, flower and vegetable. The school had recently benefited from a face lift from the Raleigh Organisation, and was blue-roofed. Inside, the classrooms were neat and conventional. The windows were clean and the panes unbroken, and the children looked and sounded as if they were enjoying school. The library was a modern building, containing few books, but the latest Gates Foundation computers.

I continued on down through the square, planted with low bushy pine, which gave shelter and shade along concrete paths and rustic log benches, which no one used. A woman was not very busy repainting the benches rust-red, and several others smiled over their shovels from deep trenches in the road. Around the square, simple wooden panels quoted the wisdom of grandparents through the mouths of their grandchildren.

> Lago Verde. Land of rivers and mountains and people of country tradition.

> People are never closer to stupidity than when they believe they are wise.

> Water. Our greatest resource. Remember not to contaminate it.

Rubbish boxes, also made of logs, stood at each street intersection. They, too, were painted rust-red and their lids were difficult to lift, but they were full and regularly emptied by volunteers. In the Patagonian tradition, popular songs were belted out of a loudspeaker in a corner of the square, and, unusually, there were few prowling dogs.

I glimpsed *La Loca* Lily's husband, now sitting in the back of a *carabineros'* truck. I was uncertain whether I should wave, but he helped by turning away. The medical auxiliary who the previous year had so impressed with his homespun wisdom, courtesy and sympathy had been posted elsewhere. The woman in charge of the library key told me, as she had done ten months previously, that the library was not open until the diesel-generated electricity supply was turned on, and although the mains supply poles had been erected back to La Junta, the wires were still missing.

With preparations for the numerous stages of our journey to make, we were to spend several nights at Doña Dora's house during which the first of the many tales she told was about her own arrival at the age of three. Accompanied by her mother, sister and baby brother, their group also comprised a judge and four men hired in Chaitén, their food larder including one cow 'on the hoof'. Doña Dora's father Juan, a *carabinero*, had recently been posted to Futaleufú, and was to meet up with them at the end of Lago Yelcho near the site of Puerto Ramirez. Since there were no roads and they could not navigate up the River Futaleufú, their route on from Puerto Ramirez was to take them past El Malito, much as Hector and I had done, as far as Alto Palena, where they were to double back north to Futaleufú.

'We killed the cow and put the meat in one of the boats, and set off up the Rio Yelcho to Puerto Ramirez. The boat was so loaded that it was only six inches out of the water. The area was very unfriendly—everything was pure *montaña* [wooded slopes]. I remember a *nalca*[1] leaf as big as the roof of a house. Each time we stopped, the judge and the men arranged a bed for my mother. We moved very slowly because the river was in flood and we were travelling against the current. It was summer, but the weather was very bad. Where we could, we walked and the men carried us on their shoulders. When we could walk no more, we got into the boats and the men pulled them from the bank with ropes they made from grass. I remember my mother cried a lot. When we reached Lago Yelcho, the

---

[1] The leaves of the *nalca* make rhubarb look puny, and the roots have medicinal qualities for reducing bruises and tumours.

men thought they would have to row, but a wind got up and from there everything was fine and we crossed to the other end of the lake, where my father was waiting with a young Irishman. I remember him well. His name was Irwen and he had lived alone in Puerto Ramirez for years. He had a bushy beard and long hair. He got into the water and lifted us out in his arms.

'From there we had to go on by horse, but my mother did not know how to ride. She was a town lady and in town they sometimes walked in high heels. My father had to teach her—how to control the horse, how to turn—until she had learnt a little, and the next day we continued on to Palena along narrow paths. We had to jump fallen trees, and I fell trying to jump one. My brother fell, too, and cried. My father never complained. And so we reached Palena.

'From there, it was easy. There was a wide track. We spent two more nights and then crossed the river by raft—horses and all—where there is now a fine bridge, and soon arrived at Futaleufú. It was already a village by then. The Plaza de Armas was laid out, but there was nothing on it. There was a lake, and at one corner was the *carabinero* post. There were quite a few people. Lots of children, but no school. We were there for five years. My mother had another baby, a boy, but he died. When I was eight, we all crossed over into Argentina and then back into Chile to Lago Verde, and I have been here ever since.'

One night, I was talking to Dona Dora about the original settlers of Lago Verde. I told her that I understood the first was Antonio Solis in 1914.

'Funny you should say that, because I heard something similar on the radio not so long ago, but it is not true.

'Antonio Solis was the head of the Solis family, which has now died out, although there may be one left. I remember this gentleman. He was from here, but he was not the first. He was waiting in Cisnes when we arrived in some trucks on our way here via Argentina. My brother-in-law to be, who was a *carabinero* in Cisnes, wrapped me in a cloak and asked this gentleman—this grandfather with a long white beard—to look after me. He lifted me into the truck and we travelled together. The road down the Cisnes valley did not exist then. That is how I met him. He was a lovely person, but he was not the first to arrive in Lago Verde, because my father-in-law to be was already here, and he helped Don Antonio get his land. At that time Don Antonio was being chased by the Argentine police, and my father-in-law hid him in a barn.

'We arrived in Lago Verde in 1941, when I was eleven. There were seven families here. The Ollasos—the grandparents—they lived below here. A San Martín lived on the other side, in an old house. Rubio Solis had an *estancia*, which he bought in 1935 from a German who was married to my aunt. There was also Daniel Solis on the other side of the Rio Pico. He was my husband's uncle. Further on was the land of the old man, Don Antonio Solis. My father-in-law had land here, from the town as far as the cordillera. He had more than he needed and gave some to my husband and some to his brother. It was all pure Solis.

'My father Juan came here also as a *carabinero*. He was over six foot and well endowed, as he used to say. He was a good man, well educated, good with people; a friendly and affectionate man. My mother was the same, but she was like a little bird; slim, short—well, not so very short. She lived a very long time and died at the age of 105. Some years ago it was, when she died, but her mind was sharp. She could not walk, but she was very lucid and gave lots of interviews.

'My husband was a Solis, born and raised here. He was a character. There was no one like my husband. Not even his brother. He was as if he had been born in a big city, because if he went to Santiago, he had no problems. He liked to dress well, to go out, to take me to some beautiful place where we could dine; where we could have a coffee, a tea or the like. He was affectionate, respectful, a worker and honourable; a special person. He was 22 and I was 16 when we married on 4 March 1944. We did not have children immediately. I had my first child when I was twenty. But God knows how to order things, because if that child had lived, I would have died.

'I was three times at death's door, until my third child. The first two died; the first a boy, the second a girl. The third—the one who is ill—he too had difficulty at birth, and it was this that caused his illness. He was a long time without breathing, and this affected his brain.

'In the first year I was married, my father-in-law gave us half his animals: 800 cattle, cows, calves, heifers and bullocks. That year there was such a snow storm that nothing was left. Seventy-five animals out of 800! Can you imagine that? My husband and I were completely demoralised. What were we going to do? How could we repay that capital?'

1944 was a year when not only a colossal fire destroyed much of Lago Verde's rich and varied timber, but a terrible winter killed off most of the cattle. Of the few horses which survived, most were in such a state that they were barely rideable.

'We decided to carry on. We started again. Conditions were precarious, with a rotten house. There was no floor. It was very cold. All the chickens died. Everything died. We nearly died ourselves. Those were very difficult times. There was not even an aspirin here. Everything came from Argentina, when the river let us cross. My husband had to take me to Rio Pico in Argentina, when I was three months pregnant and because I could not stay here. I had to have treatment. I could not eat, and neither the baby nor I were gaining weight. We went on horseback. One whole day in a snowstorm. I had a tremendous fever. Another day on to Costa, and another six hours to Esquel. There they had good clinics and very good doctors. I was well attended. It seemed that because I was Chilean, they attended to me even better. I was operated on for appendicitis. They also operated on my husband for the same thing, and later when my son was eleven and ill, we took him there too. Then we took him on to Santiago to see specialists. Don Eduardo Simon gave us a letter addressed to his brother-in-law there, and arranged everything.

'There was no school and my husband organised meetings. The alternative was to take the children to school in Argentina, but this would have been very difficult. We would have had to have a house there. Besides, the customs were different. It was decided to build a school. Everyone worked. Those who could saw, sawed; those who could make roof tiles, made them; those who had roof insulation, gave it; those who could give nails, gave them. Those who had something to give, gave it. We, the womenfolk, cooked, made bread and prepared food. In this way, we built our school. Later we built a house for the radio operator, because people were falling ill and we needed to contact hospitals.'

Doña Dora had eight children, the first two dying at birth. The third, her eldest son, was born with brain damage, and still lived with her. Three girls and two more boys followed. One of the boys, Herminio, suffered from diabetes, as had his father, grandfather and uncle.

'I was very sad, because Herminio did not want to do anything to live. He told me he was not going to die of an illness which did not let him eat. He did not want to be a prisoner of his illness, or the medicine he had to take. When his uncle became ill, no one knew that a spoonful of sugar might have saved him. He died because they did not know what to do. With my husband, I did everything they told me to do. He took all his medicines, but first he lost the use of his legs, and then he went blind. He became like a child, like a baby. For this reason Herminio did not want to go on.

'He was a special person, my son, a good person even when he was a boy. I say this not because he was my son. Ask anyone about him. He did everything. If any animal was ill, they came to him. If he was having his meal, he would stop and go and look at the horse. The same if it was a dog. Sometimes the dogs were wounded by the wild pigs, and he would stitch them up.

'It was Mothers' Day when he came to see me. He brought me a pair of slippers. He was on his way to Coyhaique with a friend.

'"Mamita," he said.

'"I want you to put these on, so you can be warm and don't go working so much."

'… "but working has kept me young," I replied.

'"That's right. I am old because I can't work. Mamita, don't you ever go away from here. You are from here, and the people love you very much. As much as they love me, although the girls love me more! You are going to suffer. I don't want you to suffer. You have been a good wife. A loving mother. A mother who has never let us down. And I am very happy, because I have two mothers, if I include my aunt."

'"That's true. She is your mother too. When one of us lacked milk, the other gave."

'The banter went on and that day we talked a long time. He was saying goodbye but I did not realise it. He had only four days to live. He died on the 26th. He was ill all night on the 25th and they did not tell me. At one o'clock he died on the road. He got as far as Coyhaique.

'In any event, he was not going to live because he had three thromboses—one of the brain, one in the leg, and one in the lungs. He always said he was not going to reach fifty.'

Rubio Solis, one of the largest landowners in and around Lago Verde, had died recently and his land was up for sale. Rumours were rife: that he had been involved in drug smuggling—a label which, even in Patagonia, attaches and tends to stick to those who have accumulated wealth; that the Tompkins were planning to buy another strategically sensitive area of Chile. Doña Dora, however, would have none of this.

'Rubio Solis brought cattle here from Osorno [Chile] via Bariloche, and into Chile via Palena. It took them forty days. When they sold them, they used to take them out via Argentina. Later the authorities would not let them cross, out of sheer bloody mindedness. They had to close their eyes and get on with it. Rubio helped Lago Verde a great deal. He brought doctors, and they came to give vaccinations, to see us all and to check the children and what they needed. They say he was good for nothing. I say that we should not be ungrateful. He gave the land for the cemetery. He cleared and gave a field so they could make an airstrip for small planes to land. We started getting news and papers. Equipment came for the school. They could take the sick out to hospitals and people to the frontier. I remember one girl they flew out. She was very ill. The whole of one side of her was dead. They flew her to Santiago and saved her life. She had a brain tumour. These are things for which we have to thank Rubio. He did not have to give anything to anybody.'

Following what seems to have been a Solis family tradition, Francisco Solis—'Don Pancho'—son of Antonio Solis, was to take himself and his family off trekking some 600 miles south-west to the Mano Negro area of Manihuales, where after years of enormous effort, he, his brothers and uncles carved out 6,000 acres of prime agricultural land. Don Pancho's reputation for achievement was equalled only by his legendary friendliness to all comers.

During our conversations, Doña Dora had mentioned the name of Eduardo Simon. I had heard of him before and that he was universally accepted as a major benefactor of Lago Verde. Now in his eighties, Eduardo Simon came to Lago Verde from a still war weary France in 1950. He had been a pilot during the Second World War and had been wounded. Over the years, he had built up a model farm at Cacique Blanco—White Chief— with prize herds. It was said that his line riders' huts, *puestos*, were the only ones in Patagonia with hot showers. I asked Doña Dora about him.

'Don Eduardo has brought much. He, too, has brought people to Lago Verde in his own aeroplane. If you were ill, then he flew you out himself. He brought medicines. The man doesn't feel the cold. He doesn't feel hunger. If he has been out in the fields and still in his working clothes, he gets in his plane and takes the sick. Not just once, he has done this many times, and he never charges. Nothing. People don't have to do these things. They are willing to do good. I have much for which to thank him. We have been good friends. He improved the cattle and sheep, bringing in semen, and his *estancia* Cacique Blanco is a model for all of us. We worked many years with him. There was never anything in writing. OK, it is not wise to do this. One should put things in writing because no one is eternal, but we never signed anything, and we worked with a lot of money and we worked well.

'He was very fond of my son Herminio. He had known him since he was a child. Don Eduardo would appear suddenly, and they would sit and talk for hours. He regarded my son as a complete man, and Herminio felt good with him. Others looked and said, 'Why with him?' It was because my son had something to talk about. They were both people with education. People with the ability to get on with anyone. They knew how to converse.'

In the first of his trilogy of books,[2] one of Chile's foremost modern authors, Enrique Valdés Gajardo, draws on his own formative years in Lago Verde and the hours he spent with Doña Dora, when they, too, 'knew how to converse'. Enrique Valdés, who died in 2010, was an exponent of 'frontier literature' and based his novels on the history of the settlers of Aysén, and those who preceded them: the Indians.

---

[2] *Ventana al sur, Trapananda* and *Calafate.*

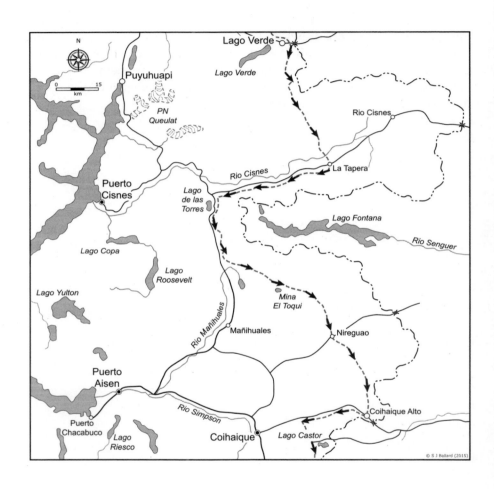

CHAPTER SIX

Lago Verde to Coyhaique

*H*ector was happy. We had acquired three mares—one bay and two black. None of them had been christened, which gave us the opportunity of learning their ways and naming them accordingly. They were each quite small, and while this suited Hector and his nine stone weight, I was less sure about my fourteen plus.

'There weren't any bigger, but they are all *mansos*—tame. The two blacks have been brought up together.'

The bay he had chosen with my weight in mind, was strongly built, her shoulders and quarters being significantly wider than the others.

'Yours was a bit more expensive, but I got the other two at a discount.'

I persuaded myself that my mare had an intelligent face. In truth they all looked bright. Her mane and tail were long, and a lighter shade. The mane had been clipped to accommodate the saddle. There were white markings on feet and forehead. A pretty horse in keeping with Hector's preferences, she was to receive many admiring glances and comments during the next months.

There was much to do. The horses let Hector bend and strap each leg up in sequence, and stood patiently on the remaining three, while he trimmed, gouged and filed feet with a machete and file. Shoe sizes were approximate, and nail ends bitten off with a sharp tap on pliers. Six new shoes took several hours. It was time to saddle up. My bay squealed and took a bite at my arm as the last inches of her girth were hauled in.

'Watch her! They said she always does that.'

She always did, and since my camera made a similar but lesser noise, within days she had become 'Olympia'.

The black mare was selected as our main *pilchero*. She had a tendency to walk across the horse behind, and whether out of pique at being nominated for pack duties or natural cussedness, she wore the pained look of the offended. Since an aged aunt had had the same crabbing tendency, she became 'Tia', Auntie. Hector's preferred black was also a pretty horse with white socks at the front and a star on her forehead. The price she paid for prettiness was in nerves. She constantly started for no obvious reason.

Some days were worse than others, when there was much slapping of rein ends, rearing, cursing and squealing. She became 'Petaka'; I know not why, but the name grew on her.

So it was that Hector and I, Olympia, Tia and Petaka rode out of Lago Verde. John Wayne and his like always left town without a backward look—the male residents always looking solemn, and many of the women weeping. I knew that the women of Lago Verde had far too many things to do, and the men were all out in the fields. The only similarity was that John Wayne and I both sat straight-backed in the saddle and did not look back—the one because the role required a macho man, the other because his back and neck were so stiff that he had no alternative.

The Virgin of Buen Aire, as the patron of horsemen, had laid her plans kindly. The abrupt re-introduction to riding was gentle as we rode beside a stream, past daydreaming cattle and the occasional hut. As we eased up a slope at the valley's end, however, I guessed what was coming, and Hector nodded. Having brought the horses back to Coyhaique after the previous year's abandonment, he knew the route.

The track was not visible until we reached it. Then it snaked upwards. The horses were fresh—too fresh perhaps—but they needed no prompting. They surged on and up, twisting first one way, then another. Soon the sweat showed dark, then foaming white, on Olympia's neck and flanks. She paused, and this was to become our routine. There was no way I could have asked for more, and we both heaved with the exertion. A gentle pressure, a nudge, and we completed the next quarter, then the last half. Finally, we could each turn, stiff neck and all, and look down with amazement at the wall we had climbed. The gentle valley and stream were now far below, and already Lago Verde was out of sight.

In those lung bursting moments, we had gained the lower level of the rolling hills I had glimpsed from the cemetery. Thereafter, the climb was more gradual. Pasture gave way to *montaña*, which in turn led to higher pasture. There were light trails through endless woods, round fallen trees of *niree*, *lenga* and *coigüe*. The wind gusted through the tree tops, rustling the leaves and bending the upper branches, but the trunks were unmoved and at ground level we felt nothing. Then Olympia sat down. Her legs collapsed under her. I was so surprised that I remained sitting in the saddle with my legs curled under me. Still stunned, I eased myself off and stood beside her. Hector had continued on ahead, unaware of our problem.

Eventually he came back to find me on my knees, whispering in Olympia's ear.

'What happened?'

'She just sat down.'

'Never seen that before.'

'What do we do?'

Already I was wondering how we could possibly expect to ride another forty days or more, with my horse collapsing on the first day, and I suspected that Hector was thinking the same.

'Get up!' he commanded, and slapped at her rump.

To my surprise and no doubt hers, she got up and shook herself. I walked her round in a few circles, then mounted and we continued. The wood soon ended, and we emerged onto an exposed plateau, dotted with blackened tree stumps. Startled cattle took off in various directions. Ahead lay another distant plateau with the skeleton shape of a rough corral and several wooden huts. This was to be our first camp site.

I had brought my tent, but the time required to put it up and take it down were such that I needed no persuasion to use our large pack sheet instead. With the corral fence as a windbreak, we stretched the sheet over a line, leaving a short end angled down. Each corner of the short end was stretched with further ropes and these, together with the other end of the sheet, were secured with tent pegs. The result was to give us space for saddles and all our bags, plus ample room for sheepskins, bed rolls and sleeping bags. Depending on the weather, there was the choice of head in or out, with the latter giving a clear view of a star-studded southern sky. Provided that we chose the correct direction to face the open end of the sheet, we were to find this method very efficient, even in thunderstorms, and with the added advantage of giving room to keep ourselves and our equipment dry until the last moment. Simple to erect and simpler to take down, 'tarp' was to replace tents thereafter.

Looking back over the day's work, I could see much of the length of Lago Verde. The lake had been almost invisible from the town, which was now itself hidden. It was just possible to follow the start of the valley of the Rio Figueroa back to La Junta, and the ring of mountains to the north of the town, were now a frontal to the ranges beyond. Clouds slid past distant peaks, temporarily blunting their sharpness, and silken skeins of pink, edging across a soft blue, forecast another warm day to come. The stillness was such that even the soft munching of the horses seemed an intrusion.

This was a vista we had not seen before. We had gazed along and across valleys, but the mountains had contained our view. For the first time we were looking to the northern limits. Ahead, we had much climbing still to do before those limits could be matched to the south.

Olympia seemed none the worse and her reaction to the tightening of her girth was as good as ever, but the first challenge of the day was almost immediate. Hector stopped and bent his head sideways and framed a square with the thumb and first finger of each hand.

'It's something a *gringo* taught me. It's a way of checking how steep a slope really is.'

I looked ahead and up. The slope looked daunting, and I knew we were going up it. I looked at it again as Hector had suggested, and he was right. It did give a different perspective, and for a moment the task did seem a little easier, and, apart from our occasional pauses, we sweated to the top to enjoy the reward of looking down on our old camp site. The views of yesterday were amplified by the extra height. Almost the whole of the lake was visible, and two smaller lakes besides. That was our last view of Lago Verde as we entered woods, ultimately emerging at the head of a steep-sided, closed valley.

A black stumped ugliness lay before us. Indiscriminate forest clearance was carried out in the 1940s, during which fires often became uncontrollable, smouldering on in the peat soil until the snows snuffed them out. There was not one tree standing, and the erosion was clear to see as we skidded our way down the valley's pebbled length. It was a relief to cross the river at its narrowest point, and change direction down the lush green meadows of the adjoining valley.

As we lay in the shade of a large tree watching the swallows and martins lunch on the wing, we were disturbed by two dogs. Typically, they did not bark, but prowled in a semi-disinterested way, checking us out. Dogs do not roam unaccompanied in Patagonia, except in the towns, where they are a plague. In due course, their bespectacled owner rode up with his *pilchero*. The simple log cabin against which we had put our saddles and equipment was his *puesto* for this section of his land; a place to sleep and cook when necessary. Another similar shelter lay half a day's ride ahead in the highlands, and in due course we were invited to spend the night there.

There were no clear signs of where next to go, and although there was someone to ask, the instructions had a certain Irish quality, so that once we had crossed the river, gone through some rough corrals and joined the river's wooded edge, we were riding by instinct again. We crossed and re-crossed the river so many times that I began to wonder if Hector enjoyed getting wet. The horses did not mind as it was hot, even in the shade. Scuffed ground on the far bank usually indicated where cattle had crossed, but there was no certainty that they were going the way we wished to go. We reached the end of the valley and switched direction away from the river and up steep wooded slopes. The soil was now a ruddy brown, and the slopes guttered by heavy rains.

Tacking one way, then the opposite, we emerged abruptly onto a meadow plateau. It was another world. The trees, the bare earth and the river had gone, and instead there was a vast expanse of thick grass, dotted with white clover and clusters of small yellow flowers, *Yuyo*, framed on each side by lines of low shrub. To our right, the upper sections of the Sierra Negra seemed to grow out of the bush line.

The Patagonian landscape changes constantly as the eye blinks and the head turns. Our view of the startlingly white peaks—Hunchback, White Chief and Needle—changed as we dropped gently down the plateau, and as suddenly as they had appeared they were gone behind trees. In their place and in an opening to our left stood the rusted cone of Cerro Steffen, appropriately marking the frontier. Numerous streams crisscrossed the meadow, hidden by the thick grass, which made them difficult to pick out until we were almost on them.

It was still warm, but we knew the sudden approach of nightfall had begun its process, and we headed for a corner of the meadow where we had spotted a small wooden *puesto*. We had arranged to meet up with our spectacled guide, but an hour later, as we sat by our fire, one of the dogs came over to remind us that his master was near, and that we had chosen the wrong place. It mattered not. The horses were staked out, our 'tarp' was up and the pasta was on the boil. Further movement was unthinkable. We were at the edge of a wood and near an icy stream from the Sierra Negra. Our nocturnal background combined a constant rustling from the trees with the infinite range of sounds that come from waterfalls. A sound sleep was inevitable.

It would be wrong to suggest that our nights were all bliss and tranquillity. Hector still had the puma's share of the sheepskins and was usually asleep by the time his head passed horizontal. I had pilfered one sheepskin to go under the hips, but it was a while before I could claim comfort. A neck pillow and a woollen hat were essential, but there was an inevitable price to pay for a pampered past and a few ageing limbs, and apparently we both snored significantly.

Mornings brought a series of chores, and it took some days to develop the appropriate methods for dealing with them. Feet were given a light airing, and after a dip in the river came the sock routine. The left foot was always a problem, even as the aches and pains reduced. The sock had to be rolled and hooked over the big toe, and as the foot was pulled down, so the sock was pulled up. Then there were the boots to put on and laces to tie, the former in the horizontal and the latter in the vertical. One part of me said 'pathetic', the other brought on an attack of the giggles.

The next day we continued our gradual descent, but saw nothing of our would-be host of yesterday or his companions. Our maps showed a largely brown area at a height of between 3,300 and 6,600 feet, and we were headed for the first of two large valleys. In between the meadows continued, broken by occasional copses of *montaña*. There were few cattle and we saw no other animals. Clearly they had been there, as the river and place names indicated: Ibis, Black Sheep, Swallows, *Gaucho, Huemules*—small deer hunted almost to extinction and now an endangered and protected species—Swan and *Contrabandistas*. The scope for smuggling remains, and we were following an old cattle route, but we saw no smugglers that day or the next.

Eventually we emerged at the edge of a deep and narrow branch of the first valley. Far below, an emerald green river seemed placid, until we noticed the scars of white breakers. The track round the perimeter was narrow and sheer to the river, and we were buffeted gently by Patagonian winds as the main valley of the Rio Loma Baja, with its cattle and a few scattered *puestos*, opened out to east and west. The slope down was steep and open and the herds took flight as we reached the valley floor at a canter. Hector headed for one of the *puestos*, which was abandoned and boarded up.

'I'm not camping there Hector,' I shouted. He looked surprised.

'Hanta virus,' I said.

'Oh. We don't need to worry about that. We will use the side as a windbreak.'

'No, Hector. We can camp over there, in amongst the bushes.'

I had done my homework and learned that Hanta virus, which currently causes national concern in Austria, is a rat-borne virus found in this particular part of Patagonia, in huts or shacks which have been abandoned. Owners usually nail them up when they are not in use, but many leave them open to visitors. The virus is a killer, and in the next valley, the Cisnes valley, there had been a number of deaths. The locals, who called it *el virus que anda*—the virus that walks—had lived with it for years without knowing, and many had built up a certain immunity, but to an outsider, the danger was even greater. The symptoms are flu-like, headaches sickness and vomiting, but by the time these are experienced, it may already be too late. The recommendations issued by the Chilean Public Health Authority are: 'Open all windows and doors and ventilate for 30 minutes or so. Inspect the interior for signs of rats. Wash down floors, tables etc. with chlorine or detergent. Similar care should be taken in open areas before camping, where a ground sheet should be used.' I had read and memorised the literature, and while no doubt Hector had done the same, I had the caution of my years, we had neither chlorine nor detergent and I was the paymaster.

Towards the centre of the valley were collections of thick bushes separated by lanes of grass. It was not difficult to find a combination which provided cover from all directions, and the cattle seemed willing to find somewhere else for the night. We found one such clearing where charred logs and a hanging empty plastic bottle indicated that it had been tried and tested by drovers. In fact, Hector was a master ecologist. It was a matter of pride to him that no one could tell where we had camped. If stones were moved, they were put back. Any rubbish was collected and stored until we came across a suitable place for disposal. Fires were always carefully dampened down, and on this occasion the empty bottle was adopted as a water carrier as its previous owner had intended.

That night we had the heaviest storm I had experienced. The rain shafted down and Thor was busy all night with flash photography, rolling back and forth over us. I could not believe our tarp would hold up, but as confidence grew, it was possible to enjoy a prolonged Loma Baja *son et lumière* and from the dry warmth of my sleeping bag smell the rain in the grass, inches from my nose. Our tarp had been completely open along its front and happily the wind was blowing into Argentina.

The early morning brought sun and a clear sky full of movement. Small finches, tyrant flycatchers and earth creepers scurried and darted at low level. Their colours were subtle browns and greys, with underside flashes of yellow and blue. There were no songsters, only twitterers. At a higher level, a variety of small kestrels coasted and swooped through the bushes, soaring back up to their hovering vigil. Their underside colours matched those of their prey, save for the absence of coloured flashes, and with a preference for blues. Their top side glamour was reserved for the sky above. It all seemed very much as Darwin had seen and noted.

We crossed the valley floor towards the distant Cordón Las Quemas, and lost our way meandering through tall thick bushes. It was difficult to work out which tracks were going our way, and even standing in the stirrups we could not see ahead. We guessed correctly, however, and broke out into the open at the edge of a stone and gravel escarpment to the Rio Magdalena. The river would have been an entirely different proposition in full flood, but fortunately was in its summer recess. Even so, we crossed with difficulty, then meandered through a wood of trees and bamboo and down a battered fence line to a corner of the valley. At this point the Magdalena had picked up a companion, and together they occupied the entire width of the narrow exit. Once again, there was no alternative but for another Patagonian rope trick up, out and over the shoulder.

The pleasure of these crazy climbs was to be found at the top, where we could pause, dismount and stretch aching limbs, and where stiff necks could survey the morning's work, picking out our now distant camp site, and where we had entered the valley the previous evening. Around us, pink daisy-petalled flowers entwined the bushes, and single scarlet honey-suckle blooms stood out in an otherwise dry and dusty background.

Each of the horses had a different pace. No doubt a more skilled rider would have imposed himself on Olympia. She tended to fall behind, and since she did not like the fast walk preferred by the *gaucho*, we were constantly trotting to catch up. I found her extended trot uncomfortable, but reined in, she produced a rocking chair canter. Hector was to try her for a few days, but he preferred Petaka, whom I never rode. Tia was therefore the change horse. She did her best with my weight, but was not really strong enough. Hence, Hector rang the changes between Petaka and Tia, and I spent most of my time on Olympia.

The land now inclined away from us, fences were new, and the clumps of poplar, signifying homesteads and corrals, became more frequent. We approached one but there was no one there, and Hector, either unsure of the way or fancying a gallop, or both, broke away and headed off towards a man he had spotted herding horses. We were on the right track, and soon we caught our first sight of the settlement of La Tapera. For a while it disappeared from view as we skirted the final bush and boulder promontory and slithered down a loose shale face to the floor of the Cisnes valley. A long ride on the flat remained and Hector appreciated my suggestion that we lead the horses for a while. We still had the Rio Cáceres to cross, our widest river yet.

'Horses swim sidestroke,' explained Hector when I asked what happened when horses were out of their depth.

'The trick is to stay on.'

Hector's instructions were normally given at the last minute, when discussion or further enquiry were impossible. If it was deliberate, it had its advantages, and as on previous occasions it proved to be sufficient. The horses swam sidestroke, we stayed on and, soaking wet, arrived on the other bank.

La Tapera was our first stop. Here we had the prospect of a hot shower, a conventional bed, some wine, and a supper not cooked by Hector. Our hostess at the *hospedaje* had won trophies for dancing the *cueca*—a Chilean dance of coquetry and elegance—but arthritis and age had taken her smile away. We had met her husband and two sons earlier on the trail, and they enthused over our traditional pack horse equipment, while we reciprocated over their homemade wooden frames.

It had taken us two days to cover what Doña Dora had done in a day.

'You have to have a good horse,' she had said. We had three.

'And you need to leave early,' which we rarely managed to do, even with our *tarpa*.

'You can do it without hurrying.' We had not hurried, and, to be fair, we were not competing either. Nonetheless, it was helpful to have a 'standard'.

La Tapera—the name comes from the Paraguayan language, Guarani, and means the remains or ruins of a dwelling—was founded in 1996. The road up the Cisnes valley, through La Tapera and past the Estancia Rio Cisnes to the Argentine frontier, followed two years later, and should have changed the town forever. There was now no excuse for isolation, but the town gave the impression of having been forgotten by the rest of Patagonia. It was a poor frontier settlement, its houses scattered over a wide area. Efforts had been made to provide some municipal facilities, with a simple, treeless park and some rustic swings and roundabouts, but they were not in use while we were there. The streets were unpaved, some with raised concrete paths, and electricity was supplied by generator with the usual time restrictions. One general shop dominated a number of smaller, front-room efforts. There was hot water eventually, and the next morning, despite limited grass, the horses indicated they had had a reasonable night.

Our route this far had taken us well to the east of the main Austral road which connects Chaitén in the north to Coyhaique in the central south. Initiated in 1976, the Austral has been a permanent project since. Some of the worst problems encountered in its construction lie between the western end of the Cisnes valley at Amengual (founded in 1983 on the site of a former military road camp) and Puyuhuapi, which was established by a small group of German *colonos* on the Ventisquero Inlet some fifty years earlier. It was the efforts of this remarkable group which laid the beginnings of the Austral through what is now known as the National Park of Queulat, and one of its members was Augusto Grosse.

Before the Austral, any attempt to connect the Cisnes valley south to Coyhaique was blocked by a lake: Laguna de las Torres. Consequently, herding stock south from Lago Verde had to be via the route we had just taken to La Tapera, thence east into Argentina and finally south and back into Chile at either Pampa Alta or Coyhaique Alto. This was the route Doña Dora's father, husband and others took.

'They had to go from Tapera up over a cordillera and across a piece of Argentina, then down from there to the frontier, crossing at Gendarmeria. It was very difficult. They had to go through the *savanna*, down vertical cliffs, *acantilados*, and across what they call the *sarandas*. These are lakes hidden under earth and grass. If the horse puts its feet in, they cannot get out and are left swimming. To cross them, they have to make *envaralados*—rough wooden bridges—out of poles. If the horses take fright in the water, you lose everything. You cannot get out of those *sarandas*. It took a month to get across. My husband said that this was no life! The cattle were filthy, covered in mud. The horses fell in the mud. Horses died. Animals died. They were all soaked and without food. They always got through, but it was bad. Very bad.'

Doña Dora did not mention the constantly changing requirements imposed by the Argentine bureaucracy and enforced by the gendarmerie, and which included the *papelitas*, duties which were little more than bribes, and the veterinary checks applied with increasing severity to all Chileans.

The first concessions to the Cisnes valley required not only the establishment of *colonos* but the building of a road to the coast and a port. In 1904 the Anglo-Chilean Pastoral Company (ACP) bought the original concession and its neighbour to the south for a twenty-year term, and ran it from London in the manner of a British colony, with first a D. H. Brand and then Angus MacDonald as administrators. It became a highly efficient and productive venture with over 40,000 top-quality sheep, but little was done to satisfy the conditions of the concession, and the ACP preferred to market its produce and maintain communications via Argentina. After fourteen years, the concession was revoked.

By then the government's attitude towards concessions had hardened, and when John Dun, former administrator of the adjoining concession to the south, the SIA (Sociedad Industrial del Aysén) put in a bid for a new twenty-year term, the conditions imposed were so onerous as to make them impossible, including buildings, barns, bridges, roads, a school, office and accommodation for a civil registry, church and police station, regional medical centre, steamer service and a feasibility study for a railway. Whatever Dun's reasons for bidding, he quickly sold the new concession on to a Chilean Company, the Sociedad Ganadera Rio Cisnes (SRC). The new owners re-employed Brand and a predominately British staff and made an effort to open up a road westwards to the Pacific, but were forced to give up after 25 miles. Thereafter they, too, returned to the priorities of their predecessors, continuing high-quality wool exports through Argentina and increasing the flock to 60,000 by 1927.

For Hector and me, the next two days were relatively gentle as we wound our way east down the Cisnes valley, following the river of the same name. Farms were extensive, their boundaries marked by new fencing, and there were even areas of vivid green wheat. The signs of order and affluence grew as we travelled west. To the north low ranges rolled out to the white peaks we had passed several days previously, but from this side their individual identities were less obvious. To our left, the brutal wall of the Loma Collar marked the intrusive line of the frontier, now running east-west. It was a lazy hot day and we made good progress. There was even time that evening to cast a fly into the lumbering river. The fact that the fly had been made in Argentina probably influenced the fishes' decision to ignore it. Eventually, however, I lost patience and attempted unwisely to gain the extra yards to that side of the river where every trout in Patagonia seemed to be breaking the surface, and my Argentine fly found a new and permanent home thirty feet up a tree. The shrill squawk of the green Austral parakeets overhead was ill timed, and the casual and repeated success of a resident cormorant rubbed more salt in the wound. That night it was tinned tuna, but we slept soundly on a small island, lulled by the sound of the river, mere inches below.

As we entered the section called Cisnes Medio, the valley dropped a level. The view below was an Impressionist dream—valley curves bisected by lines of tall poplars; river bends emerging from hidden canyons; and in between the green tones of crop and pasture, dotted brown and black by cattle. The picture was promptly completed and signed off by the sudden appearance of two Frenchmen, each riding a fine white stallion and towing a white packhorse. The packhorses were piled high and covered with a bright yellow plastic sheet. We had heard through the grapevine that they were riding our way, and we stopped to exchange greetings. They were on their way to Lago Verde, with Chaitén their ultimate destination. As we parted company, Hector exploded with laughter. Each packhorse was attached to the tail of the horse in front.

'Never seen that before,' he said.

'Crazy! They'll pull their tails off.'

From their obvious riding ability, it was a reasonable guess that in France things were done differently, but the image Hector had conjured up kept him amused for a long time.

I was half looking to see if I could identify the land which Doña Dora's father had bought. All she had said was that it was a thousand hectares (6,000 acres) 'on the other side of the river' in Cisnes Medio. She had said it was very beautiful, but that when he died, her mother had sold it to Doña Dora's brother-in-law. She had also described an incident there, during the terrible snowstorms of 1944.

'I heard my father was lost, that he had been caught in a snowstorm, and that nothing had been heard of him. The only information we had was that he had left Cisnes for Lago Verde with a sergeant. Do you know that for three months, nothing was known about them? The sergeant's father was told and he had a heart attack and died. But the two were both alive. They were trapped by the snow, but in a part of the estancia where the best cattle were kept; where there was a barn. There they stayed, but no one could get to them while it continued snowing. The sergeant's wife could not stop crying, but no one knew whether they were dead or alive until three months had passed, and they appeared. They had been unable to leave because the horses had lost much weight and others had died.'

In 1898, when Hans Steffen finally broke out of the jungle of Queulat, after two months of hell battling up the lower reaches of the Rio Cisnes from the Pacific, he found himself in the pasture and meadowland at the entrance to Cisnes Medio. The barometer then immediately plummeted and a violent storm was followed by a heavy fall of snow such that soon there was nothing to distinguish the burned wood slopes of the Cordón Las Quemas from the valley below.

We were lucky. We certainly saw enough to confirm that the area was beautiful, but it was not difficult to envisage how suddenly the weather could change things and how treacherous the valley could become.

We were to spend one more idyllic night by the Rio Cisnes, and have one more, equally unsuccessful, fishing session. This time, however, the compensation came from our first encounter with the *chucao*; a strange bird the size and colour of a blackbird, but with the erect tail of an over-sized wren and the red chest of a robin. It is one of several onomatopoeic birds, and its haunting metallic call is as evocative of Patagonia as the bellbird is of Paraguay. The *chucao* is rarely seen but often heard in the distance, and does not like to fly. In truth, it probably has forgotten how to. It scurries, and being inquisitive, tends to appear at camp sites. Just as suddenly, it is gone. Even on our short acquaintance I became very fond of the *chucao*.

The next morning, the *chucao* joined us briefly for breakfast before disappearing and bidding us farewell from the undergrowth. Being then ignorant of the local belief that if the *chucao* calls from the left, it is advisable to postpone travel to another day, neither of us took note of the side from which the farewell had come, although since our day was to be largely uneventful it would seem probable that it was from the right.

The Cisnes valley ran out in a flurry of woods thick with bamboo and typical of the abrupt changes in climate and vegetation to be found in this area. This was where Steffen and his group emerged after experiencing the very worst of weather conditions which Patagonia has to offer. For the first week of their trek up the River Cisnes from the coast they had been unable to move at all. Thereafter rapids and rocks forced them out of the river and constant *sarandas* and incessant rain made progress even along the banks painfully slow, and many more days were spent miserably wet in camp. A decision was taken to leave all the boats save those which were collapsible. Even when it was not raining, the undergrowth was so thick that each machete blow brought down torrents of water from the beech trees. Camp and rest were only possible once raised platforms of bamboo had been constructed. The men were so badly affected that Steffen decided to reduce his team to himself and eight others, and the rest were sent back to the coast.

Thirty-four years later, Augusto Grosse and Max Junge were to make a similar journey. For Grosse, a Hans Steffen fan, this was to be the first of many similar expeditions. His objective was to establish links across Aysén from the interior to the coast—effectively what the government had sought but failed to achieve through the concessions and their conditions—and his tireless efforts were crucial to the future planning of roads. On this occasion, they were accompanied by ten selected *peones*, and Grosse left the following account.[1]

> Each one carried a heavy bag on his shoulders; met by a persistent rain, we entered the wet jungle. Two men with machetes cleared the worst obstacles so we could follow with our burdens. Not even our rubber waterproofs could protect us and each gave off steam in all directions. The darkness surprised us in the middle of a swamp. With great difficulty we managed to put up our tents and later collected round a weak fire which did not want to burn. Sitting on trunks we longed for the dawn. The second day was worse. The damp forest seemed to want to flatten us. Spurred by the desire to make progress, we kept going. The mosquitoes hound us and the huge leeches which exist in abundance because the wet ground is full of them, stick to the joints of our feet and hands or get between our toes and fingers. The load on our shoulders seems to weigh a ton and once again we decide to camp in the mud. Notwithstanding all our tiredness the rain and the leeches, we cover ourselves with a roof of branches, roll ourselves in a rug and fall asleep. The two days following were harder, but slowly we reach flowing water and on a sandy beach we at last find a dry place, and, what makes us even happier, dry wood. Soon two big fires are crackling and miraculously we glimpse some stars; later the rains stop. Quickly we strip off our wet clothes and crowd round the fire to dry. Happiness replaces the depression which had taken hold of everyone.

Much later, when indulging in those reminiscences which are part of the pleasures of travel, I remembered the *chucao* and the Cisnes, and recalled that prior to their unhappy experiences, Steffen, Grosse and Doña Dora's father had each been travelling up the valley towards Argentina. Since none of them mentioned the *chucao*, they too may either have been ignorant of its folklore or ahead of its conception, but if—as seems likely—the *chucao*'s

---

[1] Augusto Grosse Ickler, b. 1902. d. 1998. *Visión Histórica y Colonización de la Patagonia Occidental*. Santiago. 1986

habitat follows the river, it may be that travellers to the Cisnes valley should be advised to travel down rather than up it.

Whatever the folklore, Hector and I were fortunate not to be going further west. I had my own unpleasant memories of travel in that direction, albeit in the comfort of a pick-up, winding up and down the precipitous Austral through Queulat to the Cisnes valley in cold unceasing rain, dense tall dripping trees crowded at their base with gigantic wet *nalca* leaves, and with one solitary moment of pleasure, standing over the spectacular Padre Garcia waterfall. While we did not welcome having to join the Austral, even for a short stretch, at least we were headed south, and the stony road we joined had been widened in parts to airstrip width since the previous year.

Steffen's detailed exploration of the headwaters of the Cisnes river persuaded the Tribunal to grant the valley to Chile, creating a significant deviation in a boundary line which otherwise meanders north-south from Futaleufú to Lago O'Higgins along one side or the other of Lat. 72°W. An adjustment then had to be made to include within Argentina the east flowing highland lakes of La Plata and Fontana, thus creating an effect similar in shape to a *gaucho* boot, one side of which forms the southern wall of the Cisnes valley—the Loma Collar. Its 'foot' was now to force us due south for several days, before we could head east again, up the other side of the boot. Neither horse nor rider enjoyed walking on the broken stone, and even less having to share it with trucks of varying size and colour. Orange or red caused the greatest offence, and always seemed to be driven aggressively. Each vehicle left a tail parachute of thick grey dust for us to choke on.

Anxious to clear this stretch, we pressed on and in due course passed round the pre-Austral obstacle of Laguna de las Torres. Black vultures— *Jotes*—circled lazily above, occasionally flapping their wings vigorously. We paid the price for an over hasty choice of camp site, where heavy rain and a steep slope made sleep difficult, and we woke to find our legs dotted with leeches. At least we had now cleared the 'foot' and could turn back up the El Toqui valley, but we had not appreciated that this was also the route to a large zinc mine.

Fortunately, we had arrived on a Saturday, which was the only day of the week when the mine was not working. We learned of our luck from a friendly young *gaucho*, Favio Salas, who guided us across the river and then accompanied us for the rest of the day up into the hills. Having politely admired our horses, Favio then put his own magnificent stallion through its dancing routine—sidestepping, twirling, rearing, alternating feet, reversing—all without any of us losing forward momentum. We were very impressed and felt sure that the trophy on offer at the Manihuales

Horsedance show that week, would be his. He lost points for overall impression only when he dismounted, barely reaching the top of his saddle.

The beauty of the El Toqui valley was misleading. There was a sense that all was not as it seemed or once had been. The imported dark grey dust and mud were the first clue. The sullen cream waters of the river below and the dead trees and burnt brown grass at its edge were the confirmation. Effluent from the mine flowed unchecked by local protest, and claims for compensation were left unanswered. The power of large international mining companies was a depressing reality. We hurried on through a deserted village encampment of blue-roofed huts, the lights and noise from the mine and a vast area of white mineral waste adding to an obscene intrusion. At least we missed the workday truck traffic. By all accounts, it would have been us who were the intrusion, and we would have been fortunate to have survived.

Reaching a new summit, we rode down one side of a long valley, dominated by a series of tall granite monoliths. To our left, a long fence line edged an expanse of water meadows, which tailed off first into a mess of scrub and reeds, and finally into a large lake. This was *saranda* country. A small wooden chapel stood in the middle of nowhere amongst its congregation of sheep. As we watched this variety unfold, so the wind and rain drove our heads down.

It is surprising how often the human body can go past the pain barrier; how many times the person inside can be heard to say 'Enough!' *Basta!* is even more expressive. Yet an hour or so later, another barrier is reached, and passed, then another. On this occasion, however, there was a bitter coldness to the driving rain, and eventually Hector heard one of my *Bastas*. We had reached a small cluster of huts. In Patagonia, the traveller does not ask for shelter. When he does, he is offering to pay. The better alternative is to wait, and the offer of hospitality almost always follows. However, there was no one to be seen and we had to try each hut in turn. Ultimately our reward was the offer of a deserted hut which was in the process of being washed down, and in which there was a stove, a supply of wood and wooden planks for a bed. The price was a rip off by Patagonian standards, but I was in no mood to bargain. We could greet the sun of the next day, warm, dry, fed and refreshed. Few can imagine how good a carton of cheap Chilean wine can taste, even after being warmed by a horse's sweating flanks, cooled by several hours of freezing rain, and then rewarmed by a wood fire.

We had found a gap in the granite wall, and turning south down a link valley we started our long descent into the valley of Nireguao. Within an hour we were standing at a high vantage point, El Gato (The Cat). To the west lay the snow-covered peaks of the cordillera Las Lástimas and Manihuales. To the east, the huge valley opened out on to the plains of Argentina. Ahead lay the ranges dividing Nireguao from Coyhaique. Our next objective was the settlement of Nireguao, which then lay out of sight behind a series of slumbering granite lions.

El Gato stands almost exactly on the line of Latitude 45, the northern extremity of a huge, open-ended triangle which has the Estuary and Rio Aysén at its western apex and the Cordillera Castillo at Latitude 46 as its southern end. Within this triangle the major rivers all flow into the short stretch of the Rio Aysén: the Nireguao, which bisected the valley immediately below us, flows west before changing its name into the south-flowing Manihuales, then west again to the Pacific as the Aysén; the Simpson travels up from the south, picking up the Coyhaique on its way, until they, too, become the Aysén. Much of what has most affected the course of Chilean Patagonia's history occurred within this triangle and during the previous hundred years. Its open side, comprising high flat lands, extends into Argentina—rolling plains, dotted by flat-topped *mesas*. In the centre, and invisible from our vantage point, the capital Coyhaique stands at the confluence of the Coyhaique and Simpson.

There was a sense of timelessness. How many generations had stood precisely at this point and gazed south over a vista that has changed so dramatically? One hundred years ago, the mountains were occupied by *huemules* and pumas. The central valleys were densely wooded, in part by thick bamboo. The Tehuelche roamed the flat plains to the east, and the Chonos and Alcalufes flitted through the Pacific canals to the west. As they slid into extinction, many of the Chonos were absorbed into the Alcalufe. Both were sailors, fishermen and fish and seafood eaters, a diet which did not appeal to the Tehuelche, and which the Mapuche in the north, looked upon with disdain. They were not considered worthy of 'araucanisation'.

The first *huinca* incursions into the Aysén triangle were made by Father Garcia in 1766 when he discovered the falls which bear his name, and he was followed some twenty years later by the pilot Moraleda. There was then a lull of nearly one hundred years before Comandante Enrique Simpson of the Chilean Navy explored a short distance up the river which bears his name. Apart from these excursions, any settlement was limited to the coast, and specifically to the commercialisation of the *cipres* tree.

In December 1896, in the dying years of the frontier dispute, Hans

A last view north to Lago Verde across forest destruction and corral site of previous camp.

Several days later, from Cordon las Quemas, across the valley of Loma Bajo and memories of a special Son y Lumiere.

On from Nireguao, the fences of the Bano Nuevo and mesa land to Argentina.

Coyhaique Alto towards the Simpson valley – still shaking after our encounter with the yellow bus.

Southern fringe of capital Coyhaique.

To avoid the Austral, south of Coyhaique, we followed the line
below the distant ridge.

Estancia La Laurita, Argentina. (Mauricio Braun.)

Cerro Castillo, where the gods do not subtract from men's lives the hours spent fishing – whatever the result.

At the foot of Cerro Castillo. No through road for horses.

Cerro Castillo from south. Hector on Petaka. Wisdom after the event.

Puerto Ibanez and Lake Gral, Carrera.

Pilchero – in retirement
2014. And with all of us
finally aboard 2004.

Passing williwaw and rainbow on Lake Gral, Carrera.

Arrival at Chile Chico.

Steffen set out to explore the Aysén area equipped with flat-bottomed boats and a collapsible canvas boat to help them upstream. Landing at the mouth of the Aysén, where the river splits in two, Steffen took one section north up the unexplored branch—which he later named the Manihuales, after the distinctive, long waxy-leaved species of the *Manio* tree—past its tributaries, the Emperador Guillermo (in honour of Steffen's emperor) and the Nireguao (after the species of small southern beech) and on to the great horseshoe cordon of the cordillera which was found to shut off and enclose the contiguous Argentine lakes of La Plata and Fontana to the east. Large numbers of guanaco and the corresponding absence of any vestige of human habitation confirmed the suspicion that the valleys had been free from human contact for many years. The other section of the expedition meanwhile travelled east down the river branch which Simpson had discovered and named 25 years previously, to its confluence with the River Coyhaique—where the territorial capital now stands—up the Coyhaique to its eastern source and thence to meet up with Steffen's section. The expedition took a gruelling six months.

Hector and I snaked our way down the hill past a small settlement comprising school, chapel, medical and *carabinero* posts and—surprisingly, since it was built in stone—a community hall. We then turned east towards the open end of the valley and a distant Argentina. The River Nireguao disappeared behind the central granite sentinels, and for a while we walked in their shadow. Fences were new and there was even a sign advertising a 'holiday centre' down by the river. These were the only indications that the valley was being dragged, struggling, into the new century.

It was another hot cloudless day. The lion sentinels took their leave, as the country opened up into table-ridged areas of scrub and thorn to one side and tufted grass clumps to the other. As the ridges flattened out, we found ourselves in tall waving grass. Ahead, the sun reflected off metal roofs and we could see distant lines of poplars. Frustratingly, a long fence line pushed us away from our objective, and forced us to approach the settlement of Nireguao from another side, so that as we rode the final straight, aching limbs demanded a break, and with Hector riding on ahead, Olympia and I reached and crossed the ford which marked the entry to Nireguao on foot.

Nireguao—otherwise Nirehuao—stands at the head of *mesa* land: a vast open area dotted with tall green tables of rock. Here, the frontier boot is on the Chilean foot, and Argentina is some way off. It was through this part that the first settlers, Juan and Guillermo Richard, came from the Welsh colony in Chubut in 1896.

Juan and Guillermo Richard located the Nireguao valley with help from the Tehuelche. They saw the potential for cattle and believed the area belonged to Argentina. Juan would appear to have been more interested in the daughter of chief Quinchamal than in his cattle and in time the stock became wild (*baguales*).[2] With the signing of the frontier Treaty, however, they found themselves on the wrong side of the border, and were forced to sell up to the owners of the adjoining concession, the SIA, and return whence they had come. Many others on both sides were to fall into the same trap.

The town of Nireguao had to wait until 1969 for its foundation, and 35 years later there was still nowhere for a visitor to stay. As important was the absence of anywhere to graze the horses. Just as the last light was fading, however, we met the Supervisor of the local school who immediately offered the grounds to the horses and the boys' dormitories to Hector and me. As the boys were on holiday, the hot water had been turned off, but even a cold shower did wonders for body and appetite, and we headed for the town's one *cantina*, where, we were told, steaks were on offer. There was a silence when we went in, and all heads swivelled. Once our mode of transport into town had been established, however, normal service and noise levels were resumed, and we were all shouting over the *rancheros* from the radio/cassette. There was a *fogón*, but it was neither the time nor place for *mate*. Beer and wine flowed, and the steaks were average.

As the number of empty bottles and glasses on the bar grew, several of the gauchos were teased off their stools onto the floor. Hairy goatskin chaps—*pierneras* or *chivas*—and jingling spurs added a local flavour. Hector had a fine voice and a large repertoire of Chilean songs, most of which I had heard from time to time, but despite his experience at local festivals he was not in the mood to sing, and the guitar was sent back to its place behind the bar. Instead, another tape was found for the cassette, and he showed some nimble footwork in several versions of the *cueca*—some seen publicly for the very first time—and there was no shortage of willing female partners.

The next morning after inspecting the school Supervisor's collection of local fossils and Tehuelche artefacts (arrow heads, spear heads, stone knives and some gigantic antlers from imported red deer) we splashed back through the ford and rode east. Our objective was to cross over the hills to the Simpson valley at Coyhaique Alto, and to leave the horses

---

[2]   Another adopted Paraguayan Indian (Guarani) word meaning 'wild cattle'.

well to the east of the city for their well-earned break. For the rest of the day and half of the next we rode the fences of one side of the huge Bano Nuevo *estancia*,[3] at 111,200 acres, one of the oldest and largest in Chilean Patagonia—and comprising originally one of the two eastern sections of the old SIA concession. Passing the outskirts of Nireguao, with substantial wooden farm buildings and paddocks of massive idle bulls, the lush open plains were strangely devoid of the cattle they would normally contain. Hawks and a pair of condors patrolled the skies, the former busy and agitated, the latter floating in enormous circles quickly to disappear out of sight. The peaceful surface of the reed-bordered lakes was disrupted by the clatter of many and varied duck, geese and snipe, which circled briefly before returning to their interrupted feed.

As evening approached, we found ourselves in the middle of nowhere—or so it seemed—until we noticed a small *puesto*, tucked under the lea of a hill and almost hidden by its protective semi-circle of poplars. This was the home of the gaucho responsible for the boundary fences and stock in this corner of the *estancia*—the *puestero*. Following the custom, we paused at the gate and waited.

'*Hola! Buenas tardes! Hay gente?* Anyone there?' shouted Hector.

A man appeared with two small children and a number of dogs.

'*Están de viaje?*' It was fairly obvious that we were travelling, but the question formed part of a certain ritual.

'*Si, señor. Viajamos hasta Coyhaique.*' There was little likelihood that we were going anywhere else, but given the hour there was also no prospect of our reaching our destination that day. Impliedly, therefore, we were putting ourselves forward as candidates for the night.

'*Bueno. Entonces desensillen.*' This invitation to unsaddle amounted to an invitation to join him as his guests, to stay the night and to put our horses out to graze. The alternative, *demonten*, would amount to an offer to hitch our horses to his fence, to sit round his fire and share his food and hospitality. Had our conversation then continued about trivia, but without the invitation to unsaddle, our prospective host would effectively have been inviting us to continue on our way. These are the formal codes of the gaucho, and today, while the exact terminology can vary, the meaning and message remain the same.

Hector and our host led the horses off to good grazing nearby, and a stable was offered with a wood burning *fogón*. Our host busied himself collecting wood, brushing down the stone floor, removing harness from wall pegs to an adjoining store and laying hay-filled sacks on the wooden

---

[3] The name, meaning 'New Bath', is derived from the large sheep dip constructed there by the SIA.

119

boards which would form our beds. He could see we were equipped to camp, but it did not seem to enter his mind that we should do so. A joint of prime beef was sliced from a hanging carcass and offered as our supper. Then it was our turn to fill the kettle and prepare the *mate*. While Hector prepared our supper, we sat round the *fogón* to exchange news and pass the *mate* round. All the time, our host's wife and the two children hovered in the background. Their supper preparations had been interrupted by our arrival, but only when our meal had been prepared did Juan our gaucho friend leave to join them. Not for the first or last time, I felt greatly humbled.

As we finished our meal, Juan returned with the two children Victor and Jasmine. Both Hector and I were now *Tío*, uncle, in the custom of Patagonia. As we sat round the *fogón*, Juan told us the tale of the *Tuerto*, the man who was blind in one eye.

THE TALE OF THE TUERTO

'No one remembers his name. Still less his surname. Perhaps even he had forgotten it behind one of the many gates that had closed behind him during his life. He had earned the name *Tuerto* from this vacant eye, which was a permanent reminder of his adolescent life on the Estancia Elsita, over there in Argentina, and of when he came to blows with his 'trainer', who with one blow of his whip closed his eye for ever.

'He dressed in the old way: black beret, neck scarf, a discoloured poncho, *bombachas*, concertina boots, and his inseparable *chivas*—goatskin leggings. His only possessions consisted of a *malacara* (literally 'bad face'), a horse with a predominately white face, generally regarded as inferior, his *pilchas*—saddle bags—and a dog as old as he, and which helped him earn his bread, because the *Tuerto* was a drover. A drover without a dog is like a Balmaceda without wind, or a Coyhaique without snow in the month of May. He was a dog, a mixture of an infinity of breeds, like all the dogs he had had; he was a stray; found on his wanderings and known as well as his own soul. The dog was half of himself, his only companion. Sometimes when he went down to the town and stopped off at some bar, the dog waited patiently for him. At the end of the day, the *Tuerto* would leave, usually drunk, and go to sleep anywhere. The dog would sleep, too, offering the warmth so needed in those lonely places. They shared their poverty, the sorrows and the small happinesses that filled their lives.

'They came and went through the country, always alone and always silent; moving constantly from one place to another, as if a herd of memories followed them. They understood each other perfectly. One whistle, and the dog moved to the front, stopping the flock; another different whistle, more strident and high pitched, made the dog turn with his ears down and tail between his legs, as if expecting a punishment, which only rarely he received.

'The puff of the wind changed, and the drover raised his face to the sky, scanning the clouds, which announced the fall to come. First it was a large tear, which slid down his poncho, and without changing the pace of his *malacara*, he let the first snowflakes fall, before a whistle drove the dog at the faltering sheep. There were still a number of miles to their destination; this time it was the land of one Sanhueza in Dos Lagunas. That morning, after *mate*, he had left with his dog and the fifty sheep on their way to their destination. Payment was agreed on a handshake, as had been his life code; any sheep missing, no payment. He had never lost a sheep. Not even a lamb. He kept his word.

'In the distance, he spotted the lights of a truck, and he gave a whistle to the dog to bunch the sheep together. The snow, which a moment before had started to fall, was forming a carpet which covered the road.

'The vehicle was closing rapidly, revving its engine. Perhaps for this reason, the lead sheep was startled and ran madly in the direction of the truck. The others, true to their nature, followed. The *Tuerto* saw a tragedy unfolding. He whistled twice: two short blasts that left his lips almost without thought. The dog flew into the road, cutting the sheep off, and turning them to the side. Only the lead sheep remained, defiant in the middle of the road.

'The dog turned to look for the stubborn animal, but it was already late. The heavy vehicle ran over the two animals, the dog and the sheep. The *Tuerto* stood, his whistle frozen on his lips. Not one shout. Not a tear. Slowly he moved towards the road. He lifted his old companion. The head hung loose, and the eyes were glazed, already unseeing. He seemed smaller then. He looked for a bush and left him there, patting him lightly. Without looking behind, he went back to the road to lift up the sheep, the cause of the accident, and continued on his way. He would keep his word.'[4]

---

[4] This version was found in Spanish in the Coyhaique library, but the author's name was not noted, and subsequent enquiries have failed to reveal it

We guessed that Victor and Jasmine had heard the story before, but there was not a dry eye in the house.

We left Juan and his family with regret, but even the freedom to which we had become accustomed created its own limits and pressures. We wanted to be in Coyhaique within the twelve days we had set ourselves. The fence line continued but we started to wind our way upwards and out of the valley and plains. The condors joined us again briefly before sweeping off towards Argentina, and we overtook an armadillo, travelling in the slow lane. Apart from traditionally forming the sound box of the *charango*—a small double-stringed instrument not unlike a small guitar, and found in the highlands of Peru, Bolivia and northern Chile and Argentina—the first and largest armoured ring of the armadillo's tail is used by gauchos as a toggle for their neck scarfs.

Strangely, Hector had not seen one before, and while he dived after it, I recalled doing the same many years before. We both assumed that being slow, it was an easy matter to catch them, but the armadillo goes underground a great deal faster than it runs, and within seconds the pursuer will be fortunate if he is left even with the last ring of its tail in his hand. In any event, while the smaller version makes a reasonable meal, cooked in its shell, the larger variety, which Hector was so keen to catch, is considered inedible.

At the head of the pass we paused for lunch and a final view of the Nireguao valley. The town was out of sight behind a promontory, and our panorama was of the green plains and their *mesas* to the north and east, extending far into the horizon haze. Ahead, the land continued to rise gently and it was several hours before we reached the next summit, this time dominating the Simpson valley to the south and west. As we started our long descent we rode by a small sheep farm, the farmhouse set in a sheltered hollow, and the adjoining corrals milling with protesting sheep awaiting their summer cut. Beyond, the fenceless countryside rolled away from us, and was completely deserted, save for the distant figure of an approaching rider. Half way across, we stopped to check that we were heading in the right direction and learned that the rider was on his way to help with the shearing. It was clear not only that he had come a very long way, but that he did not count the cost of his neighbourliness in either time or distance.

As the slopes flattened out, so the fencing started, and it became clear that we were passing a substantial and mechanised *estancia*. In this western approach to Coyhaique, there are a series of connecting valleys, each divided from the next by high ridges and descending in long fertile steps to the elbow where the town itself is sited. These valleys contain some of the best land in Patagonia.

Eventually we reached the *carabineros'* frontier post beside the gravel road to the Paso Coyhaique and Argentina, where we were given directions to a suitable site to camp off the road at a bend in the river. It was a good choice, the horses had good grazing and we were up at first light for our final lap to Coyhaique. For Olympia and me, it was almost our last. I had just remounted after a 'photo opportunity' and we were approaching a hidden bend, when a bus appeared out of nowhere. Not only was the bus accelerating and revving loudly, but it was bright yellow and big, and the story of *El Tuerto* was still fresh in my mind. I recall holding the reins short and turning in towards the bank. Olympia did the rest. When I opened my eyes, I found myself still astride but approximately twelve feet above the road on a narrow ledge. Of the bus there was no sign.

'How did you get up there, Jon?'

I had no idea how Olympia had managed an almost vertical jump, and Hector had been far too occupied in trying to prevent the other two horses from going over the sheer drop on the other side. I was sweating profusely and could not stop shaking. It was several minutes before I had recovered sufficiently to curse the bus driver.

Ian had organized some grazing for the horses on a small farm outside Coyhaique. Since the next stage of our journey was to take us south, this meant that we could avoid riding both into and then out of the town traffic, and give the horses better and cheaper feed than the town itself offered. As we turned them out into the paddock, we shared their pleasure as, freed of their saddles and us, they rolled repeatedly in the dust and chased each other over the hill. They had served us well. For Hector and me, four days of rest, hot showers and good food lay just half an hour away.

CHAPTER SEVEN

Coyhaique and the Simpson Valley

*I*t was the Tehuelche who gave the name Coyhaique[1] to the river which flows west from the frontier marshes to link up first, with the Simpson from the south, and then the Manihuales from the north, and thence to the Pacific. In time, the two distinctive areas through which the Coyhaique flows have come to be known as 'Coyhaique Alto' in the highlands—whence we had come—and 'Cohaique Bajo' in the valley—where we were headed. Although the site selection and building of the current capital of Aysén were not to start until 1929, the original name for its first nine years was Baquedano.

Following the Arbitration of 1902, which in terms of central Aysén, showed a preference for the Chilean 'division of waters' thesis but left neither side entirely happy, and once the surveys had been carried out, the border markers placed and the border Treaty signed, both countries moved to consolidate their respective positions. Thus began the era of colonisation, a process which continues to this day. For many years, the policy applied was to issue long-lease concessions to large areas of land, and European immigrants and capital were encouraged. Individual settlers (either *poblador* or *poblador espontáneo* or *colono*) were left largely to their own devices to fill any gaps. Each term came to carry certain deprecatory inferences. In Chile, *poblador* is also a slum dweller, and in other parts of South America *colono* is an Indian tied/bound to an estate. In the absence of such inferences, *poblador* is an independent 'squatter', often Chilean/Argentine, and *colono*, an approved settler, usually foreign.

Punta Arenas at the southern tip of Chile quickly became a key centre for both sides of Patagonia, and it was almost inevitable that the first bids for the concessions should come from there, and further that they should come from the recently arrived European *colono*, the remarkable Mauricio Braun, who had arrived in 1874.

The names Braun and Menéndez are inseparable from the history of

---

[1] In Tehuelche, Koi, Coy,Coi and even Coig each mean lake, and Aiken,Aike and Aique, a good place to camp, with plenty of water, wood, grazing and fauna, and a good climate. The alternatives have given rise to as many alternative spellings of Coyhaique.

Patagonia and crop up repeatedly in the context of the concessions on offer in central Chilean Patagonia. Over time, while intense arguments continue as to whether they benefited or delayed development, they were the seeds from which Patagonia was destined to grow. Some claim that the Companies and *estancias* were essential. As many others say that it was precisely the *estancia* system which obstructed the process of colonisation by excluding or discouraging families. More recently, the Tompkins maintain that continuous overgrazing in the Chacabuco valley has brought about an ecological disaster area, which it is their mission to redress. They may yet inherit the poisoned chalice which the Braun-Menéndez held for so long.

From their unrelated arrival in Punta Arenas in 1874 and 1875, it took the Braun and Menéndez families some fifteen years to establish themselves, by which time Mauricio Braun was 25 and still single, and José Menéndez, some 19 years senior, had married Maria Behety and accumulated a family of nine. In 1895 the families were united by the marriage of Mauricio to Menéndez's daughter Josefina. Their rivalry, which had been intense at times, was to be continued beyond this marriage, which produced a further ten children.

While there were others who were prepared to put up the initial capital to obtain the land concessions—seeking a quick profit on re-sale—Mauricio Braun was looking further ahead. He had gained experience from many successful partnerships and joint ventures throughout the southern provinces of Santa Cruz (Argentina), Magallanes (Chile) and Tierra del Fuego (part Chile, part Argentina), and colleagues had confidence in his vision, organisational skills and drive. Braun himself was drawn to the Baker area and convinced of its future—a significant conviction he was to maintain throughout his long life. He perceived that companies were the appropriate vehicles to exploit the concessions, and he had the personality and magnetism to attract the quality of pioneers capable of implementing their development plans. Thus, first the SIA, the Sociedad Industrial del Aysén, and then the CEB, the Compañia Explotadora del Baker, came into being.

The concessions acquired by both the SIA and the CEB differed from other land ventures further south, in that they carried obligations to prepare the way for *colonos*. The areas were larger and more isolated and communications non-existent. For the Baker concession, the original requirement for 1,000 families was reduced to forty on some 1.2 million acres, but with the requirement that a shipping link should be established between the Baker and Punta Arenas. By the time the CEB collapsed in 1908, a port had been established in Bajo Pisagua at the mouth of the Baker, but it was way off the main south-north shipping route and never took off. It did, however, spawn today's strange fishing village of Tortel round the corner.

In the context of Patagonia as a whole, Mauricio Braun's priorities were sheep and cattle, the land required to rear them and the technology and organisation to market the produce internationally. He did, however, extend his operations into communications and local (Punta Arenas) infrastructures. José Menéndez never lost his initial interest in shipping, but added mining, finance, electricity, fishing and insurance as well as ranching. Both joined forces to create a commercial arm, La Anónima, with branches throughout Patagonia even today. These were general stores, selling and buying a wide range of products, and providing locals with credit and services similar to those subsequently offered by banks. They took bankers, merchants, farmers, miners and sailors into partnership or lent them capital in return for a shareholding.

After centuries of legend and speculation over the existence of the City of the Caesars and Trapananda, real gold was discovered in the far south during the last fifteen years of the nineteenth century, and a gold rush followed. Its long-term significance, however, was dwarfed by the white gold which the sheep carried on their backs. Gold digging required only a pan full of luck to make up for the hardship, but one Patagonian sheep needed at least two and a half acres of grazing, and the Braun-Menéndez had many thousands of sheep. Inevitably, they also had a finger or two in the gold pans.

By the 1920s it is estimated that Mauricio Braun owned or occupied on one or other side of the frontier, a total of over 7.5 million acres and was a shareholder in a further five million. José Menéndez had more modest holdings, principally in Argentine Tierra del Fuego. However, they also owned the marketing and shipping infrastructures, which all landowners and sheep farmers needed for the export of their wool, as well as the many-tentacled La Anónima. Inevitably Patagonia, which had looked to the Braun-Menéndez for leadership when matters were going so well, also turned to them when at the end of the First World War demand for wool and its price started to collapse. By then, many original state leases were coming to an end, and at law one half of the land acquired had to be returned to the Treasury. Against this background, social unrest, which had simmered and then exploded in the north and centre of Argentina, now broke out in the form of strikes on several *estancias* in Santa Cruz, and by 1921 the whole province was affected by boycotts and all work ground to a halt.

The opposing factions polarised, with on one side the landowners and their managers—the Patriotic League, the Rural Society and the League of Commerce and Industry plus the Santa Cruz governor—and on the other the town and country workers—the Workers Federation (later Workers Society) plus the state judge. Authority and law enforcement rested with the police, whose bias towards the landowners was legendary. President Yrigoyen, the first democratically elected President of Argentina, albeit by male suffrage, saw reds under every bed. There was some justification, since apart from a number of Argentines, the Workers Federation included Chilean, German, Paraguayan, French, Russian, North American, Scottish, Portuguese and Spanish members, many of whom made no secret of their anarchist beliefs. One of the Spaniards was Antonio Soto, and another, José Maria Borrero. Soto did the talking and Borrero the writing. Once he had gained the leadership, Soto took the strike out to the remaining *estancias* in Santa Cruz, but he was now riding a *potro* he was unable to control, and although he had experience as a circus performer, he was never much of a rider.

Unsurprisingly for those times, neither the landowners nor the authorities had social vision. They therefore reacted to each situation as it arose, and initially that reaction took the form of repression. There were arrests and detentions and the vocabulary of the two sides reflected their prejudices—'agitators', 'foreign plague', 'anarchists', or simply 'black beasts'. In fact, the proposals and counterproposals of the two factions showed marked areas of agreement, which in another age would have cried out for meetings, discussions and conciliation. Instead doors were slammed shut noisily on further talks. José Menéndez had died in 1918, leaving Mauricio Braun head of the united family Braun-Menéndez, the natural focus of the landowners and the chief target for the workers' wrath and abuse. Borrero was happy to oblige, since he had worked for the family in Rio Gallegos and had gained some insight into their operations before he was dismissed. His articles in the local press were remarkably blunt and acerbic, and indeed there was much social injustice to write about. The landowners responded similarly through their press. Violence was inevitable and with it another bloody chapter in Patagonian history, which Borrero converted into a book *La Patagonia Trágica* in 1928. There have been many accounts since.

The Braun-Menéndez relied heavily on Europeans for their managers and foremen. Some foremen became managers and some managers became joint owners and partners. Some were French and Spanish, a few Chilean and virtually none were Argentine. It was, however, predominately the British and Germans to whom they turned. In an age of the *patron*, the values of Victorian paternalism fitted well, as indeed did Victorian architecture, dress and social mores. Most were pioneers rather than *colonos*, they had capital and/or relevant skills, and many came with the intention ultimately of retiring back to their native country. None of them could

128

function without a labour force, which was drawn from a number of sources.

Some sources were local. The gaucho had always been a loner and traditionally a rider. His preference was for cattle, and he did not take kindly to the mundane backbreaking tasks associated with sheep, which often meant he also had to walk. As the fences expanded, many gauchos formed carting businesses or became itinerant horse tamers. The Tehuelche Indian was also a natural rider and horse tamer. Some of the mainstream Tehuelche became skilled sheep shearers, but for most, the organised life and demands of a sheep *estancia* were not to their liking. It was alcohol and the white man's diseases, however, which caused the most havoc amongst them; measles, diphtheria, TB and whooping cough drastically reducing their numbers, just as they had done to the Fuegian Indians. This therefore left a number of east and west Europeans, Argentines and Chileans. Of the latter, by far the most numerous were the *Chilotes* from the Chilean island of Chiloë, descendants of the Huilliche.

The role of the *Chilotes* in the development of Patagonia has been greatly undervalued. Many became *pobladores* or *colonos*. Characteristically, they were humble, hardworking and uncomplaining. They and the other workers were called *peones*, a label implying a lesser status in an age when class distinctions and pecking orders were marked, and inherited from the humble foot soldiers of Imperial Spain. They bore the savage brunt of Patagonia's weather and conditions and, unlike the Indians of the Peruvian highlands, they had no coca leaves to chew to dull the pain, only *mate* and the inevitable alcohol. Originally they were fishermen and potato growers, but quickly became skilled shepherds, sheep shearers, horse and stockmen, uniquely tolerant of the most extreme conditions. They accepted seasonal separation from their families in Chiloë, since from the *estancia* managers' point of view, single male workers provided the best returns. Isolation by distance, weather and poor communications made them the more dependent on their employers, and such dependency laid them open to the abuses of the tied shop and debt. For many there was to be no return home.

These, then, were the agricultural workers whom Soto sought to lead and Braun-Menéndez and other landowners to employ. Many hundreds went meekly to their execution with an Argentine army bullet in the head in 1921—between 120 and 180 behind the shearing sheds on José Menéndez' Estancia La Anita near Lago Argentino—while Soto escaped to obscurity.

The Sociedad Industrial del Aysen (SIA) was set up by Mauricio Braun and acquired a concession to 1.2 million acres of land within the eastern half of the Aysén Triangle in 1903, and John Dun or Juan Dun Walker was appointed manager. Born in Scotland in 1875, Dun and his parents migrated to New Zealand, and he had travelled to Punta Arenas in his twenties, where he had attracted the attention of the Braun family.

Dun believed that since the SIA was a Chilean Company, its wool products should be taken out via the Pacific—a view that was to become a requirement in subsequent concessions. He it was who established the main *estancia* at the junction of the Rivers Simpson and Coyhaique, slightly to the north of today's provincial capital Coyhaique, an additional centre higher up in the Nireguao valley named Baño Nuevo and a coastal base, which Mauricio Braun named Puerto Dun, and the paths linking them. A fellow Scot, Angus Macphail joined him the following year to run the Nireguao section.

The men faced many hazards, not least the crossing of the River Manihuales. One of their earliest attempts proved disastrous. At a point where the Border Commission had left a cable and raft and Dun had appointed a ferryman, the river was high and the ferryman new to the job. Just as the last horse had clambered on the raft, it tipped, throwing Dun's assistant Fohman and two horses into the river. Dun spotted some bubbles under the stern and reaching down grabbed Fohman and pulled him on to the raft. Fohman had been hanging on to one of the horses with one hand, but when the horse gave a sharp tug on the halter, this dislocated one arm, leaving him hanging on to the raft with the other. Meanwhile, fearing that the ferryman was about to be strangled by the stern rope, Dun went to help but as he did so the raft tipped again and threw him and another colleague Garcia into the water. Garcia was a good swimmer, Dun was not. Weighed down by his boots and the revolver in his belt, he went under three times before managing to grab a bamboo stalk and pull himself ashore. For a while he was unable to move, exhausted and trembling with cold, but gradually his strength returned and he went back to find Fohman and the ferryman frozen but alive on the raft. Of Garcia there was no sign. Dun's horse drowned and Fohman's was found later safe on an island some five hundred yards downstream. Garcia's body was recovered a month later, trapped in the overhanging roots of a tree.

'They say that when one is about to drown, all the sins of one's life flash through the mind. I have to say that when I came to the surface for the first time and saw my new hat floating down river, my first thought was … there goes another hundred pesos. Perhaps my Scottish nature was predominant at that moment.'

It probably was, but his instinct for survival was even stronger.

Extensive fires, whether caused by accident or electric storms—as Steffen had reported earlier—had long been a feature in Aysén, even before the disastrous policy of torching the forests in the 1940s. In John Dun's case, he appears merely to have been rather match happy. In 1905 he tossed a match into some dry bamboo, thinking the fire would be contained by the greenness. The fire lasted three months and the smoke crossed the continent to Comodoro Rivadavia. He claimed that the trees were mostly rotten or worm ridden, but two years later, another match destroyed four square miles in less than twenty minutes. In each case, however, the vegetation seems to have returned with the first rains.

By 1914, when Dun resigned and the SIA was sold to an Argentine company, there were 110,000 sheep, 7,000 cattle and 2,000 horses. As noted previously, Dun was subsequently involved with the SRC in the Rio Cisnes valley. He died in Puerto Montt in 1958 at the age of eighty-three.

Dun much admired the *Chilotes*, regarding them as having qualities few men have. 'The success of the Company is due to a great extent to the loyal cooperation of these hard working companions.' Yet for all the hardships Dun shared with his employees, he was neither *colono* nor *poblador*. He was a pioneer, and one of the best, but ultimately he was well paid for what he did, and had the comfort of knowing that if he survived there was the prospect of a comfortable retirement. Whilst the *sociedades ganaderas* brought development to Patagonia, it was inevitable that their interests should conflict with those of the *pobladores* and that social and economic problems should follow their demise. However, the SIA was one of the most successful examples of the concession system, and brought order, infrastructure and communications to an area of great potential, and the site of its central administration was to become the location of the capital Coyhaique. These legacies survived for the benefit of all.

During my extensive travels round Argentina in 1968 I was fortunate to obtain an introduction to the Braun-Menéndez empire and was given a bundle of visiting cards to a number of their *estancias*, each urging the appropriate manager to afford me the hospitality traditional to Patagonia. After visiting several in the far south, including 'Sara' in Tierra del Fuego and 'La Anita' near Lago Argentina, I was waiting for a lift on the forecourt of a filling station in the small town of Sarmiento, which lies in the centre of Argentine Patagonia at approximately the same latitude as Coyhaique. I had been waiting most of the day and custom for petrol was bad. A pick-up truck pulled in and the driver stepped out. He had a freckled and sun-reddened face and blue eyes.

'Grandfather Berkshire shepherd,' I thought, and asked if he was going north.

'Where are you going?' he replied.

'I want to visit the Estancia La Laurita.' He looked surprised.

'I have a letter of introduction to the manager, a Mr. Morley.' He looked even more surprised. 'Can I see the letter?' he said.

I gave it to him. He read it and then excused himself to go back to his truck. I then noticed there was someone else in the front passenger seat.

After a short while he returned and suggested that I put myself and my rucksack in the open back. I did so and sat there while he refuelled. Without any further exchange, we then drove off and continued for over an hour at breakneck speed before leaving the pebbled road and dropping down into a valley along a poplar-lined driveway, past stores, simple wooden buildings and a rough football pitch, over a cattle grid and into the tree-shaded area surrounding the main *estancia* house and its gardens. The truck came to a halt and I lifted out my rucksack and climbed down.

A couple who had been sitting in the front came up to me, the man extended his hand, and in excellent English, said, 'Welcome to my *estancia*. I am Mauricio Braun and this is my wife Anita. You can cease your wanderings for a while and instead be our honoured guest.' The driver also stepped forward, offering his hand and introduced himself as Morley. I never made a note of his Christian name. He was the manager, and this was La Laurita. I was thankful that at least I had pursued a policy of shaving and washing myself and my few clothes each day, but was suddenly conscious of the holes in my trousers. Mauricio Braun-Menéndez was the seventh of the ten children of Mauricio and Josefina Braun. He strongly resembled the pictures I had seen of his father—the same moustache and smiling eyes, but shorter and stockier. La Laurita was one of the three *estancias* he owned and his favourite. An agronomist and expert in sheep and cattle, he was the farm inspector for the family, which he told me then numbered 96 grandchildren. True to tradition, the Braun-Menéndez continued to deal in big numbers.

'Don Mauricio', as others and I called him, had been born in Punta Arenas in 1904. He knew Patagonia well, and his three *estancias* intimately. His was a natural welcoming warmth which reflected the love he felt for this land. He was at ease with himself and those he met.

La Laurita was clearly very well organised, and Morley was obviously the man responsible. His father, a Scot rather than a Berkshire man, had been the previous manager, and Morley had been there thirteen years with his wife and two sets of twins. The *patron*'s visit had no doubt influenced the amount of fresh paint on view.

Outside on the prime pastures were the stud rams, the dairy cattle and horses. Away from the shade of the poplars, the land was dry, there having been little rain in the previous three years. While the area totalled nearly 170,000 acres, the terrain supported only 24,000 sheep. The Rivers Genoa and Senguerr provided water from the north and west, although their tributaries were currently dried up, and a canal had been dug to bring water to an adjoining valley some miles from the *estancia*. A winter 'camp' of 18,500 acres lay some hundred miles away in the cordillera foothills, and the sheep were wintered there, being brought down in the summer to fatten up.

The next day Don Mauricio drove me out to the far valley where the men were rounding up cattle, Argentine steppe style. This tends to be fairly impromptu and lengthy, since there are no corrals. The men were mostly *Chilotes* and were gathered round an *asado*, or bonfire barbeque, when we arrived. They then attempted to cut out the barren cows and bull calves. There was much whooping, shrieking, whistling and waving of spatula leather whips. One calf escaped and set off towards the distant cordillera followed by two riders. They had disappeared from sight when another calf made a break in the opposite direction. This time tactics were adapted and two more riders merely stopped it, while eight more drove the rest of the herd to absorb the truant.

In the afternoon the calves were roped, and those destined for the butcher were branded. The smell of scorched hide mingled with the sweet odour of smoking manure, which in the absence of firewood served as peat for the fires. Later it was loading time and the calves were driven, pushed and threatened into a 'neck' which reduced their entry up the ramp into the waiting trucks to a single file. The men whipped their horses into surges of speed, then checked them abruptly and pushed their chests against the calves' rumps, now stained with faeces. The skill of man and horse was a violent poetry, against which the separated mothers set up a mournful protest.

'They keep that up for days,' said Don Mauricio.

Our evenings were spent in conversation round the fire. Don Mauricio talked and told tales. I listened and asked questions. Doña Anita busied herself with her stamp collection. I learned much of the family and *estancia* histories. Don Mauricio felt the harsh judgements and criticisms of the family as deeply as had his father, but he dealt with my questions as only an honest man could do.

'Why?' he asked. 'It all seems so unnecessary.'

My last sight of this gentle man was of a figure slightly bent by the years, a favoured shawl draped over his shoulders. He waved and turned back to his beloved La Laurita. He will now be lying in the small *estancia* graveyard where he told me he would be buried.

From Chilean President Balmaceda's resignation and suicide in 1891, the country was governed by a small elite who had inherited either wealth from the mines in the north or land in the centre, or both. Lack of interest in Aysén, which had been a feature of government policy prior to the Arbitration, meant that Simpson's recommendation for a road into the interior was not acted upon for over thirty years, and then only just in time for Holdich's inspection in 1902. This was the road which Dun was to complete. After Arbitration it was deemed easier to let the concession bidders exploit and administer their land, subject to conditions that any *colonos* should be Anglo-Saxon or European and that the concession holders should create the basic infrastructures. While avoiding any cost to the public purse, the consequence was that no attempt was made to integrate Aysén or to install the basic elements of national administration. In many instances, purchasers of Chilean concessions also owned adjoining *estancias* in Argentina and became the de facto controllers and enforcers of rights in the cross-border areas, and in some cases it was they who paid the police wages.

Prior to 1927, when the province of Aysén was created, the official Chilean authority over any Chilean citizen south of Puerto Montt and north of Ultima Esperanza, was shared between the former's Province of Llanquihue and the latter's Territory of Magellan, and individuals often had to guess which had authority over which set of circumstances. The only means of communication was by telegraph to Comodoro Rivadavia (on Argentina's Atlantic coast) and the nearest Chilean Consuls were in Argentina's Esquel or Bariloche. In practice, any formal representation had to be made on horseback via Bariloche and across the cordillera, or south to Punta Arenas--in either case a huge and arduous journey through often hostile Argentine territory. The absence and ineffectiveness of Chilean representation had already allowed Argentina to play her 'only local effective authority' card at Arbitration and was to cause further problems throughout the twentieth century

In the market that developed round the sale of concessions it was who one knew which counted most, and there were quick profits to be had simply by selling the concession on. As it happened, both countries were fortunate that there were not only those with vision and capital to take on the concessions, but others with the administrative capacity and pioneering spirit to turn them into a commercial success. The SIA was one such example, and it was on SIA land that Coyhaique was to be built, but many other concessions failed. Those that succeeded could expect some of their conditions to be relaxed, but for those that failed there was no follow up plan, no administrative structure in place, and the land involved, often of considerable potential, was an open invitation to all comers, whose numbers were constantly on the increase.

Prior to the 1902 Arbitration, the Chilean *pobladores* to the east of the cordillera, whose existence had come as such a surprise to Hans Steffen and others, received some recognition from a Law of Repatriation (1896), which provided facilities for their return, but once their occupational status had been overridden by the Tribunal's decision those who chose to stay faded back into further obscurity. Pioneers they were, but to officialdom they remained squatters. In time, a significant number of Chilean *pobladores* collected in the Argentine region round Alto Rio Mayo and Lago Blanco, where—the cordillera having all but disappeared—the frontier was at its most porous, and where today there are no fewer than five official border crossing points. Out of this number the first to cross were a number of Huilliche Indians (including the brothers Miguel and Juan Hueitra), the Finn Olof Lundberg, a Briton John Brooks (who worked with Lundberg) and Paul Richard, who may have been either another British citizen or a German. They all settled near the site of Balmaceda and it was not long before others, including one José Antonio Silva Ormeño (José Silva) joined them. The wider area came to be known as Rio Huemules or Simpson Valley.

The SIA's concession initially covered both the (higher) Nireguao valley and the northern part of the (lower) Simpson valley as far as the frontier, but the basin of the Rivers Simpson, Palos and Blanco to the south—including Rio Huemules/the Simpson Valley—formed part of an adjoining concession of some 115,000 acres granted in 1903 and subsequently assigned to the Sociedad Ganadera de los Tres Valles (STV). Despite obtaining a three-year postponement on the start date of its twenty-year term the STV was always under pressure in trying to meet the conditions of its concession, and turned to a Swedish aristocrat Carlos Von Flack[2] and his brother for help in securing possession. Von Flack duly arrived at the STV concession with a small herd of cattle and immediately set about forcing the Huilliche settlers out. His methods were brutal and he sought to impose his own rule of law by dressing himself and two of his men in quasi-military uniform and calling himself 'Prince of Patagonia' or—on days when modesty prevailed—*Comisario del Baker*. From that moment he

---

[2] Otherwise known as Carlos Juan Flacher in Argentina, where he appears to have run up debts to the extent that Chile would have seemed a more desirable place for him to be.

and the *pobladores* became sworn enemies, but the STV was running out of time and both the *pobladores* and the SIA knew this. Even Von Flack seems to have had his own agenda of trying to acquire the concession for himself and operating it as a 'joint venture' with the Braun empire, and he was to reappear several years later in the town of Chile Chico and the Baker area with similar objectives and even more violent consequences.

The STV duly failed to meet its colonisation deadline in 1911, and despite a last minute request for a suspension the concession was cancelled on 18 June 1914. Shortly afterwards, a group of Chilean *pobladores* led by Juan Foitsick, set out from Rio Mayo and crossed the frontier, taking a new and direct route via Lago Polux. After hacking their way through dense woodland, and a further nine harsh days' travel, they arrived at the SIA's Estancia Coyhaique where they were met by the general manager Angus Macphail. In contrast to the meetings between Von Flack and the *pobladores*, this meeting was friendly and welcoming and the group were provided with food and lodging during their stay. Having assumed that they had come via Coyhaique Alto—the route which Hector and I had taken but for which the SIA's prior permission was then required— Macphail was amazed to learn of the route they had actually taken, but when told that they and many other Chileans in Argentina were hoping to occupy the land of the failed STV concession, he had to advise them that their journey had been in vain because the STV land had just been granted to the SIA. In fact, the decree authorising the SIA to take over the best of the STV land in the Simpson valley in exchange for land to the north of Manihuales, which the company had never managed to occupy, was not issued formally until later in that year.

In the meantime, José Silva emerged as the *pobladores'* natural leader, setting up a 'Chilean Colonisation Committee' and petitioning the Minister of Agriculture in Santiago for the formation of a Chilean colony in Rio Huemules. A severe winter prevented personal delivery of this petition and it was sent to the nearest Chilean Consul in Esquel, who did not reply. Over a year later, a similar note was sent to the Minister of Colonisation, and a copy to the press.

Little is known of José Silva's background except that he had served in the Chilean Army and had spent much of his subsequent life building up a general stores business with his brother in Argentine Lago Blanco. He was politically astute and well aware of the power of the press, and capable of expressing himself in the colourful and direct language of his time. These were feisty times and produced feisty people who—in the Spanish idiom—called bread, bread, and wine, wine.

Apart from supporting his fellow *pobladores*, José Silva pursued a dream of establishing a new town some three miles inside the frontier, which he hoped would rank in importance next to Punta Arenas and which was to be named Balmaceda, after the former president and Chilean patriot. By 1918 there were 250 *pobladores* in 35 (mostly) brick houses, and two years later these had grown to 91, a mail and passenger service had been established between Balmaceda and Comodoro Rivadavia and a hotel built. Described as an 'idealist', José Silva acquired no plot or interest for himself. Ultimately Balmaceda was to lose out in priority, first to Puerto Aysén and then to Coyhaique, and has since achieved status only as Coyhaique's airport. José Silva, however, still had a significant part to play in the 'War of Chile Chico' further south.

By 1915 José Silva was corresponding with the president and a number of ministers and the provincial governor—with copies to the press in Puerto Montt—all signed by an ever increasing number of *pobladores*. The content was clear, concise, courteous and confident: the Simpson valley was occupied by more than 400 *pobladores* whose investments exceeded half a million Argentine pesos: they were not going to leave and there was now an urgent need for a civil and legal administration in the valley, a proposal which the Llanquihue governor himself endorsed. It was a clear 'wake up call', and at last a response was to be forthcoming.

First, John Dunn at the SIA offered to settle all the *pobladores* (in effect now elevated to *colonos*) on their then legal entitlement of 100 acres each, plus a further 50 for each son over twelve. Three months later, a new subdelegation was announced of the Llanquihue province, called 'Rio Simpson', its boundaries defined, and the first subdelegate leader was appointed. Olof Lundberg was named the first judge and told that no one was to be evicted without a court order.

Frederick Olof Lundberg, aka 'the Russian' or 'Long Fred', had been born in Finland when it was part of Russia, and had set himself up first in the Ultima Esperanza area to the immediate north of Punta Arenas. When the boundary was resolved, his land was put up for auction and he moved north, marrying Elizabeth McEwan in 1905. He crossed over into Chile, and the following year established the sheep-rearing Estancia Helena south of Balmaceda. His wife joined him from Puerto Dun in 1907. While Elizabeth always carried a revolver and would not allow any stranger into the house when her husband was away, she often invited employees to join her for afternoon tea. In the year of her husband's election as judge, and when he was absent from the *estancia*, Elizabeth invited two men who had been working there for some time—a Brazilian and a Chilean, Evaristo Miranda—to join her for tea. While she was pouring the tea, the two men grabbed her, raped her and then cut her throat before running off, leaving her dead on the floor. Subsequently an Argentine police lieutenant tracked the two men down. Removing his uniform at the border, he crossed into Chile posing as a *peon* looking for work, and eventually found both men, one working as a shepherd and the other looking after horses. He then shot them both, before crossing back into Argentina. Elizabeth Lily McEwan's white gravestone still stands in its own isolated wooden corral and bears the inscription:

> There is peace in the valley of blessing so sweet, and plenty the land doth impart. And there is rest for the weary worn travellers' feet, and joy for the sorrowing heart.

For Lundberg there was to be neither peace nor joy. He retired as judge and sold his *estancia* to the SIA in 1918. Shortly afterwards, he took poison and died in Buenos Aires.

In 1920 the Chilean government sent José Maria Pomar to Aysén to inspect the Simpson valley and the SIA, and in 58 days he covered 500 miles on horseback and in all weathers. He met and recorded the views of 155 *pobladores*, plus the administrators and employees of the SIA, *carabineros* and officials, and his report was delivered the same year. Three years later, he published his notes, observations and maps. Written against a frank historical exposure of the area and many of the individuals he met, he left a unique picture of life in Aysén at that time—what was happening and who was who. He collected data on areas and stock counts, which allowed comparison between the SIA and the *pobladores*, and he attacked the injustice they faced in having to decide either to apply as *colonos* for a maximum of 100–250 acres—which was hopelessly insufficient—or to seek an auction with the probability of being outbid and then evicted. He supported the local estimate that a family could not subsist on less than 3,500 acres, and while praising the SIA for 'having introduced civilisation to these remote areas', he nonetheless recommended that its concession should not be renewed beyond its expiry date of 1933.

Although the government which had commissioned the report appeared not to know what to do with it, in time his recommendations were followed almost to the letter, and included the creation of an autonomous territory of Aysén, with its own governor and administration, and the building of a new town Coyhaique at Pampa del Corral on the junction of the Coyhaique and Simpson rivers, where the SIA had its administrative centre. In due course, each Chilean father or widow was permitted to apply for 1,250 acres, plus 1,250 for each child over one.

Meanwhile, the Chilean people as a whole were becoming tired of a government that was both oligarchic and plutocratic and which President Alessandri seemed intent on continuing. Pomar was not alone in expressing concern that after all the years of frontier trauma there was a real danger that Chile would lose even the territory it had secured. Argentina had made huge political and economic advances, and although the 1920s brought much social unrest to the south, she had already earned a status which few, if any, South American countries could match. The Argentine people walked tall and looked down at their western neighbours, and Chileans felt a certain envy and a sense that they had underachieved.

Change, when finally it came, was messy. Because the main political parties boycotted the 1927 elections, Colonel Carlos Ibañez del Campo was faced by only one opponent—a communist in exile—and the only surprise was that he secured a mere 98 per cent of the vote. President Alessandri and his elected successor were forced to resign and Ibañez was elected. For the next four years, Chile was to have a dictator who ruled by decree and with an iron fist, and whom some have called Chile's Mussolini. Under slogans of 'national refoundation' and 'A New Chile', a new territory (later revised to province) was created of 'Aisén del General Carlos Ibañez del Campo', its limits defined and with its centre in Puerto Aysén. For the first time, Aysén was officially separated from Magallanes in the south and Llanquihue in the north, and Luis Marchant González was appointed its first governor.

Marchant landed at Puerto Aysén, which he described as 'a wooden sheep greasehouse—miserable and in a deplorable state'. Given the swampy nature of the area and the fact that it had operated for the benefit of the SIA who founded it, this was understandable. Nonetheless he ordered the building of a drainage system and the surfacing of the streets. A proclamation was issued, setting out his objectives and priorities, admitting past failings and promising an administration in which 'honesty, justice and good customs' would prevail. A commission was established, consisting of his secretary, the newly appointed mayor and his police chief, to distribute his message to every corner of the territory. Marchant then rode off to the SIA centre at Pampa del Corral, eighty miles inland.

Pampa del Corral was a plateau set aside by the SIA as a playing field, *cancha*, for horse racing and football. The only buildings were two wooden *casas brujas* (witch houses), so called because they had been put up overnight to avoid asking the SIA's permission, thus leaving the SIA with a *fait accompli* the next morning.

'What a beautiful place to build a town!' exclaimed Marchant.

That night there was a meeting with the SIA Administrator, Thomas Anderson, who gave immediate authorisation for the project, thus avoiding the delay of a formal application to his board in Valparaiso, and Marchant's team were instructed to draw up the plans. The surveyor Hector Monreal later produced a design for the central Plaza de Armas in the form of a pentagon, said by some to represent the badge of the carabineros, of whom Marchant was a Colonel, and by others to symbolise 'the chileanisation of a European town'. There is consensus that the act of foundation was signed on an empty crate of sheep-dip, although the actual date remains a mystery.

During his three years in office, Marchant travelled extensively throughout the new province, founding towns and schools. Sub-delegates were appointed from the *pobladores* for each of four communes; a postal service and savings bank set up; a police presence established in 22 locations; administrative offices including agricultural extension created in Puerto Aysén; and a start made in identifying and measuring land for future colonisation. He emphasised the absolute need for all to be involved. To the *Ayseninas*, 'Work and more work' was hardly an original slogan, but they now had a plain-talking leader who gave them a collective identity. It was they who built the schools, opened up new paths between settlements, to Futaleufú and Lago Verde, and who built the Plaza de Armas in Baquedano/Coyhaique.

Over the previous ten years, I had watched Coyhaique continue to grow in size, stature and confidence. Boasting a wide range of modern buildings, many with a distinctive Aysén architecture—none higher than four or five storeys, and now including an impressive provincial library—the town has shrugged off Santiago's sneers of 'gaucho garnish', and today presents itself as the window of *la mística aysenina* (Aysén mystique) and Chilean pioneering pride.

On this my second visit, my priorities were to report home by email and plan the next stages with Hector, Ian and his team, while enjoying the simple but welcoming hospitality of Juan Carlos and his family. While it was a pleasure to walk everywhere, dodging the glare of a hot sun along the chunky pine-lined pavements, in no time Hector and I were visiting the supermarket where he had been employed to purchase our food requirements for the next stage to Chile Chico via the Simpson valley and Cerro Castillo.

The final section of our journey between Cochrane and Villa O'Higgins was likely to be the hardest and to take thirteen days, and we were going to need extra supplies and the option of resting one horse each day. Hence, we decided to increase our complement of horses to four with the return of Cuervo, who had been enjoying a year off on Ian's farm. Hector was to ride him over to our grazing, and we had taken the precaution of catching and tethering him the day before. Hector had observed that horses have prodigious memories, and although there was no nod, wink or extended foot, there were gratifying signs of recognition, but the difficulties we had in catching him suggested that his memories might not have been as happy as mine. He was showing some of the characteristics of a grumpy old man I knew well, and I wondered whether we could carry more than one. I then remembered the events that had preceded his shooing in Futaleufú.

'Pass friend and be recognised.'

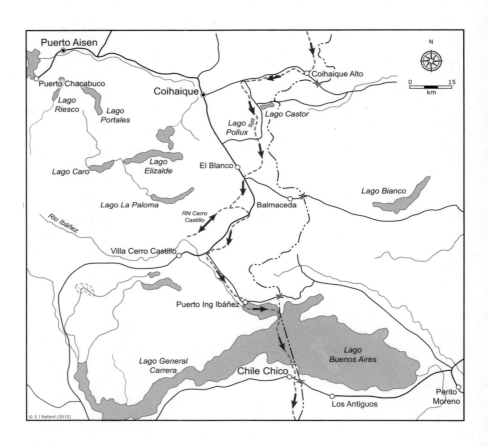

CHAPTER EIGHT

Coyhaique to Chile Chico

*T*he Austral is at its asphalted best in the Simpson valley, and the stretch south to beyond Cerro Castillo, while perfect for driving is hopeless for horses. Apart from the traffic and its speed, the verges are narrow and tightly fenced, and such farm buildings as exist are set well back from the road down padlocked tracks. Our plan, therefore, was to cut south from where we had left the horses, well to the east of the Austral, as far as the village of El Blanco, and thence via the Cerro Castillo National Reserve and Ibañez valley to Lago General Carrera.

Olympia, Tia and Petaka had benefited from their four-day break, as indeed had we. Initially reluctant to be caught, they were now even more reluctant to be separated. Cuervo, we decided, should lose some weight playing *pilchero* for the first few days. The terrain was relatively flat, but there were fences everywhere. We soon spotted our first intended short cut, and wandered down a sandy track for an hour before coming upon a locked gate. The gate and fences allowed no alternative route, and Hector walked towards a collection of wooden buildings to enquire, returning with the news that there was a guardian, but he was acutely deaf and he had no key.

'He says he's sorry but his boss is in Coyhaique and never leaves a key. He says his boss is a bad tempered bastard. He would like to help but cannot without a key.'

'But the map clearly shows that this is a path. He can't just put a gate across it and leave it locked.'

Clearly he had, however, and not only was there no point in arguing, there was no one to hear our argument. We had no alternative but to go back.

Some miles later, and having re-joined the main track, we met a *carabinero* on a moped, and I asked Hector to wave him down.

'How is it that this man is allowed to put a locked gate across a public path?' I asked, and the *carabinero* looked at our map.

'It's not a *camino vecinal* (neighbour's path),' he explained.

'But it's shown on the map as an official path, and the map is prepared by the National Institute. What better authority can there be?'

'I'm sorry *señor*, but there is nothing I can do.'

So that was it. This area in and around Coyhaique had passed into the hands of landlords or owners who could lock gates across official paths and then disappear. We had not met this situation before and we were to meet it again.

Our short cut should have taken us past Lago Frio. Instead we were forced to take the longer route to the east, past the larger Lagos Castor and Pollux and the route taken by Juan Foitsick, and his group for their meeting with Macphail and the SIA.

It had taken Foitsick a while to raise the finance for his return, but by the time his expedition set out, they knew not only that access over SIA territory would be denied but that the SIA had extended its fences, and such gates as existed were all locked. Whatever their feelings about fences, however, the *pobladores* would not cut them. That was for rustlers or criminals. Instead, Foitsick applied a simple but effective method for crossing them—a method which came to be adopted throughout Patagonia and entered local legend as 'the passage of Foitsick's carts across the wire'. Whenever they came to a fence, a ramp was formed from wooden poles up one side of the fence and down the other and the carts were passed over the 'bridge' created. The cattle and other stock, meanwhile, were driven across the unfenced rivers.[1]

Other groups were to follow and eventually the SIA was forced to propose—and the government duly accept—a reversal of the exchange under which it had acquired its Simpson valley land five years earlier: the failed STV concession. This then left the SIA with only one section in the valley, whence the small number of *pobladores* who had managed to settle there were unlikely to be removed.

---

[1] Accounts of Foitsick's journey were given by Pomar in his *La concesión del Aisén y el valle Simpson,* and by Foitsick's daughter Segunda in Danka Ivanoff Wellman's *Huellas de mujer: memorias y testimonios de Aysén,* in which Segunda describes her father as 'very machista and my mother, very humble. She bore the greater part of our sufferings.'

Although we had no carts, and the rich Simpson valley had long been cleared of its timber, there was often a strong temptation to do a Foitsick, but at no stage in our travels did Hector even consider crossing wires, let alone cutting them. Nonetheless in an area so lightly populated and with so many landowners absent for long periods, the use of wire and locked gates was out of tune with the Patagonian code of hospitality and free movement. A recent Chilean project entitled Sendero de Chile (Chilean Footpath) was intended to create a simple path some 4,700 miles along the length of the cordillera, and we were to meet national and international volunteers engaged on parts of this path. With the multiplicity and combined political weight of its owners, the Simpson valley was likely to take longer to incorporate into the scheme than the more isolated areas.

We eventually found the small farm where we had hoped to spend the night. The invitation had been extended by a relative of the owners in Coyhaique, but she had no means of warning the occupants that we were coming. Hence, the ritual conversation preceding the invitation to dismount took longer than usual, although the result and the warmth of hospitality were the same. A young family with little land and a few sheep did not have more to offer than an open lean-to stable, but in no time the horse was turned out, the cowpats brushed to one side and our tarp was extended over the logs missing in the roof. We then joined everyone in the kitchen for a shared supper. That day we had not seen a single suitable place to camp. Each of the lakes had been fenced, and while any one of them would have been idyllic, there was no way down to them. The verges were all narrow, and if there was water, there was no grazing. At least traffic had been confined to one police moped.

The next morning started with my first ever wake-up call from a chicken, who came within an ace of also giving me a peck on the cheek. Otherwise the day was to be similar to the last, with the jagged peaks of the Cerro Castillo gradually taking shape ahead. Towards evening we stopped at an isolated shack where an old man was leaning on the remains of his gate. He was the first person we had seen all day. We asked whether there was any water and grazing nearby, and shaking his head, he invited us to dismount. A quick glance and a few short questions revealed that he could supply none of our basic needs, and indeed little of anything apart from the company and conversation he sought, and we felt guilty in turning down his offer—the first and only time we were to do so.

In fact, the old man had been right. There was no water or grazing ahead. The verges between track and fence remained narrow, and copse followed fenced copse until we both felt it was pointless to go any further. There was a high bank to one side and a trace of water on the other. This would have to do. The horses were staked out down the verges, our tarp attached to the fence and enough water was trickle teased to fill our pan. After all, it was a comfortable night, apart from the activities of an amorous bull which took place sufficiently close for me to speculate on possible headlines for the *Coyhaique News*.

'*Gringo* Gored: was this a case of mistaken identity?'

'Randy Bull Flattens Foreigner.'

'Never heard a thing,' claimed Hector.

An hour's ride after breakfast and we could see vehicles skimming the Austral, with El Blanco just beyond. On reaching the road and picking gaps in the traffic, we cantered diagonally across from one safe piece of verge to another. Pausing below a bridge until all traffic had ceased, we then made our final dash over.

From El Blanco to Cerro Castillo, there were two alternative cross country routes, and we learned that the better option was believed to have a locked gate. Our first task was to try to find the owner and we were not surprised to find that he was away. The alternative now meant a further mile's ride beside the Austral, albeit this time with the protection of wide grass verges, before we were able to cut south up into open country. The ground was now soft and sandy, but little effort had been made to clear away the black skeletons of former trees. Nonetheless, the cattle found rich pasture in between the stumps, and our view of Cerro Castillo was now uninterrupted. We were aiming for a point on our map called Las Horquetas, and stopped an old gaucho to confirm we were on track. His back was straight and his eyes bright. He said he was in his eighties, that it was likely to remain sunny but he had no idea where Las Horquetas was.

We topped a rise and the land ahead fell away in all directions into what could only be a series of river canyons. Far below there was a hut and a thin plume of smoke revealed it was occupied. We urged the horses forward. The hut proved to be one of a family of three, and as we reached the wooden fence of the third Hector decided to have a violent nose bleed. His timing was perfect. In no time he had attracted the sympathy of the occupants and we had the offer of the finest grass in an enclosure set aside for hay close to a stream, plus fresh bread and cheese and an invitation to join the family after supper. We were all ecstatic. Even Cuervo managed a smile. A bathe in a pool below a small falls was tempting, but by the time we had finished unloading, put up our tarp and collected wood and water the sun had slipped behind the looming crags and the temperature had dropped to a level where the heat of a fire was a greater attraction. It was dark when we started eating and one of our hosts slipped noiselessly in to join our conversation.

The best night yet. Sleeping bag on a thick grass bed. A soft blue light against which to pick out the flight of the bats. The gentle splashing of running water and the soft munching of happy horses.

We had gone slightly off our route and fortunately one of our hosts knew Las Horquetas, so we retraced our steps and then climbed a ridge to a green plateau. From there we could look north to the snow line round Coyhaique, and south to the Cerro Castillo range which now seemed to enclose us in an extended arc. Swarms of small orange butterflies dipped and zipped. Each of a succession of lagoons carried its own preferred breed of duck, all of which were unmoved by our passing. Ahead lay the shade of a thick wood. It had an ancient feel and Hector pointed out the knots on the thick trunks which identified the trees as Ñiri. They towered far above us and there were few casualties to negotiate, but Hector seemed to be in a hurry and as if on cue, I felt a light 'plop' on my hat. I reached up to brush whatever it was off, when he stopped me.

'Careful! It's one of those caterpillars.'

Hector had a way of explaining matters by first making a statement which invited a question, and I obliged.

'What caterpillars?'

'The furry ones. They give a nasty burn which lasts a long time. They like this area, but there was a plague of them last year round La Tapera. Everyone got bitten.'

Inevitably the wood lost some of its attraction, and our pace upped a gear until we came out into the open and within minutes we were on the edge of a deep canyon. The look on Hector's face indicated clearly where next we were to go. It had been some time since we had performed the Patagonian rope trick, and even longer since we had done it going down. I was riding Cuervo, it being Olympia's rest day. He had lost weight, but while still grumpy he knew what he was doing. Previously I had found it comforting to think either 'Thank God I am not going up this bit' or alternatively 'Thank God I am not going down', to suit the occasion, and the ploy still worked. We slithered to the apex of the zig, turned, and then slithered to the apex of the zag until suddenly we were side by side with the turquoise blue of the River Bravo, its borders foaming white over an endless bed of rounded, multi-coloured boulders. Then it was 'Thank God we are down'.

We were now in canyon country. Trails were difficult to read, and we crossed and re-crossed the river so many times that I lost count. On some bends the current built up to such an extent that there was no alternative but to look for a shoulder to cross, and we had to match our crossings to the side with the appropriate shoulder. While my confidence in Hector did not flag, I believe we were both pleased to meet two gauchos who knew their way out of the final sections. Few words were exchanged on our meeting. They simply took over and we followed. Showing great patience, I could only admire the ease with which they soared up vertical passes and waited patiently at the top while Cuervo and I lumbered up behind. Occasionally the younger gaucho would drop back to walk alongside, his eyes taking in Cuervo's every detail. The older gaucho, once again in his eighties, was known as Tío. He kept to himself and would disappear from time to time with his dog, suddenly reappearing ahead. There were flat areas alongside the river, which were the pastures for the cattle, and as we proceeded so we drove the accumulating herd ahead of us. Eventually we reached a larger section containing a corral and the main herd. We all dismounted, and the initial glances at our horses then converted into comments on matters of importance.

'Fine horse. I like the saddle. Where did you get it?'

Once again our traditional saddlery proved popular and, fleetingly, I was taken back in time to childhood visits to the local cattle markets, when the sole topic of conversation was the condition and lines of a particular animal or the quality of workmanship in leather or ironwork. I had been absent too long, but these observations were so natural and central to the world we had entered that to reciprocate was instinctive.

We were left to our lunch while our guides went back to their interrupted business. Within minutes we both heard the gentle ploppings on our tarp and knew that any thought of a siesta would have to be abandoned. The caterpillars were indeed hairy and seemed to know what they wanted, and we moved back into the open until the gauchos returned. The final exit up a steep slope out of the canyon was invisible from below, and Hector agreed that it would have taken us some time to have found it on our own.

As we emerged into the open, the Austral and the bend called Las Horquetas came into view at the end of a short, steep-sided valley. A small mobile sawmill spewed waste cuts down to the river below. Nearby was the gauchos' simple shack, more plastic sheeting than timber. This was as far as they were going and we were directed across the river to a paling fence on the other side.

'At the fourth post from the right, there is a gate. Go through there, up over the top and you will be in Cerro Castillo.'

We did not spot the relevant post until we were almost on it, but we had managed to cut a large corner and without realising, we were already within the Reserve.

Chile's protected areas are many and each is extensive. The principal ones are either National Parks or National Reserves, the latter allowing some sustainable economic activity. Usually there is a particular natural focus, and in the case of Cerro Castillo it is the soaring peaks of the

Cordillera Castillo, flanked by three large glaciers, and with a total area of some 450,000 acres. In another it might be a single peak, a volcano, forests or a specific tree, plant, flower or animal. Guards ensure compliance with basic regulations within the Parks and Reserves, patrolling and maintaining paths and giving guidance to visitors.

We had a detailed trekking map of the Reserve, but never managed to come to terms with it. The entry was simple enough and we followed a peaceful river until we glimpsed one of the peaks ahead. For once we were spoiled for choice of camping site, and picked a space within a copse and a few yards from the river. We had water, good grazing, a view through the trees and plenty of time to watch the sunset sharpen the peaks. As light failed, the martins feasted and there was a flash of luminous blue as a *martín pescador*, kingfisher, jinked his way downstream. When he touched down at his usual fishing pitch opposite, he too had a short, erect Patagonian tail. Later it was the turn of the night shift: the twitterers, warblers and soft hooters.

At ground level it was difficult to identify which peak was which, and in the morning their snows dazzled under the sun. Our map seemed to suggest that we might cross to the left of Cerro Castillo itself, at some 8,900 feet the highest of the peaks, but first we would pass Cerro Peñon and its glacier, to the north-east of Castillo and a mere 6,500 feet tall. We set off through woods, weaving round the fallen trees, past small groups of foraging cattle and a swamp which our map claimed was the home of black swans. If there were any, they had business elsewhere that day. Hector then suggested a diversion to a small lake for a swim.

Remembering the old saying that 'the gods do not subtract from the allotted span of men's lives, the hours spent in fishing', I had other thoughts.

The lake, a neat sphere, was set in a clearing. We tethered the horses to bushes on the sandy beach and looked across a mirror image of green on white on blue, containing even the detail of the spires and serrated ridges behind. This image of near perfect peace was then slowly blurred by the ripples left by a family of russet headed teal and the widening circles of rising fish. While Hector stripped to his underpants and tiptoed through the gravel, I unpacked my rod and guessed at the appropriate fly. Fingers trembled at the expectation of an arching line and the thrill of playing a fighting fish of mythical size, but an hour later, right arm aching and feet protesting at the harsh gravel and freezing water, I handed my rod to Hector. This time there were no excuses, and what was left of a delicious optimism slowly ebbed away, leaving only a perverted satisfaction that Hector had done no better, and resignation at the prospect of yet another tin of tuna for supper.

A further short distance through the woods and we dropped down a steep bank on to a wide valley floor of rounded stones and boulders. A bend to our right took the Rio Turbio off into its own canyon while we picked our way over the stones towards the first of several wooded islands. Cerro Peñon's huge glacial pendant hung far above us and ahead stood the multiple pinnacles of Cerro Castillo. Patagonian mountains tend to reflect urban terminology. However, while Cerro Castillo reflected cathedral spires rather than castle turrets, apparently 'cathedral' had already been taken elsewhere as a name. Whatever the name, though, the view was one to absorb with wonder.

Hector was convinced he knew the way and we continued up the valley before starting to climb alongside a descending torrent. At intervals we were forced to cross and continue up the other side. The river fell through a series of waterfall steps, and our crossings were via platforms of spray, boulders and deep pools. It was slow tortuous and steep. After a while our progress was blocked by a small glacier through which the river had hollowed a tunnel too small to take us. We twisted and turned our way vertically up a rock wall and away from the river course. The horses skidded, paused and exploded upwards to break out onto an open slope littered with book-sized scree. They had not enjoyed the torrent or the abrupt break-out, and enjoyed the scree even less. They had nothing firm to grip on and they and the scree were constantly tipping and slipping. We tried to traverse on foot and eventually reached a thick, tough undergrowth through which we had to slash a path with machetes. We paused, sweating profusely, and looked ahead and up.

Cerro Castillo was temporarily out of sight round the corner of a rusty lesser brother, whose flank now formed a wall to our right. Ahead and at the top of a near vertical slope, the upper horizon was a ridge of deep snow. Between the ridge and the scree on which we had struggled to stand was a long climb over smaller sized moraine. The river we had followed had disappeared, leaving only a steep gulley between us and the rusty mountain flank.

If this was indeed the route over, then it was going to be difficult enough on foot, let alone with four horses. If we managed somehow to reach the top of the moraine, could we cross the snow ridge and what would we find on the other side? Where would we camp and could we be sure that the horses would have food? It was already mid-afternoon.

'Hector, if this is the route, I can't see how we are going to make it today.'

I was very aware that Hector and the horses had given their all, and I was not keen to see their efforts wasted.

'Why don't you see if there is any better way up the other side of the gulley?'

It did not seem likely, but at least it would give Hector time to assess whether the crossing was feasible. He was gone for some time, and on his return he shook his head. We turned the horses and led them back down the way we had come, managing to find a gentler alternative to the river route. Back on the valley floor, we tramped on past several islands until we found one with all our needs, and that night after supper, we went over our maps. We were both now doubtful that we had found the correct route and were determined to explore the only other alternative in the morning.

We had picked an oasis of thick grass and that night the trees formed a circular frame to a star-studded sky. Small sunken streams bustled through the meadows and pebbles on either side of our island, providing tufted seats for foot baths and basins in the purest of drinking water. After breakfast and as we returned our fire boulders to their original place, we agreed the route for our next attempt. This time we would head to the north of Cerro Castillo's peaks, up the one remaining side valley. We were not optimistic as our maps appeared to show no reduction in height such as might indicate another shoulder. We had also suffered our first loss. In all the twisting and turning, scrambling and climbing, and perhaps when we were cutting our way through the bushes, my fishing rod had gone missing, and there was no prospect of our finding it. However unsuccessful, fishing had been a welcome diversion, and had given time for the mind to concentrate on matters which otherwise tended to go unnoticed.

Next morning we headed back up the main valley, crossing its dividing river and up into woods, finally emerging on to rocks broken by patches of grass. The green was dotted with a variety of tiny flowers—reds, golds, yellows and violets—and crisscrossed with hidden streams. Once the green patches ended, rock and pebbles were replaced by boulders and moraine, making progress extremely uncomfortable for the horses, so we left them to graze and went ahead on foot. It was a long haul to a dirty grey glacial lake. Skirting this, we reached the valley end. There was only one way to look. Up. On both sides, a vertical wall of moraine led to large glaciers hanging far above our heads. In between was the sheer rock face of an adjoining peak which we were unable to identify on our maps.

If there was a way through, it had to be the route we had tried the day before, and thus we concluded that there was no way through Cerro Castillo on horseback. It transpired later that our trekking maps were for the ambitious climber. There was no alternative but to go back the way we had come to Las Horquetas. While there was a deep sense of disappointment, once the decision had been made it was possible to pause and take in the wild ruggedness surrounding us. It seemed extraordinary that in that piece of Patagonia where so much beauty was in stark greys, whites, browns and black, there should also be a place for flowers and the darting, delicate grey yellow pipits and bobbing wagtails. We were able to witness such contrasts solely because the season had gone soft on us. A glimpse of a shy *huemul* or a coasting condor would have completed the scene, but we saw only tracks, and we had met nobody.

Our return to Las Horquetas was not quite the same but it was familiar. Squabbling pairs of orange and dove grey butterflies soared and dipped until one broke off and spiralled away. The black swans were still away, and the cattle had hardly moved. I also learned that if the reins were held fractionally tight when approaching a tree trunk, Olympia would jump it. It was a rude surprise but a reminder that for all the constant diversions, concentration was vital. Happily, instincts and muscles had developed sufficiently over the previous weeks to offset such mental lapses, and we took off and landed as one.

We were now dreading our journey down the asphalted section of the Austral, but it passed without major incident largely due to there being little traffic. The road occupied most of the narrow winding valleys— appropriately named Las Mulas and Los Mallines (Mules and Marshes) and often there was barely room for road and river. Verges were a luxury, but at the hidden curves there were only narrow strips of loose gravel beyond the metal crash barriers. Understandably, the horses liked neither the barriers nor the strips. Most of the time the sun was overhead and there was no shade. On the whole, Patagonian drivers respect horses, slowing down to pass, but many ruined their thoughtfulness with a blast on their horn as they moved away. Some did not slow at all, and occasionally, when we were caught out by their speed, we had time to form our defensive box.

There were glimpses of what was to come through the trees, as we wound down a series of defiant S bends, but the impact of our first sight of the Rio Ibañez valley was similar to that at El Gato. Part of that deep pleasure from surprise views are the timeless moments spent in recovering from them, scanning backwards and forwards, up and down, and focusing on selected detail.

Ahead and extending into the heat hazy west was a wide green valley, coursed haphazardly by the arteries of a river—some blue, some sparkling as they caught the angles of the sun's rays, and here and there the hint of small lagoons. A wall of snow-topped peaks enclosed the valley along both sides and at its far western end. Closer to where we stood, the back side of Cerro Castillo soared sheer from the valley floor. We had viewed it from north and east, from near and afar, but unquestionably the southern side was the most awe inspiring of all. It was not possible to pick out the shoulder we had tried to cross, but if we had had the view we had then, we would never have made the attempt.

Our first impressions of the way ahead were misleading. Save for the fact that the Austral went that way, our initial preference might have drawn us to go west. That inviting green valley, however, had been the scene of a volcanic eruption in 1992 which had clogged the main channel of the river, creating the many arteries we could see. Instead of the meadows we thought we were seeing, the area was a waterlogged cemetery of dead trees, whose blackened bare trunks stand fifteen feet out of the water, reeds or swamp. Invisible from our *mirador*, the Austral skirts the valley's southern side, compressed volcanic ash taking the place of asphalt, and then cuts south unmade through the densely wooded and wet Murta river valley.

Our chosen route to the south was to take us along a wide ridge from which we had only glimpses of the valley or the Rio Ibañez below. Seemingly less affected by the volcano, this route had good pasture but continuous fencing. We made good progress and the horses earned a reward, albeit at a cost, when a Señor Fox was to provide us with a suitable sheltered spot and a topic for some gossip from Hector.

'Is that his real name, Hector?'

'Yes, I think so. I seem to remember something about the family. I think the grandfather killed someone's son, and so the son's father then killed one of the grandfather's sons, and so it went on. I cannot remember what the final outcome was, but I remember the name.'

'Did you know any of them?'

'Oh no! I just remember the name and the tale.'

The next morning, and since we had asked for our site, the moment for payment presented an opportunity to find out more.

'*Señor Zorro* ...' I said, using the Spanish for Fox.

'No, *señor*, my name is Fox,' was his reply, also in Spanish.

He was puzzled, but there was a hint of something else which suggested that the matter should be left there, and so after expressing our thanks for his paid hospitality, we rode on.

Mount Ap Iwan frowned down on us from a backseat in a long unnamed range to our east. Llwyd ap Iwan and his Welsh companions from Trevelin had not only found the River Fenix—out of our sight behind the ridge in Argentina—and the mountain which bears his name, but one of them, Evan Roberts, had poked his head round the corner, spotted the Ibañez and baptised it as the River Evan. Whoever later decided to convert 'Evan(s)' into its Spanish equivalent, seems to have been stumped over applying a similar treatment to Ap Iwan, but since poor Llwyd was to meet a violent and undeserved end at the hands of the American outlaws Wilson and Evans, when they tried to rob his store in 1909, some form of rough justice seems to have applied to preserve his memory in what proved to be a vital point of reference for the Arbitration Tribunal. It was in that Ibañez valley that the Indian *pobladores* came after their eviction from Balmaceda by Von Flack, thus creating a uniquely Huilliche/Indian settlement.

The last stretch before the lakeside port of Puerto Ibañez was high, flat and open. The wind gusted and blew dust in our eyes and we were down to our last bag of nuts. We would have welcomed a direct ride into the town, but the planners forced us to take the long scenic route. The poplars protecting each residential square or *manzana* all leant the same way, but the wind which had blown into our faces on the higher ground was a mere breeze compared to what blew down the tunnel formed by the lower section of the Ibañez valley. It was a place for tightened chin straps. It was also where we needed to persuade the captain of the ferry to take our four horses across the lake to Chile Chico. The first omen seemed optimistic. The ferry was called *Pilchero*.

We were in good time, but we needed to unsaddle the horses, water and graze them, and for once the *carabineros* were unhelpful. Eventually we found someone willing to store our belongings and saddlery for a few hours, and having tethered the horses on a vacant lot we had time for a shower and lunch. Hector believed that all negotiations with the captain should be left to him, but when we met on the quay some hours later our position was still uncertain. Vehicles and passengers were building up and the scheduled hour of departure was closing fast. The captain clearly ruled his ship with an imperial rod, and despite several approaches from Hector he refused to commit himself, and the horses and our baggage remained some distance away.

Suddenly Hector raced back smiling with his thumbs up, but we were now under real pressure. A pick-up truck offered to take us back to collect our belongings and saddlery, which freed Hector to bring the horses, but we both still had doubts as to how Cuervo would respond to an invitation to board, especially one made with such indecent haste. To our surprise and delight, they all walked quietly up the ramp and into the tiny sloping area which had been set aside for them. The metal door was raised and clanged shut behind them. Hector and I joined them as they struggled to find their footing, but they seemed to draw comfort from being together and soon we were able to go on deck to watch our progress across the enormous Lake General Carrera.

The shores we had left in soft sunlight took on a certain hulking threat as they faded behind and lost their form. Then a last view of the distant white spires of Cerro Castillo reappeared to define the horizon again and remove some of the menace. It was a clear evening and the lake was being kind to us. To its Argentine east, it widened to an infinity, the boundary line between its 'Buenos Aires' and 'Carrera' parts invisible to all but politicians and the ship's radar. A sense of brooding remained in the waters and air—a sense that at any time the calm of this inland sea could be shattered. Conversation was spaced between satisfying slurps on the plastic straw to my backpack water bottle, primed with the best carton-wine on offer. After two hours, Chile Chico began to take shape ahead.

Our arrival was a local event which was repeated daily except on Sundays, and the quayside had a crowded seaport feel. Despite the ship's name, however, horse passengers were something of a novelty. An extropero, who had had to exchange four legs for two wheels, had already attached himself to us. Having cycled back and forth to check the horses while we were awaiting the captain's decision, he now offered to find us grazing for the horses and 'hospedaje para el gringo'. Hector was looking forward to spending a few days with friends and family.

We were in the mood for another break, and Chile Chico had an immediate simple and welcoming charm. Sheltered by a long arid ridge to the south, the lake's brooding was behind us and a soft breeze brushed the upturned smiling faces. That same breeze was to greet us each day and keep the town free from flies and tábanos.

Chile Chico owes its existence to several Chilean families, notably the Burgos and the Jaras, who travelled over the newly defined frontier from Argentina between 1906 and 1908. It was here that they and José Silva crossed swords with the Flack brothers in 1916 in what has since become known as the War of Chile Chico, details of which appear in the author's book *Patagonian Odyssey: A History of Frontiers Won and Lost*. Since that turbulent beginning a long period of prosperity was halted abruptly in 1991 when the Hudson volcano erupted. The fruit orchards and benign climate for which the town had achieved fame received an overdose of volcanic ash. It now seemed to be resting and in no hurry to do much else, and shops opened and closed at the proprietors' whim. Unlike in Puerto Ibáñez, the poplars which boxed the streets stood erect and the breeze merely rustled the leaves. Ancient adobe walls and crafted wooden tiles mixed with modern styles and materials, and the cement surface of the main streets was slowly extending down the dusty stone arteries.

There were many interesting people to meet in Chile Chico, although we were not going to have time to meet them all. Eduardo Rasche ran the popular restaurant El Corralito with an unlimited supply of classical and popular music. His formula was simple: intelligent and sensitive attention to all, with good food, modestly priced. Success was guaranteed.

Eduardo's father had served on the German raider SMS *Dresden*, which had been the only German ship to survive the First World War Battle of the Falklands. She was chased back and forth through the Chilean fjords before being caught and scuttled. Papa Rasche stepped ashore and stayed. A regular visitor to El Corralito was Dr. León Ocqueteaux — lawyer, poet, former cultural attaché in France under President Allende and an old friend of Pablo Neruda. He came from Cochrane in the south and exuded a certain mystery. I struggled through one of his poems which Eduardo lent me, but after a friendly meeting he left the impression that I had exhausted my relevance to his world and that there were chapters in his life which only few were permitted to share, and an itinerant *gringo*, even an itinerant *gringo* lawyer, was not one of them.

Ferdinando Georgia was unmistakeably 35ish and of Italian origin. His father Pascual had settled in the area and established a small brewery which had been very successful. His mother had produced him in mid-winter in the isolated mountains to the south, where she and the family lived. Climbing was his love and he knew those mountains as no one else. One route to them lay through the Reserva Nacional Lago Jeinemeni, which was to be part of our next stage. He warned that there had been severe landslides in some valleys, which had left sandy deposits — *aluviones* — some of which were quicksands. He was uncertain whether there was still a way through. For good measure he added that there had been incidents of Hanta virus and large poisonous black spiders in the dry lands adjoining the Reserve. I duly passed this information on to Hector for filing.

Hector was more interested in trying to fit in his first ever trip to Argentina. There were a number of items we needed — nails, shoes and spray or cream for saddle sores — and Chile Chico did not have them. It was said that Los Antiguos, just across the border, had at least one store selling such items together with saddles, bridles and other equipment. Most harness and saddlery was still being made by the gauchos and traded among themselves, and there were very few specialist businesses in Argentina, and in Chile even fewer. Since many of the Chile Chico residents crossed the border daily to work, it seemed probable that the fact that Hector had no passport would not be a problem. So it turned out, but at a cost in time, as the *carabineros* had to run a criminal check on him. We had had a similar experience in Futaleufú, when a friendly Major had quietly done the same. He had given Hector a hard time, before commenting — with a broad smile — that in fact he had to be at least twenty years younger than the Hector Soto who had tried to assassinate the President. Either Chile Chico had different records or a different sense of humour, but Hector had his pass and there was no interrogation.

The side trip took all day, and while we found our immediate requirements, there was no store for harness or saddlery. Los Antiguos operated
at a different speed and gave the appearance of a thriving community,
notwithstanding the trough into which the Argentine currency had fallen,
but we were both glad to return to Chile Chico and the task of re-shoeing.

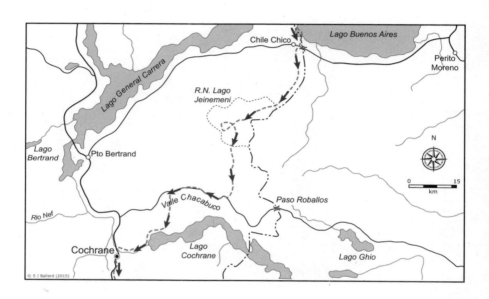

© S J Ballard (2015)

CHAPTER NINE

Chile Chico to Cochrane

The morning after our trip to Los Antiguos, we took our saddles and equipment to the horses in the back of a decrepit horse-drawn cart. At a guess, the driver was marginally older than the horse, and the cart many years older than either. The driver spoke with phlegmatic punctuation—most of it downwind—and it was clear that they worked to a well tried routine. Every few minutes the old man raised himself on tiptoe and cracked his rubber tyre whip on the horse's skinny flank. The horse then broke into a laboured trot for a few paces before resuming its preferred walk. The fare was the equivalent of two bottles of beer, with a tip of one more for the horse, and worth every drop.

Tia, Petaka, Olympia and Cuervo were well rested and fed, and after going through their usual routine of playing hard to get we were saddled, packed and ready to go. Our route was east out of town, south to the Jeinemeni Reserve, through the Paso La Leona to the Chacabuco valley, and thence via the Tamango Reserve to the town of Cochrane. We cleared the last line of poplars and wound our way up hill to the raised ground and the town's airstrip. Olympia shied suddenly at a large collection of plastic bottles which had accumulated at the side of the track. Some had dead flowers in them, but there were so many that the first thought was that we had stumbled on an impromptu bottle bank or tip. In fact we had passed a piece of local legend.

It happened that they had to cross the whole Pampa, she with her recently born baby. The baby was suckling, taking milk even though the mother was dying and had nothing to drink and started to die of thirst. The baby was saved, but she died, and because of this they always put bottles of water at the roadside shrine to the dead Correa ... so she does not lack water, and has more than she needs. Here almost everyone leaves water, this is why there are so many bottles. They serve to protect people so even we will not lack water ...[1]

---

[1]   See Appendix 2

We did not know or we would have left our bottle too.

As we reached the level ground, we could see what Señora Correa had crossed. The many shades of green were all equally misleading. Ahead and all around were prickly mounds with yellow flowers, thick clumps of *coironales* and taller thorn scrub. To our right, rolling folds of a lighter green rose to a continuous ridge of blunted grey knives and chisels against a cloudless sky. It was very hot, but a soft wind drifted over us from the lake behind, clearing the heat haze and reducing the temperature to a tolerable level. Various members of the Seedsnipe family—the smaller variety resembling partridge and the larger a chestnut grouse—burst from beneath us. For several hours there were no trees and no sign of water, until we saw some small poplar oases tucked into the base of the ridge line and astride small streams. The only sign of life was a distant but solitary horse and rider.

The frontier area south of Lago Buenos Aires/General Carrera as far as Mount Fitzroy remains today one of the least populated and most inaccessible in all Patagonia. Neither Steffen nor Moreno visited and Holdich relied on Captain Robertson, who did, and the border was drawn down the river valleys of Jeinemeni and Meyer, where there was thought to be a limited potential for settlements and ranching. Some *pobladores* were to leave Chile Chico, south along the Jeinemeni or west along the shores of Lago Buenos Aires, but today the area is a National Reserve to which there is currently one track.

The ridge ended its easterly run, allowing us to switch direction and climb steadily, parallel to its southern side. With a final glimpse of the lake and Cerro Castillo, a new arid world opened up ahead. Far below was the narrow gorge of the frontier Rio Jeinemeni, and it was soon clear that if we were to find our camping priorities of grass and water, ultimately we would have to go down to join it. The track took us through a succession of hairpins which seemed to go on forever, and Hector decided to take a short but steep cut to avoid them. This worked well for a while until he bit off more than any of us could manage. He had gone ahead on foot with three of the horses while Olympia and I took our time behind. Suddenly the land fell away to a sheer drop. I saw Hector lose his footing and slide almost out of sight and out of control. Something stopped him with his feet and lower body over the edge. After a long struggle, he managed to pull himself back up and stop the horses following him to a worse fate. The slope was loose shale and pebbles and there was a wild scramble and flurry of legs. Cuervo slipped and slid onto his hind legs and only with a massive heave regained his balance. Olympia and I were twenty feet above, helpless and with a ringside seat. It was one of the few moments when I had time to be annoyed.

'Come off it, Hector. Back off!'

But he was already back and off up the slope. I let Olympia loose, slapped her rear and she took off skidding and slithering to join the others, leaving me with the option of doing the same or trying to traverse down by another route. I chose the latter and was fortunate. Grasping at thorny bushes for support, I found a rabbit path down to the bridge over the Rio Quebrada. It took the others some time to join me following the hairpins again, by which time I had recovered both senses and breath.

In fact, we had lost so much height that the Rio Jeinemeni and its narrow banks were now clearly visible. We chose to make our final descent, traversing left then right until we reached a small green area near the remains of an old adobe *puesto*. The green area was under water but had good grass. On the higher ground adjoining the *puesto* the grass was golden and so tinder dry that we collected extra water to cover the possibility of fire. I remembered Ferdinando's warnings about dry land, but the area had a forlorn feel of abandonment and there was a sense of such unfriendliness and foreboding that we camped well clear of the *puesto*.

It was not surprising that we had an unsettled night. It was also very cold and we were both glad to climb out and away the next morning. At least we had yet to see a black spider. Once we had regained the high ground, the landscape continued its brutal, treeless monotony until the valley started to narrow and we had our first sight of distant white peaks ahead. The Rio Jenemeni, meanwhile, had dived down a personal canyon, cut deep into the flat plateau where we rode.

With the narrowing of the valley came the first views of poplars, fences, grass, cattle and inquisitive horses, and ultimately a succession of small lakes. Lago de los Flamencos should have been home to quantities of pink and white flamingos but they were elsewhere, which was as well because there was barely room for them amongst the hordes of Caiquen geese, duck and waders remaining. It was a further piece of still life water colour: the bird-speckled waters of that small lake, set among soft green meadows, themselves dabbed with brown waterlogged cattle, and behind, the long graded staircase of a slender valley curving away and upwards to the shimmer of snow fields and rumble of peaks: the Cordón La Gloria. Clearly someone else—a long time ago—had been impressed.

We moved on down the main valley towards the Jenemeni Reserve to camp by the Rio Sucio, the name (Dirty Waters) a reference to reflection rather than content. The horses were left to roam free while we prepared a fire and discovered we had a subversive member—Olympia. We had suspected that she had a mind of her own, but when I went to collect them, instead of standing still or moving towards me, they moved away. As the spirit of independence grew their pace quickened and suddenly all four, trailing their tethers, were cantering then galloping over the hill towards the setting sun. Only Tía showed any hesitancy. Since I had neither the energy nor the enthusiasm to go after them, I returned to the fire and suggested that I should stir the pot while Hector had some exercise. He set off at a trot and an hour later returned astride Petaka with the other deserters roped Indian file behind. That night they were each firmly staked out, Hector gave a short lecture on how to recover recalcitrant horses and our pasta was slightly burnt.

One of the supports for our tarp was a tall bare tree. As I lay with my head under the Southern Cross, I was aware of a gentle throaty warbling from above. The night was cold but I was warm. Only when nature's call became imperative was I forced to stumble my way to the bushes, and as I emerged I saw the gentle warbler looking down at me, perhaps wondering what it was that dared share his nocturnal perch. His name was *Bubo Magellanicus* and he had prominent tufted ears which stood out against the night-lit sky, and he was large. He was also completely unfazed by my sudden appearance, and by the time I returned to the warmth of my sleeping bag, he was warbling again. It was very comforting to know we had acquired a feathered night guardian, but by the morning our Magellanic Horned Owl had gone.

The nails in Cuervo's rear shoes had worked loose and needed replacement, and Cuervo did not like being shod. Ultimately this meant that he had to be hog tied, thrown to the ground and his head held down. He liked that even less, but eventually stopped struggling and we noticed his uppermost eye did not seem to follow our movement. Cuervo's patient curiosity became clearer. He was going blind in one eye. Since it promised to be a gentle day, I rode him. It gave me an opportunity to try to communicate my sympathy, while our 'walk out' leader Olympia was given pack horse duties.

The final approach to the Reserve was down a series of giant half mile-long steps, with our view of the Cordón La Gloria unravelling at each. We crossed the river and followed its course through wooden glades until we emerged into the open at the head of Lago Jeinemeni. Perhaps the sun and cloudless sky helped, but the waters were a brilliant blue. We clattered over a solid wooden bridge and walked along the lake's sandy edge. The valley curved first one way, then another, so that one array of colours slowly opened on to the next. Save at the open eastern end, where the view included the distant snow-topped peaks, the upper parts of each near vertical side cascaded their mineral contents in a succession of pink, white, orange, lucent greens and granite greys—colours that sparkled and shifted shades under the sun's glare and with our progress. Jeinemeni was an altogether softer and more intimate Reserve than Cerro Castillo. Its beauty and colours were to be savoured slowly, and we were in no great hurry. As evening approached the only sound was the noisy plop of rising fish, and it did not seem to matter that we no longer had a rod.

We had decided to devote at least the next morning to exploring the Reserve and set off with Olympia and Petaka, leaving the other two staked out at our camp site. The valley floor was boulder and rounded stones, cut by several rivers and a number of minor streams. We were looking for the Reserve's tricolour lakes but found them only with difficulty after following small marker cairns—*monolitos*—which suddenly ran out. Lago Verde, the first lake, fed its green water into Esmeralda, which had only a short distance to run into Lago Jeinemeni, yet the difference between the green, the emerald and finally the blue was marked and immediate, as if nature had drawn a line in the water.

Returning to the other horses, we packed and headed for the Paso de la Leona, which would lead us south to the Chacabuco valley. All the information we had had pointed to probable difficulties, and since it was uncertain that we could cross the pass in one day, we decided to make a start and camp before we reached the reported landslide. Thereafter it was likely to be difficult to find grazing. The entrance to the pass was narrow-necked but confusing. There was no clear route and no obvious reason for preferring one side of the river to the other. We crossed and re-crossed, often having to double back when the woods and undergrowth became impossibly thick. We knew that a group had come through recently on foot from the south, and the sight of an occasional footprint was reassuring, but we also knew they had taken three days. Gaps in the trees gave glimpses of the vertical sides and occasional cascades of water, but there was no view ahead.

After some time we passed a small lake which was not shown on our map, and found ourselves on sandy flats. Dead trees sprouted from the sand and we dismounted. There was no alternative to crossing the sand, and Hector went ahead leading Petaka, with Tía the day's *pilchero* and Cuervo on his rest day following. I led Olympia some fifteen yards behind. Passing a group of buried trees, Tía suddenly sank to her belly. She struggled frantically, but the more she did so, the deeper she sank. Soon only her head and the top of our blue tarp were visible. I turned to lead Olympia back and tied her to a living tree. As I moved cautiously back to Tía, Cuervo too sank. He was carrying nothing, but was by far the heaviest of the four. Being Cuervo, he also struggled and sank deeper.

'We've got to get the load off Tía!' shouted Hector.

As I moved to help, a bubble of sand exploded to my right, then another to my left. It was as if some hidden power was belching over its meal. It was impossible to guess where it was safe to tread. We both reached Tía and struggled to reach the buckles deep in the wet sand. It seemed to take forever, but eventually the straps were free and we could lift the bundles off one by one and rush them to stable ground ahead where Petaka had been tied. With the weight removed from her back, I moved to Tía's front to locate her reins and help pull her free.

'No, Jon! Leave her be. She'll get out on her own.'

We both stepped back as Tía pushed, floundered, twisted and turned and eventually staggered free. That left Cuervo.

'Come on, Cuervo! Come on! Move, you b*****!'

Cuervo, as always, took his time. Suddenly he exploded. Wet sand flew everywhere as he seemed to find some purchase for his chest, then front and finally back legs, then he burst free. The craters where Tía and Cuervo had sunk formed over and soon there was no sign of where they had been or that anything had happened, save for the obscene belching bubbles. Soon they ceased, too.

We were all now trembling. I tiptoed back to collect Olympia and brought her back at a run, following my footsteps. Tía, Cuervo and our baggage were covered with wet sand, and we led them to a nearby stream and washed them down. While I fumbled for the wine carton, Hector relieved his tension with a lecture on procedures to be adopted in the event of quicksands.

'Never go where the trees are. Keep away from them. Get off the horse as soon as possible. Never try to pull a horse out. Just get the loads off and let them get on with it. You can't help them pulling on the reins. They need to be free.'

I promised to try and remember the next time, but my mind also went back to another missed photo opportunity many years before in East Berlin. It was as clear then as now that my prospects of ever making a living as a professional photographer were not good. Self-preservation was still the prime motivator.

We were all relieved to find a clearing among the trees where the ground was firm and dry, and that night the river chattered incessantly and the twisted roots of a long-fallen tree took the form of a seated companion with whom to share my silent thoughts.

By mid-morning the next day we had completed the first section of the pass and stood at an open valley Y junction. By far the most inviting alternative lay down a long green valley, but our route lay south through a clutter of broken rock. This was the first of a new series of rockslides; the quicksands had been caused by another. This time the debris formed haphazard angled slopes of flat stones which tipped and moved underfoot. For the horses, this was another nightmare as they slipped, slid and struggled to keep their balance and cut their legs repeatedly on the sharp edges. Being bare rock, there were few signs of any route except when patches of earth or sand revealed the odd footprint. High above us the sheer sides threatened fresh cascades of loose rock, and isolated pinnacles pointed warning fingers to the sky. Small unmarked lakes continued to appear, their grey waters witness to their recent creation and uncertain future. Eventually, however, the valley sides leaned back and opened up a view of distant peaks—the Cordón Chacabuco—and underfoot, light pastures, small lagoons, gravel and sand. At this point the direction of the waters changed and the streams now ran gently away from us. We had crossed the summit, and savoured the moment by standing across the continental divide, noting that we were still some distance from the frontier.

Conscious that the day was slipping by, we started on our long descent. This, too, was formed of distinct parts. The first took us down through woods by the side of a river. *Estero* in Chile is a brook or stream, neither of which did Estero la Leona justice. Starting gently, in no time it was a river of a thousand steps marking our route down. Many steps gave us the option of crossing, but there was no way of knowing how much progress we could make down the other bank before being forced to re-cross. All the time the valley was widening until the woods and steps ceased and the waters disappeared down a deep hidden chasm. Each side of the valley now fell steeply inward towards the chasm, their length unfolding away from us in rolling cadences down towards the Valle Chacabuco ahead.

We had emerged on the right hand side of the valley and were to stay that side for most of our descent. Our progress was in the form of V-shaped traverses of each succeeding fold abruptly down to the apex of the V, with a sheer drop to the river thundering far below, then as abruptly back up to the start of the next fold. We struggled to maintain our height above the river chasm along narrow sheep trails cut into the slopes. Our direct view of the Chacabuco then became partly obscured by the white rounded head of the Cerro La Leona which guarded the southern entrance to the pass. Our route over the final section was across a plateau—part wood, part pasture—formed by La Leona's mighty feet. As we levelled out for a while, a pair of spotted woodpeckers, known in Chile as the postmen of the woods, greeted us with their version of postman's knock. The final descent was long and steep, and as light started to fade, we reached the bottom and the door to the Valle Chacabuco opened.

I had been waiting many years to set foot in the Chacabuco valley, which has become synonymous with an age of large-scale ranching and the name, Lucas Bridges, the 'Señor' of the Baker. Here he ended his pioneering days[2] at the Estancia Lago Bertrand in partnership with his loyal friends and longstanding business colleagues, Mauricio Braun and Francisco Campos. These 'three gladiators, who survived in the arena' were the survivors of the original eleven shareholders in the Sociedad Posadas de Hobbs y Compania (Hobbs & Co.), which had acquired the 1.2 million-acre concession to the Baker in 1914. Mauricio Braun had also been behind the earlier failed concession operated by the Compañia Explotadora del Baker (CEB) between 1904 and 1908.[3]

In 1941, and after 27 years of operation, Hobbs & Co. obtained a twenty-year extension to a reduced total of 568,000 acres, but decided to abandon its centre in the middle Baker valley at La Colonia and the 212,000 acres adjoining, and move its stock and equipment up to the Chacabuco. The new company was to be known as the Sociedad Anoníma Ganadera 'Valle Chacabuco' (otherwise 'Lago Bertrand') and the balance of its concession, an area of 355,000 acres, extended from the frontier down the Chacabuco valley to the River Baker. Mountain ranges to the north and Lago Cochrane to the south provided natural barriers against invasions from the *pobladores*, which had caused many problems in the Baker and which lay behind the decision to abandon La Colonia. Instead of the enormously difficult and costly task of transporting its produce down the Rio Baker, Hobbs & Co. had already put in place all the infrastructure for routing it across Lago General Carrera to Puerto Aysén. Additionally, the easy communications over the frontier to the company's Argentine *estancias*, Posadas and Ghio, remained. That Lucas Bridges himself felt that the move to the Chacabuco was closure on the Baker is suggested by the title he chose for his synopsis, 'Work done during 28 years in the Baker' and in its final sentence: 'I feel that a victory after a desperate struggle brings more satisfaction than anything else.'

He was then 67 years of age and had already had an extraordinarily active life, of which the 'desperate struggle' of the previous 28 years had been merely the latest titanic instalment. Apart from sharing the privations of the men he employed and led by example, he had faced a sequence of disasters where he alone had to decide the next steps to be taken. The

---

[2] Lucas Bridges died in Buenos Aires on 4 April 1949 at the age of 74. He had suffered a heart attack a few years earlier, but had continued the administration of Lago Bertrand from a distance, while writing his classic book *The Uttermost Part of the Earth*, first published in 1948.

[3] An account of the history of these ventures appears in the author's book *Patagonian Odyssey: A History of a Frontier Won and Lost*.

decisions he had taken were ultimately to prove crucial to the peaceful development of Aysén. Yet throughout this period it was the Chilean government who remained owners of the land, and the CEB and Hobbs & Co. were only ever custodians, with Lucas Bridges the pioneer in residence. Furthermore, while the companies and their shareholders had continued to invest capital, they had received no dividend return.

Lucas Bridges barely drew breath before launching himself straight into the implementation of his plan for the new Chacabuco (ad)venture.

The plan involved a fencing of the valley into 48 sections for a flock of almost 75,000 sheep and 400 cattle, itself a monumental operation. A sawmill had been brought up from La Colonia—a task no less difficult than installing it there in the first place—and it proved vital in the building of all the new facilities: houses for the *puesteros* of each section, the corrals, barns, offices and other buildings, together with a number of bridges over the Rio Chacabuco. A touch typical of the man was to name many of the sections after the *puestero* responsible.

With its administrative centre at the western end of the valley, a simple house, similar to that which had been built in La Colonia, was erected for Lucas Bridges and his family at the other (eastern) end, around the corner from the Paso La Leona and looking out on an unnamed mountain 7,000 feet high. Inevitably, it was only a matter of time before Lucas Bridges decided that the mountain needed to be climbed. Setting out early one morning on his own, there was no further sign of him until 6pm, when those below were comforted—no doubt as he had intended—to see a large fire burning on the summit. Appropriately and in due course, the mountain was named after him.

Estancia Lago Bertrand was a financial success and for the years until Bridges' death in 1949, the 'gladiators' each drew an income. Bridges' share was then purchased by the two survivors and the *estancia* continued until Mauricio Braun died in 1953. At that stage, the government reduced the holding by more than half to 170,000 acres and the Braun descendants continued with Francisco Campos until the concession finally ended in 1964. It was then carrying 30,000 sheep. The following year the company was wound up and the stock sold to the Corporation for Agrarian Reform.

The next fifteen years saw various attempts to initiate land reform programmes in the Chacabuco valley. While these demonstrated that groups of *pobladores* could work together successfully in terms of collective land and stock management, the reform organisers failed to appreciate that the participants had been attracted to the area by the prospect of owning their land, and no one had told them that ownership was not on offer. Ultimately the experiments failed amidst much recrimination, claims for unpaid salaries and with a huge unpaid debt. Some participants left, taking their stock with them, others even dismantled their former houses and took the materials away, leaving a ruined valley to the main creditor, the State Bank.

At this point, and for the first time in its history, ownership of the Chacabuco valley came up for sale in 1980, and was purchased for 28 million pesos by Francisco de Smet, who formed the Estancia Valle Chacabuco (Valchac).

The de Smet d'Olbecke brothers, Paul and Jean-Pierre, and their respective families formed part of a small group of Belgian immigrants who came to the Baker between 1948 and 1953 to settle a forestation concession in the Murta valley. Paul acquired part of the former Estancia Lago Bertrand concession when it was reduced in 1953, and his son Francisco bought Valchac. The Belgian colony brought considerable benefits to the area, not least the forty-ton steamship *Helga* which was hauled across Argentina from the Atlantic and which provided vital services to the growing number of *pobladores* and miners who had settled along the shores of Lago General Carrera.

The de Smets gradually re-established the *estancia*, taking the sheep head count back to the 1964 level, when it was discovered that the original holding carried a debt of unpaid contributions due to the Treasury amounting to three and a half times its sale price. How such a sum had been accumulated unseen (even to the Treasury) for so long is not known, but according to those who had occupied land during the period of Agrarian Reform they had paid their contributions regularly to the 'Centro de la Reforma Agraria'. Fortunately for the de Smets, a compromise was reached whereby 40,000 acres were handed over to CONAF, the National Forestry Agency, to cancel the debt.

After twenty years, Francisco de Smet, despite fierce opposition from his brother Carlos, who had administered the *estancia* for the previous ten years, decided to sell up, and received an attractive offer from Kristine McDewitt, wife of Douglas Tompkins. A group of descendants of the Braun-Menéndez and Campos families offered to improve on any other offer made, but de Smet preferred the simplicity of the McDewitt offer, and for the second time in its history the Chacabuco valley passed into foreign ownership, this time for US$10 million.

The de Smets were still in charge when Hector and I turned east down the valley and a gusting wind picked up speed and began to chill. There was no obvious place to camp. The side of the valley containing the Rio Chacabuco was securely fenced, and the other was open but featureless save for scrub. Eventually we spotted some poplars and a small *chacra* hut under the lea of the valley and rode up to the gate and waited. A man appeared, and after the usual formalities we were invited to dismount and led round the back to a grassed area heavily protected by tall, dense thorn hedges. Six dogs, having completed their noisy guard duties, lay down and watched us unsaddle and take the horses off to an adjoining paddock. They had suffered badly during the ten-hour trek through the pass. Cuervo had an unpleasant swelling on his back and was becoming increasingly irritable. Tía and Petaka had both developed limps, Olympia's saddle sore had not healed and all had cuts to their lower legs.

We returned to find our host had already collected wood and lit a fire. Chickens of assorted colour and size wandered in and out of the thorn hedge and were joined by a large marmalade cat. Around us were a number of fruitless trees draped with drying sheep skins, which we were told over *mate* were 'useless and beetle ridden'. Our host was a tenant and lived alone. His hospitality was immediate, warm and generous, but conversation was stilted, and before long he bade us goodnight and he and the dogs disappeared. It was to be the last we saw of them. The chickens went to roost in the trees and the cat stayed by the fire.

Morning was spent tending to the horses' ailments. The spray we had bought in Los Antiguos had been very effective, and a hole cut in the sheepskin cover kept wool and saddle blanket off the wound, but we felt that Cuervo's swelling was the more serious and earned him a good dose of spray and the day off. I would ride Olympia again, Hector would continue on Pataka, and Tía, whose leg seemed to have improved overnight, would continue as *pilchero*.

During the night we had heard rustling in the hedges, and in the morning this continued. We then heard a bird call, and before long a pair of *huet-huets* emerged to watch us. Similar in colouring, scurrying habits and erect tail to the *chucao* but larger, these too were onomatopoeic and reluctant fliers. Both cat and birds knew the bushes and each other well, and played out their respective roles as hunter and hunted in such a casual and even good humoured way that it was clear that both expected to be doing the same thing tomorrow and the next day.

We saddled up and left a deserted *chacra* and followed sheep tracks through the scrub. The valley narrowed and the Rio Chacabuco joined us for a while. The sun, which had taken the chill out of the wind, reflected off a distant rust-streaked peak. As the river wound away from us into a wide bend, a steep cliff intruded on our side, setting up the first of a series of surprise Patagonian 'corners'. On the river side, the line of the far bank was defined by poplars and the near bank curved back towards us to form a large pool dotted with wild duck. As we came into view, they took off splattering across a perfect pastoral canvas. Almost at the same moment we rounded the cliff corner, and pastoral became pastorale as the full Patagonian wind section hit us in the face and blew my hat off.

For the next hour we tried to hug the nearside valley wall, but one cliff corner followed another, and as we rounded each our hats received the same treatment. It was difficult to see through the tears, and even the river seemed to have lost its way and become confused by its own tributaries, which in turn became lost among large areas of marsh-reeds. We glimpsed flat grasslands on the far side of the valley which would have been our preferred route, but once again they were beyond the wire. We were also in some danger from constant rock slides. The horses heard these coming long before we did and seemed to know which way to jump, so that the rocks hit the track behind us. Eventually the corners had to run out and surprisingly the wind dropped. The river sorted itself out into one channel and ahead lay the full width of the Chacabuco valley, its centre now dominated by plateau on plateau of Hereford cattle. The plateaux were interrupted at intervals by the stumps of giant fingers extending back through humped veined hands to the snow peaks beyond.

Extra strands had been added to the fences, and the carcases of several long-dead guanacos hanging over the lower strands provided the reason. Even an armour-plated armadillo seemed to have been persuaded to stay out. High above us a condor watched from his crag, waiting for someone or something to drop dead. On the side where we rode, the slopes were dry and tufted and the home of many herds of guanaco. The shrill chatter of their sentinels contrasted with the mournful bellows of the Hereford. The guanaco were difficult to pick out at first, their colours providing a perfect camouflage, and perversely it was often those on guard who gave their presence away. These stood apart, warning their herds of our approach and leading a mad dash to another site. Every now and then they paused silhouetted against the sky, apparently unable to resist the opportunity of posing for the camera, before bouncing away at great speed. 'Long-necked four-legged brown woolly pogo sticks' came to mind.

After pausing for lunch under our tarp in a rainstorm, we rode up to another level of the valley, leaving the lower cattle pastures out of sight. Ahead the land folded away past a series of lakes, their edges heavy with reeds tinted in greens, browns, golds and rusty orange. Each lake was a reserve for assorted water fowl: black-necked swans, duck, geese and divers. As the pasture improved, the guanaco gave way to herds of sheep. We stopped at an isolated *puesto*, set back from the fence. We had some letters and photographs to deliver to several men stationed elsewhere on the *estancia*, and learning that the main Estancia Valchac buildings were several hours ahead, we made them our day's objective.

The view ahead was now of the Cerro Aislado in the middle distance with the white carpet of the Northern Ice Field beyond. The sky was darkening and with the rains came the wind. Both were icy cold, and once again horses' and riders' heads went down, and stayed down. The heavy woollen Chilean poncho, while not waterproof, is an ideal garment for such conditions, but it does not protect the legs. *Pierneras* do, and Hector had his on. I preferred my waterproof trousers, but they were stashed away at the bottom of our dry bags, and inevitably therefore the water from my poncho ran down my trousers into my boots. It was half past eight before we topped yet another rise and saw the *estancia* laid out below—a village of green huts with corrugated iron roofs set in its own end valley. Once again, the horses had never flagged.

We tied the horses at the entrance gate and dripped and slopped our way to the off-duty administrator's hut, where with profuse apologies we were offered the visitors' hut. We were delighted. The horses were turned loose in the large open space between the lines of huts, we humped our baggage and saddles into the dry and soon we were basking in the warmth of a blazing *fogon* with our wet clothing steaming dry overhead. The hut comprised a number of dormitories with slatted bunk beds, and the walls were lined with rules urging us not to burn down the building and telling us how best to enjoy our stay. Warm and well fed, we were interested only in sleep.

Next morning brought back a clear sky. We acquired fresh bread and some pasta from the *estancia* bakery and stores.

'No, *señor*. We do not want payment.'

I had wanted to go south through the Tamango Reserve, noted for its protected species of the small deer, the *huemul*.[4] Hector was in favour of the route west round the Reserve. He had lost faith in the local trekking maps which had caused confusion in Cerro Castillo, so we consulted them with one of the estancia *puesteros*.

'Go through the gate marked 'No Entry'. It is not locked. Then follow the fence line until you reach the *puesto* overlooking the lake. There turn right.'

It seemed simple enough and Hector was persuaded.

---

4   The *huemul*, an endangered species, is found on both Argentine and Chilean sides of the cordillera, and appears with the condor on the Chilean coat of arms.

I was to recall and contrast this visit and the warm hospitality extended when in 2014, and after a gap of some ten years, I returned to the Chacabuco. The fences which had kept guanaco, cattle and sheep apart, and pumas and foxes out, had been removed. Only small groups of cattle remained. The *chacra* where Hector and I had spent our first night had gone. Most of the wooden buildings of the former administration 'village' and the *puestos* had disappeared and been replaced by fine, modern, locally quarried stone constructions, which included a luxury casino/restaurant. The traditional route down from Jeinimeni via the Paso La Leona had been replaced by a new route up the Rio Avilés to the west. I entered the new buildings wearing my old boots, which were probably carrying the same amount of Chacabuco dust as they had previously, and was asked to take them off. Given the nature of the beautiful new wood block floor imported from the Tompkins Pumalín Reserve, it was an understandable request, but I stayed long enough only to collect the literature on offer.

I read that the new owners had designed a work programme which included the process of reconversion of a traditional cattle *estancia* into a—world category—National Park of some 190,000 acres which would eventually link the two existing National Reserves of Jeinimeni to the north and Tamango to the south, thus forming one gigantic National Park of some 620,000 acres. The intention was that this project would contribute to regional development and particularly to the neighbouring communities.

By way of introduction, it was explained that some eighty years of badly managed farming, associated with economically unsustainable over-pasturing, had had catastrophic consequences for the ecosystem of the valley: erosion, loss of the original *coirón*—perennial tufted grass, much favoured by animals—coverage, burnt sectors and the invasion of exotic species such as the *rosa mosqueta*. In the 1920s this fragile area came to carry more than 80,000 sheep. When the current owners acquired the *estancia*, there were 25,000 sheep and 4,000 cattle, figures said to be way above the carrying capacity of the area.

Even for a project with such commendably pristine objectives, and with access to seemingly unlimited technical and financial resources, it was recognised that the support of local and regional communities had to be earned, but I was to encounter much upset. Smallholders complained that their stock had been decimated by pumas, and they believed some had been introduced to the Chacabuco to make up the numbers and restore the balance of natural selection among the guanacos and the *huemul*. Many had sold up, some at derisory prices. The residents of Cochrane complained that the project had provided little or no local employment, and since their traditional source of meat had been removed, supplies were scarce and prices prohibitive. Private aircraft were said to have brought many visitors to the valley's new airstrip, but they had little contact with the community. There was a growing suspicion that all the objectives of the project had yet to be revealed.

During the past fifteen years huge efforts have been made to record Aysén's past through the collection and preservation of life testimonies of the original pioneers. These accounts not only include valuable historical detail, photographs and reflections on past events, but also amount to a referendum of hopes and concerns for the future. Thus, the Austral figures as the region's most significant development. The hydroelectric and dam projects receive mixed, often guarded, views based on a supposition that they will bring employment and that an alternative to pylons will be found. While the Tompkins have voiced their own strong opposition to the dams, their Chacabuco valley project has attracted widespread opprobrium. There is a clear inconsistency between preserving the history and the symbols of sacrifice and achievement of those who forged Aysen and destroying physical traces and denigrating such history and symbols; and the fact that it is all being done at the behest of foreigners adds insult to local injury.[5]

We retraced the previous day's route for a while, this time with our heads high. The gate was indeed unlocked and we cut south. Guanaco herds continued their chatter from a safe distance and the scrubland dipped and rolled taking us past several small rust-reeded lakes identifiable on our maps. We were looking for a small river, the Elefantita, and a waterfall which would lead us to a lake of the same name and shape and thence into the Reserve. Instead we passed a long thin lake which some might have called Giraffe but no one would have labelled Elefantita, and our maps could not help.

Curiously we did not feel lost. From high ground above the lake's steep sides we had our first sight of the blue of Lago Cochrane and the white

---

5   Douglas Tompkins' adventurous life was tragically cut short on 8 December 2015 when his kayak capsized while he and five others were attempting to cross Lake General Carrera. Aged 72, he had already given much and promised even more to a land he had adopted as his home, and Patagonia has lost a modern pioneer it will be difficult to replace.

Cordón Esmeralda beyond. A solitary blackened tree stood guard at one end, its knot hole blasted by fire to several times its original size providing an oval frame to part of the scene behind. Cochrane, the town, lay at one corner of the lake and we sensed that we had not far to go. Our day's objective seemed assured.

We rode on down long wooded slopes until we came to a clearing in the middle of which stood a *puesto*. Whether it was *the puesto*, we never knew. The tall meadow grass suggested that it had not been occupied that year but it was an idyllic spot for lunch, and freed of their saddles the horses rolled over in delight.

All indications were for us to continue on to the lake's edge where for a while we were able to follow a narrow gravel beach, the clear waters shelving abruptly away from us. Then the beach ran out and ahead the cliffs were sheer. The only way forward was up and the maps indicated a rise of some 2,000 to 2,500 feet. Olympia was in one of her better moods and willing to give it a try and follow the others, but after five minutes she was in difficulty. There was no alternative. I dismounted, sent her off with a slap on the rump and became a *peon* again. And a very slow one at that.

'What kept you, Jon?'

I had earned the undeniable right to collect my breath and admire the view at leisure. Lago Cochrane now lay far below. Small rocky islets cast light halos on an otherwise impeccably dark blue. The lake itself curved off to the distant east and its invisible Argentine section named Lago Pueyrredón. There was no sign of life. No boats. No glinting metal roofs. No tracks. No one. Not for the first time one sensed what it was to be a pioneer, and Cochrane, the town, was still invisible.

Somehow we had connected up with identifiable features on our map, but were now on the southern side of the Reserva Tamango. The path ahead was an endless backbreaking switchback, interrupted by gigantic boulders which forced us vertically up one side and then vertically down the other. The simpler logic of edging past below the boulder was never on offer. Eventually we emerged into the open, but of Cochrane there was still no sign even though we had passed the end of the lake. Bed, food, shower and rest had been the day's magnet, but as we topped a long rise it was 8.30pm again, and we learned that we had four miles still to go. Expectation was rapidly turning to acute frustration when we reached the hut of the Reserve guard, who returned from patrol just as we were struggling to put up our tarp in a clearing. Immediately we were offered beds and the now familiar routine of *mate* and a shared supper, and tiredness slipped away as conversation continued into the night.

By definition giants are tall, but Javier Subiabre was a solid five-and-a- half-foot giant—a man to have at your side in any tight corner –and the *huemul* of the Tamago Reserve were fortunate to have him to look after them. He had started his life as a ranger in 1993 with CONAF in Cerro Castillo, where there were two groups of *huemul*, each comprising some eight animals. The *huemul*, apart from being an endangered species, will not survive in captivity. Javier's interest in them really kicked off, however, when after four years he was transferred to Tamango, which remains one of the principal tourist and scientific centres in Patagonia for the *huemul*, with a current population of 72. Man, as one of the traditional hunters, has become the defender and observer, and the puma population, although reduced, has been complemented by stray dogs from Cochrane. There is no fencing in the Reserve, and the *huemul*— excellent swimmers who can cross any lake or river including the mighty Baker—are free to move, and indeed some have recently started to vote with their feet.

Javier told how the deer divide into groups in the winter. Among fifty animals there may be as many as seven groups, with a maximum of eleven per group, partly for reasons of food and partly because of the position of the sun. A stag may break away from one group after serving its members, and move on to serve another group and so on. The does produce only one offspring each year, and these remain with the mother for part of their second year alongside any new calf, until the mother orders them out. The life span for both sexes is some fifteen years.

'I believe the *huemul* recognise me. They are very docile by nature, but I am the only visitor in the winter, and I make noises they recognise. Some are friendlier than others, but they all want to know who it is, at the same time making it clear that close is close enough. One day I was on horseback with a colleague. We were following a group of *huemul* in a straight line some metres back, when ahead I saw a puma—a female with two cubs—also tracking the *huemul*. By the time the puma had closed to within fifty metres of a stag I had narrowed the gap between us and then decided to intervene and ride between them. The *huemul* had probably neither heard nor sensed the puma. The same year, another male *huemul* was killed some 200 metres from this hut, I suspect by the same puma.

'On another occasion I saw the extraordinary ritual of a stag mating with a doe. The stag drew himself up and emitted a sound I have never heard before or since. This is something very few if any have witnessed, but I had neither photographic nor sound equipment with me.'

While it was to be many weeks before I actually saw a *huemul*, it was some years later, on my return to Cochrane, that I went looking for Javier and eventually found him. I was uncertain whether he would recall our previous meeting, and started:

'Javier, I don't know whether you will remember, but some six or seven years ago, we had ridden all day from Chacabuco and I was exhausted when we reached your hut ...'

That massive paw, which had gentled his horse to within metres of *huemul* and puma, was extended and gripped mine ...

'You had got lost and come up the cliff from Lake Cochrane. Nobody does that on horseback. You were in a pretty foul mood, so I thought you needed a bed for the night. Yes! I remember,' and his smile, too, was very much as I remembered it.

Javier's interest in the *huemul* remains, and is central to his plans for the extension of the area where they can continue to exist in peace.

CHAPTER TEN

Cochrane and a Meeting of Old Pobladores

Cochrane, the town, was spawned by Hobbs & Co. in 1929 on company land at Las Latas, where Marchant had a school built for day pupils and boarders. The boarders were housed in a simple lean-to between September and April or May. Recollections of those times are mixed.

'We played a lot outside—the girls with cloth dolls and the boys with hobby horses.'

'I didn't learn anything.'

'I learned to read a bit but I can't write or do sums.'

'The teacher was called Guerra—Humberto Guerra. He then went north and took a boat from Aysén to Puerto Montt, but he never arrived. He just disappeared.'

It was all too close to the Hobbs *estancia*, however, and when eventually a decision was taken in 1954 to inaugurate a new town with ten houses, the site chosen was on the banks of the River Cochrane and to the immediate north-east of the lake. In 1970 the department of Cochrane was created.

With the town's 50th anniversary approaching, a meeting was called between some of the original pioneers.

It was hot, too hot for those in their eighties, and there were a number in the room. Clodomiro Reyes was one of the oldest. He stood up and rubbed a grimy knuckle across his streaming eyes. The smoke from the fire curled upwards seeking a way out. He nudged a smouldering log gently with his boot and watched as the flames moved to engulf it. He then pushed open the top half of the stable door. The rain shafted vertically down outside, forming a transparent, beeded curtain. A cool draught met the curling smoke sucking it out of the hut.

Some sat on split logs. Some on simple benches. The old blackened kettle hissed and Clodomiro reached forward to lift it from the embers. He paused before pouring into the *mate* he held in his left hand. The silver 'straw' stood upright as he bent his head and his lips touched the metal, sensing its heat and he sucked deliberately. The old fingers curled round the gourd, nails streaked with dirt, their ends chipped and split. He cleared his throat noisily, inclined his head to one side and spat into the dusty floor. There was another, longer, pause before the kettle was raised again, the *mate* refilled and the lip test re-applied. The chattering ceased expectantly. Clodomiro turned to his neighbour, extended the *mate* to him and sat back on his log.

'I was born in the province of Valdivia—up north.'

His voice was quiet and the others strained forward to catch his words.

'I went across to Junín de Los Andes in 1911 and then down to Esquel for a time. I kept moving south looking for somewhere warm. I was in El Oro for eight years. I came here because I killed two men for having big balls.[1] Well, they wanted to kill me. So I came here running away from the law. I worked for myself. Contract work. Life was very difficult. I had to go to Cañadón Verde or Perito Moreno to find goods to sell. It took ten to twelve days there and back with five or six *pilcheros*.'

'Don Clodomiro,' interrupted one of the listeners. 'Do you remember Don Lucas Bridges?'

'Yes. I knew him well. For me he was a good man. Friendly. There were others who did not like him. 'Oh, *companerito*', he would say, 'how are you?' 'OK. OK, Don Lucas. And you?'

'Oh, I'm OK too. I have come here looking at a bit of land. Do you know that if one can grab a star, you grab it. If you cannot grab it, you leave it.'

'He was quiet spoken was the *gringo*, but straight speaking. He had his office in Cañadón Verde. At that time all this land was virgin. Don Lucas grabbed land as far as he could see. 'Oh *companerito*!' 80,000 hectares he rented from the State at five pesos a hectare. That was why he grabbed so much land. Of the 80,000 hectares in his contract he had to choose all these hectares in just one area. At that time these lands were empty.'

'I remember Señor Bridges,' interrupted Maria Luisa Cruces. She explained she had been born in Confluencias in 1921, where her father had worked for 'the Company' as a *puestero*.[2]

'We were many years in the River Salto. My father started working for Lucas Bridges. He was well trusted because he did his job. Later friends started to hate him. They became jealous because there was no one like *Compañero* Cruces. They called him *Compañerito* but instead of patting his back they stuck a knife in it.

---

[1] References to testicles (*bolas*) or eggs (*huevos*) in their various forms are used throughout South America, and particularly in Patagonia. The words and hand signs (cupped upwards) are used to describe someone who is stupid or idiotic, or who has behaved or spoken stupidly. In some circles either reference can cause offence, but the user can usually be presumed to know where and when.

[2] A Segundo Cruces came to the Baker as a herder for the CEB, leaving for Argentina when the company collapsed, but returning to Las Latas in 1918.

'I remember in 1937 I became ill. I lost the use of part of my body. I still cannot walk. Now I cannot walk round the house any more. First my sister fell ill suddenly. She was only four and she died within four days. Then it was my turn. The only person who knew a bit about medicine was Don Manuel Huelet. He made me some callipers and later they spoke to Martínez the *carabinero*. He prepared some remedies and told my parents to take me away from there. They took me out on horseback to where Marín used to live. Then they took me by cart to Entrada Baker and later Mister Bridges took me to Aysén in a grey coloured *camioneta* which I called 'the wolf'. He asked me, 'what colour is this? What are we going to call it?' and I said 'Wolf' and that stayed its name.

'In Aysén I spent the winter. My mother left me in a house. The following year she came to find me and took me to Puerto Montt. We stayed in the house of a man called Cogotin. He walked on stilts as high as the roof.[3] His wife was a spiritualist. She told my mother to leave a photo so she could prepare medicine for me.

'That was the only time I have left here. Sure, we have lived in other places, but round here. I married Adan Vera in 1946, I think.'

'My father too used to work for Mister Bridges,' said Maria Graciela Fuentes.

'Mister Bridges sought my father out when he heard he was a sawman. That was his profession. He had come to Huemules and started working on an old sawmill high up in the Pampa Castillo. He had to rebuild it from scratch. It was burnt out. Mister Bridges improved it, added a turbine and brought in some belts from outside. Mister Bridges was a very good man. Very polite to everyone. He felt no superiority. He worked alongside his *peones* in the *campo*. He was always visiting us at home. He was tall. A big man. When summer came, he brought his family and when winter started, they went. He had grown up children, but at that time they were small.'

There was a break in the conversation. Light was beginning to fade. The rain had stopped but there was a chill in the evening air. Clodomiro pulled himself upright to shut the top door, throw a log into the fire and refill the *mate*. He handed it to Maria.

'Don Clodomiro,' said Maria. 'How old was Doña Maria when you married?'

Clodomiro looked surprised.

'She was very young, was the old girl. I was maybe 45 and she was 22. To this day I have nothing to say against my woman.'

'Is it right that you stole her?'

If Clodomiro was upset by the question he did not show it.

---

3   Stilt walking has long been a local custom in Chiloë.

179

'Yep. I did steal her. Her old woman didn't want to give her to me. She wanted her to marry someone with a bar or with more than 1,000 cows. I only had thirty cows. I had 200 sheep. I had enough to keep her and the silly old woman. We never made friends after that; whenever she met me, she ranted at me. But me raise my voice to her? Never. Not once. And so I got married. And they called the police. They took me prisoner to Chile Chico for 'Kidnapping'. They said I had stolen her. What a load of shit. One can't steal a woman because a woman is as rational as a man. They go where they want. If they go and hide from their elders, that's OK, but don't say that I stole her, because they are not animals. We are not animals. We are rational animals.

'Now I have ten children—four are girls—and grandchildren. I have a soft spot for those cheeky little devils and I love them all equally.'

Maria handed the *mate* back to Clodomiro, who refilled if from the kettle. No one needed prompting. They knew the procedures even with their eyes closed by the smoke. He handed it to Margarita Romero.[4] It was her turn.

'I don't remember when I was married but I was fifteen and we went to live in La Colonia. It was in the hills. Pure hills and woods. The sky was all one ever saw. I stayed on my own when my husband went out to work. I wasn't frightened. No one went out that far in those days. There were plenty of deer but we didn't kill them. There were lions [pumas]. I saw them. They passed very close to the house and you could see their droppings. There were mountain cats. We hunted them and took the skins to Argentina where they paid 4,000 pesos a skin. A good price.

'It was a good life. Not difficult like now. My husband brought eight cows with him and we added to them with others he received as part payment. We started to accumulate capital. We never lacked food and the men who worked earned enough to live. We never lacked meat. There was no shortage of animals or crops. Supplies we brought from Argentina together with clothing.

'I remember once I went to Coyhaique. My daughter Susan was six months old. She is forty now. We went on horseback. It took fifteen days. We went by La Leona to Chile Chico and then to Los Antiguos. We left the horses in Coyhaique and went to visit family in Puerto Aysén in a vehicle. We did not know vehicles. I was terrified. It seemed as if we were going to turn over. I didn't say anything. I felt dizzy and when I got out it seemed that where I was, was not this world. On the way back the vehicle broke

---

[4] One of the *poblador* families to settle outside the Baker concession at the junction of the Baker and Colonia rivers was Antolin Romero Barros and Cardemia Castro Rajas and their children who included Rosalia, Margarita, Jose Ricardo and Rosamel Romero Castro.

down. I do not know what happened but we could not continue. We had nowhere to stay and it was raining. It was awful. That was the worst that happened on that trip. The food was different. I didn't like seafood. I ate water melon and apricots. There was a lot of business in Coyhaique but I could not wait to come back. I did not feel at ease even though I was on my own. There were lots of people but I was bored.

'I came to Cochrane to live ten years ago. Since I came I have had no wish to go back to the *campo*. Here I find things better and if I need anything I have only to go and buy it. If I had to go back fifteen years, I would return to work as I did before. I was happy with no thought of going to town. Simply to work and look after the animals.'

Old eyes were reddened. Old limbs ached. The flames had yielded forgotten faces which had smiled and flickered in the smoke and shadows. The shaking of heads and the mumbled 'Gracias' now finally indicated that the *mate* circuit had closed and an evening of memories was at an end.

Our horses had been left in a paddock at the edge of town. Petaka's right foreleg was badly swollen and a visit from the vet confirmed our fears. She was not fit for further travel and we could not wait the estimated two weeks for her to recover. Cuervo's saddle sores were improved, but he had become increasingly difficult, particularly as *pilchero*. Only by constructing a restraint round his neck out of wire coat hangers was he persuaded to keep up, the contraption biting into his neck whenever he pulled back. It was not a remedy of choice, but he was undoubtedly feeling his age and the strain. Olympia was always willing. She too had suffered badly from saddle sores, but these had benefited from the magic spray. Tía had been got at by a passing stallion who had somehow managed to enter the paddock. It had all happened in a few seconds. Hector assured me that her pregnant state would not affect her riding performance, although I had some reservations.

Ahead lay two weeks across some of the wildest parts of Chilean Patagonia, and we needed at least two *pilcheros* to carry sufficient food. The season was moving on and while our days in Cochrane were dry and hot, warmer clothing was going to be necessary. An extra horse was needed to replace Petaka, and Hector was to ride one of his own over from his father-in-law's farm near Puerto Bertrand.

The days passed peacefully enough. I slept at El Fogón, which was also a restaurant capable of producing excellent meals. The town spread out from a pleasant pine tree-shaded central square, which housed a spired modern church, bank, a large general store and the *carabineros*. Most of the principal streets had been concreted and many more were in the process. Almost every street had one house devoted to the sale of something—food and groceries being the most popular. Some had become small meeting centres where marketing was an afterthought. Chickens were free ranging as were packs of randy dogs, and horses predominated at certain times of the day. The local school was modern and housed the library and computer centre. The centre was state-of-the-art and the local hospital, while of somewhat dejected appearance, was cottage-style friendly. The rolling Rio Cochrane skirted the extremes of the town and during days when the temperature rarely dipped below 30°F, hardy children frolicked in its freezing waters.

During my rest days, I spent time in the library and paid visits to the Baker, Tortel and Hector's home in Puerto Bertrand. The latter was fla-voured by an 'international' fishing contest, a knees-up cum barbecue/ *asado* and a horse race finale. Patagonian horse races tend to evolve. A date is fixed well in advance, so that rivals can hone themselves and their horses in readiness while pretending that they are too busy and uncertain about when the event is to take place. Yet for all the practised indifference, horse races are eagerly awaited. Significant reputations can be made and broken, and a wholly disproportionate amount of money changes hands. I had hoped to see Hector race. He had his father's reputation to follow, and by accounts he was not far behind. On this occasion, however, he had been appointed end referee, and I guessed his father-in-law had decided he needed to be held in check. Since he was an official, he could not also ride, but—more significantly, since I had just paid him—he was not allowed to bet.

The course was a sloping piece of open land above the village. The background was an exquisite combination of wooded slopes, Lago Bertrand and the white peaks of the Cordón Contreras illuminated by an evening sun. A pair of condors had appointed themselves observers, and circled against the blue sky. Each race had two competitors, the riders riding bareback. There was much milling and circling and as many false starts, as each strove for advantage. These were the moments when tactics played their part. Eventually and by mutual agreement the pair hurtled off in a straight line some 250 yards uphill, where Hector determined who had arrived first. His decision was final but the arguments were intense, and it was not difficult to imagine how provincial wars have broken out in the past. Privately I was pleased that the first winner was Hector's friend from Cochrane, who owned the land where our horses were grazing. But it was very close!

Local legend recalls a similarly close finish to a race held in 1938 at Las Latas, before it became Cochrane. On that occasion, not even the judges, Rosario Gonzalez Cerda (Chililo) and Bernardo Silva Colipan could agree, and nearly came to blows. When eventually they parted company, each swore to kill the other the next time they met. Some time later, Chililo was sitting in the kitchen at the rear of the only store in Pueblo Nuevo (as it was then called). Although drunk, in his subconscious he heard Silva's voice. Staggering into the store, he invited Silva to join him for lunch and a few drinks. Those that later saw them together described them as two good friends enjoying a reunion. After their meal, Silva loaded his pilchero with purchases and was about to climb into his saddle when Chililo came out to join him. Words were exchanged, then two shots echoed and two bodies lay in the dust. At that time there was no church or priest, and no parting words or prayers were said as they were buried in the same grave. Today, neither the children who play nor the residents who walk on the grass pavement covering the old cemetery have ever heard of Chililo or Silva.[5]

I had not heard the legend before, but then I had not expected the day to end on the balcony of a smart French timber restaurant, eating vegetarian food with two Canadian kayak instructors, watching the moon's reflection shimmer on the lake and listening to Hari Krishna music, but Patagonia never loses its capacity to surprise, and it gave ample opportunity to ponder what lay ahead.

South of Lago Cochrane the cordillera resumes normal business at Mount San Lorenzo (12,000 plus feet), and thereafter, apart from two interrelated breaks at the Rio Mayer and Lago San Martin,[6] it continues to the foot of the continent in the revised guise of the Southern Ice Field. The sheer remoteness of the region has meant that its discovery has been largely accidental or incidental to longer journeys. Perito Moreno and Carlos Moyano were among the first *huincas* to set eyes on the Lake in 1877, a few others including Hans Steffen and Captains Thompson and Robertson travelled along the Argentine side, but the region excited little interest.

On the Chilean side, access was limited to crossing from Argentina

---

[5] The legend was resurrected by Rosa Gomez Miranda in her 'Por las Sendas de la Patagonia' published by the Cochrane Municipality in 2010

[6] Even following the Arbitration and the lake's division, its original name San Martín remained in common use until 1960, when the Chilean part became O'Higgins. To avoid repeating the two names, Lago San Martín and Lago O'Higgins will be referred to as the Lake. A glance at the map will show the octopus shape of the Lake, its many *brazos* (arms), its division, the Peninsula Florida and the Isla Central, which provides a bridge between the east and west shores.

either at the Rio Mayer and thence to the Lake, or by the Lake itself. One large concession, the Freudenburg, had been granted in 1903, but never took off and finally expired in 1917, leaving settlement almost exclusively to the individual *poblador*. By 1945 only 109 Chilean settlers had crossed, most of them via the Mayer, and had just about survived at subsistence level, employing barter and living in houses made of tree trunks. The town of Villa O'Higgins was not established until 1966, and the section of the Austral, connecting it with Cochrane, was only completed in 1999.

The route Hector and I were to take had been discovered by the *carabineros* in the early 1930s. Closely following the frontier across the wildest terrain, it had been little used and had played little or no part in the early settlement of the region. Hector had ridden part during the previous year and estimated a thirteen-day ride, but thought that in the later and more difficult sections we would be obliged to ride significant distances in a single day because of the shortage of camping sites. The time of year promised unpredictable weather and we could expect to meet very few locals. To add to difficulties, we then received news that the winter timetable of the boat I was hoping to catch across the Lake, had kicked in, reducing our available travel time to eleven and a half days. Due to strict quarantine rules and a particularly sensitive section of border, it was not possible to take horses across into Argentina. Those who defied the rules could expect their horses to be shot from under them before questioning started. Hector and I were to part company at Villa O'Higgins, he to bring the horses back to Coyhaique by truck, and I to proceed on foot.

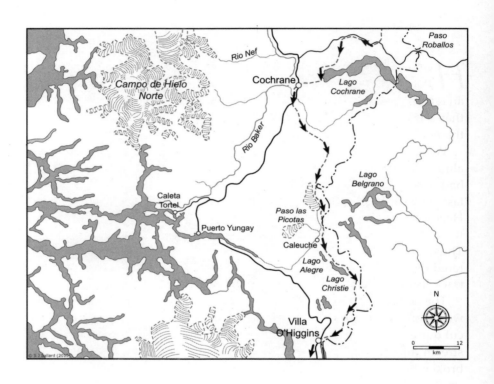

CHAPTER ELEVEN

Cochrane to Villa O'Higgins

*H*ector scrapped his plan to ride one of his own horses over from Puerto Bertrand. He had made enquiries and located some horses at an *estancia* one day's ride down our planned route. There was a suspicion that social demands had sapped his enthusiasm, but he was confident in the new alternative and it was his mount we had to replace.

We spent the morning buying provisions. Our food requirements were almost double what we had needed for the previous section, but we both had a better idea of personal preferences and which products tended to last longest. We then turned to the inevitable horse shoe replacements. Hector had arranged for a friend to help, but the friend did not show and it was to take him most of the morning to complete re-shoeing on his own. Thus it was half way through the afternoon that our team of three clattered over the concrete roads and pavements and on to the dirt and stone track leading south. We were determined to make a start.

The aches and pains, which for so long had been a daily feature of life, were noticeably less troubling. Within two hours light was fading and we cut our way down a sheltered gulley to make our first camp beside a small stream and protected by willows and bamboo clusters. The silence was broken by the typewriter tapping of woodpeckers, the twittering of many small birds, the watery call of a *whet-whet* and the occasional screech from a flock of green parakeets.

In the morning the pine plantations to the south of Cochrane came to an end, and we started to climb through dry scrubland. Looking back, Cochrane was out of sight and only the lump of Tamango was visible. Ahead and to the west a double-page vista opened out, revealing fresh detail with each step. In the foreground and below us lay Lago Esmeralda, its own natural colour intensified by a cloudless sky and its edges spilling across the page into green swamps and rusty reeds. Behind, one snow-covered peak led to another, each more stunning than the last. Cerro Colonia fell onto Cerro Puno—at 7,200 feet the highest—followed by the pride of Lions (León): Head, Teat and finally Tail. This range formed the eastern edge of the Northern Ice Cap and the backdrop to a magic vista devoid of corners. It was not difficult to understand why the CEB and its immediate successors selected the Colonia area as their base before transferring up to the Valle Chacabuco.

A *caracara* stood tall on a post, its dark crest a black pirate patch betraying its regal hawk profile for the scavenger it is. It was interested either in a hare lying on the track or a skunk which had garrotted itself on the wire fence, and was in no hurry to make up its mind until we had passed.

We then turned south again to follow a switchback of dips and curves along the Rio del Salto. One moment we were looking down on glacial green waters confused by twists and turns and small islands, and the next we were level with its sand and gravel banks. From the last rise we dropped down an ancient tree-lined avenue which would have graced the finest man-made park, and emerged to the stunning impact of Mount San Lorenzo. Set back from its lower sharp-peaked companions but linked to them by towering ice bridges, it formed one of the natural border markers in the southern cordillera. As we crossed the Rio del Salto by a sturdy metal suspension bridge, San Lorenzo was lost from view. Torrent ducks busied their brown selves crisscrossing at the base of the falls. We had reached the Y junction formed by the long del Salto valley and the shorter east-west valley of yet another Rio Tranquilo. The latter, leading up to Lago Brown, had already been described to me as a 'paradise', and appropriately for such a place it was reasonably well populated. Our route south, however, was to take us to a Garden of Eden: poplar-bordered squares of lush grassland, reeded lakes and, fittingly, a number of apple trees. This was where we were to pick up our replacement horse, but while there were cattle and horses in abundance, there was no sign of any hut or human.

It was an area of such peace and warm tranquillity that there was no urge to hurry, and we meandered down endless earth paths until eventually we came on a hut housing the *estancia* foreman. He was a strange man—his twelve-year-old son even stranger. They were the only inhabitants.

'No.' He had not received any instructions from the owner to sell us any horses, and...

'Yes.' There were plenty of horses but ...

'No'. He was very sorry he could not take it upon himself to sell us one without the boss's permission and ...

'Yes.' There was a radio on an adjoining *estancia*, but he was not sure if there was anyone there.

We were not going to make any further progress that day, and while Hector went off to find the radio, I unsaddled the horses and prepared our camp for the night. I could hear the foreman's son chatting to himself in the bushes nearby, and fleetingly saw him sitting cross legged surrounded by a number of primitive dolls. Hector returned to say he had found the radio but had been unable to contact the owner who had gone away. Our prospects of reaching Villa O'Higgins in time were fading fast, but without an additional horse we were completely stuck.

We decided to leave our horses and supplies and head back to the suspension bridge in the hope that we might meet a timber truck heading back to Cochrane. As we waited a young rider came by and a long conversation took place. He had a small farm not far away and gradually Hector teased out of him that he had two spare horses which he did not want to sell, but one of which he might be prepared to hire provided we brought it back from Villa O'Higgins. A very reasonable price was agreed and the next morning he would shoe the horse and bring it to our camp.

It had taken nearly two hours, but Hector had shown great tenacity patience and skill, and he had conjured us our missing horse out of a hat which had seemed to be empty. I was even more impressed when he said he would be responsible for the rental and the cost of transporting the horse back by truck.

There was much movement and noise that night. The twittering and hooting were welcome and friendly, and when eventually I woke to the sound of alarmed cocks there was a heavy dew and a ridge of mosquito bites revealed the gap I had left in my sleeping bag. We sat warming ourselves in the sun, the only sounds a distant saw, an occasional bellow or bleat or a 'Look what I've found' from an excited hen.

As promised, our piebald fourth team member was delivered—a big stallion. Over breakfast we learned a little of his idiosyncrasies, which apart from a 'strong mouth' were modest. We were delighted and spare nails and horseshoes and the rental changed hands. There was no time for formal introductions to the other team members—one of whom was now to have a free day each day—and with Hector astride 'Piebald' we broke camp and headed out of the Garden of Eden. We had lost perhaps one day.

The owner of Piebald had given Hector a new route which took us round the steep sides of Laguna Confluencia and saved time. Sheep scattered as we reached the end of the lake and entered the first of many woods. This wood, however, ended almost without warning on the down slope, and before I knew it, we were in the Rio del Salto.

Being outside the concessions to the Baker, this area was open to both *pobladores* and *colonos* and their families, the majority of whom were Chileans from the region between the Rio Bío Bío and Llanquihue. Today the pressure to occupy the last valley seems to have gone into reverse, and only the hardiest remain, their families installed in the relative comfort and security of Cochrane, while the breadwinners struggle with the environment, access and ever reducing returns.

Hector's customary late warning—'Watch out, Jon, it's deep!'—came when we were already in the Rio del Salto beyond our boots. Lack of concentration had meant I had forgotten that the river was due back, and while advance planning had equipped us with short length rubber boots, poor execution had left the boots on the packhorse and each of us in normal footwear. Mine filled up rapidly as the horses surged across.

'Why are your feet dry, Hector?' I asked, to cut short any post-mortem on the far bank.

'Because I took them out of the stirrups.'

I spent several minutes working out that he had managed to cross his feet over Piebald's neck—a manoeuvre I could not have achieved even with a week's advance warning.

The Rio del Salto had slipped by unseen and its summer course was now confined to passable channels, leaving a wide mega-pebbled valley floor to speak volumes of the forces prevailing in winter. We tacked our way up its length, crossing from one isolated poplared oasis to another. The valley sides were abrupt and bare, broken by occasional waterfalls from glaciers, and the upper reaches were dusted with snow. At the second and last oasis we paused for lunch and were joined by the owner, who told us he had had enough and was moving out. Apart from isolation, it was clear that his paddocks, if lush, were small and could only maintain a modest quantity of stock. Importantly, from our point of view, he gave us a piece of information.

'When you get to the "Paso de las Picotas", go for the white rock. You'll see it high up on the right.'

It was to prove invaluable advice.

Among the many problems of tracing a route through Patagonian Chile is the use of names. Maps bear names applicable when the map was first printed. Our maps were the 1987 edition and contained no reference to Paso de las Picotas, and many of the names had changed. Even those who lived locally use different names. Fortunately Hector knew where the 'Paso' was.

Ahead, the terrain was looking increasingly formidable. The end of the del Salto valley was a wall of rock, and the snow-covered mountains beyond gave no clues as to how they could be reached. We continued across the pebbles, which the horses disliked intensely, until we met the river on its last curve. We were now near its glacial source and the current was fierce. This time Hector stopped to give his advice.

'Don't look down at the current,' he warned. 'You can lose your balance and fall off. We'll cross the first bit at an angle but we may have to switch direction half way over.'

My level of confidence in Olympia was high, and I now had muscles which could guide her with the pressure of my thighs, which added significantly to my still modest riding ability. A bow wave built up round the horses' chests. Their feel for a pebble floor hidden from the rider's eyes was instinctive. We switched direction before turning into the current again and we were through. I even had time to look at the current briefly and sense the justification for Hector's warning, particularly when crossing at right angles to the bank. My boots and trousers were soaked, and so I noticed were Hector's. This time, we both grinned.

Past a short passage of thorn scrub and pebble and we were at the foot of the valley end wall. We climbed violently and along a series of narrow rock paths, then violently again, first one way then another. Suddenly we were looking down not only on the valley length behind, but on a huge grey glacial lake to one side—one of the sources of the Rio del Salto. Even on that bare rock, constantly sprayed by the freezing water, there were small yellow, pink and white flowers and clusters of wild strawberries. From the frozen wall of ice feeding the lake rose the massive twin towers of Cerro Los Mellizos: the twins. Ahead and at the new level we had reached, a mass of woodland—*montaña*—stretched as far as we could see and sloped into a deep gulley down which our new river companion, the Pedragosa, thundered.

For several hours we weaved our way round and over fallen trees and across streams. The constant change of direction was tiring and the tracks at best faint, but the horses did not flag. Eventually we emerged onto a high clearing and a simple wooden hut. By now the drizzle had become rain, and while there were a large number of rat traps hung round the hut, each big enough to hold a cat or small dog, exhaustion overcame my fear of the Hanta virus. A few yards from the hut was a fast-flowing river, where during a break in the rain it was possible to sit on the grass bank, and wash teeth and body bits. The shock of the grey/white freezing waters re-awoke the senses in face and feet, which later tingled with pleasure round a roaring fire in the hut. In one corner was a raised wooden platform, where I slept uncomfortably, while Hector snored gently on his sheepskin couch on the earth floor.

We spent the first hour of the next morning crossing and re-crossing rivers, pebbles and rocks before dropping once again into the endless *montaña*. When visible through the trees, the mountain sides were heavy with cloud. Otherwise the woods were so thick and the change of direction so frequent that one quickly became disoriented. There was a total absence of sound, save for the click of hooves on stone and the rush of nearby water. Of birds or animals there was no sign: an occasional blue bi-planed dragonfly, and when we stopped for lunch, a dark green frog with vivid yellow lines from head to toe. The tree trunks wore chevrons of light green moss, called locally 'old man's beard', and their falling was indiscriminate. Wind or perhaps the weight of snow brought them down, roots and all, some so big that a substantial detour was necessary. Others the horses could step over. One such—a little higher than usual but not enough to go round—I approached with the reins too tight. Olympia took this as an invitation to jump, and did so. A frantic message from brain to muscles arrived too late for the latter to react, and I somersaulted out of the saddle to land on my shoulders and complete a forward roll. The fact that I was wearing waterproofs, hat and bumbag probably cushioned my fall, and I remained sitting—shaken and stirred—and scarcely able to believe that nothing was broken. Hector's face said it all. It was not a place to have an accident.

We emerged at last into an open rocky valley in which there was little vegetation. Ahead lay a valley wall scarred by a falling stream. To the left a series of peaks towered upwards cascading snow and ice into a huge glacier, from which melting waters plunged vertically down a rock tube gulley. The lower levels of that side and the central wall were a steep mess of broken rock and moraine. The right side was a black wall, at the top of which—unmistakeably—was a large whitened rock. We had reached the Paso de las Picotas, otherwise La Cruzada.

Aurelio Quelín, Jacinto Delgado and Heraldo Real are three pioneers whose names were not amongst those who had first settled in the area during the period between 1910 and 1930. Aurelio, almost out of his eighties, but who has since died, was the eldest and Heraldo, at 62, the youngest. They knew the pass because they have had to drive cattle through it, and because they have created and maintain a path for others to use. 'Pass' however is a misnomer. 'Wall' describes the problem feature better: a wall of rock, moraine, water and ice.

'I came to know the way from Cochrane to Villa O'Higgins shortly after leaving Don Lucas Bridges,' Quelín was later to tell me.

'I am proud to say I was the first to take cattle down this route. That was in 1950. There was no track. Pure highlands. To take animals, one had to make a path as you went. Sometimes we went via Argentina, by way of Murta. We had to go a lot of the time on foot. There is one bad part, which is called "La Cruzada", which is a pass at the birth of the Rio Salto, where there is a glacier. It's really bad; it's narrow and you have to go down and up a sheer wall; we *pobladores* made a path that would be more or less sixty metres down in a curve. There are some picks which we leave there so those who pass can clear a path. This is why it is called "Pass of the Picks".

'In summer it is nothing, but in winter, when there is ice, it's a different matter. The path does not collapse in the winter because of the sand and clay there. Those who have to work most are those who come through first. It would be worth making a small diversion because there is space for one. People do not realise the sacrifice made so that others can get through.'

Jacinto Delgado came to Cochrane in 1952 and five years later settled in the Bravo area. He too later gave me his account:

'There was a man called Alberto Mena nearby. Then the Brunels, Don Armando Aguilar. Don Aurelio—Quelín—was there. Now I live in the Mayer and have someone looking after my land in the Bravo. I used the Paso de las Picotas. We left picks there, which some stole. They are there as a public service, the same as the axes. All these paths have been made by those who have driven cattle through or the *pobladores*. It makes me mad that you now have to pay for the right to bring animals through a route we ourselves have made.

'Las Picotas is where Tiznado Fuentes died. That was in February 1988. He was bringing some cattle through with his two sons—one fourteen and the other twelve. He died for lack of a good path. I too suffer a little from blood pressure. I don't dare climb through without one two or three rests on the way—more when one is constantly turning and going back and forth. Looking at that precipice makes it even worse.

'*Es cosa seria!*

'If this path had been repaired, this man would not have died. The boys said that they were driving the cattle on foot, and had started to climb with four of them but could not get them to go onto the path and that was what killed him. They saw their father sit down, and when he did not turn up they went back to see why, but he was dead. The boys did not know that the way back was shorter but fortunately they met two men from the area. If they had gone on to the flatlands above in those clouded days, they would have been lost and would have woken dead as well. There is no one who could help up there. It's pure mountain. You could not imagine. It's like going from here to Guadal or Mallín. No path, no road, there is nothing. Pure lava beds. And a boy of that age loses his bearings. What's more, sometimes the day is fine, but then suddenly it's gone.'

'You need to take one animal at a time, herding them on foot,' added Quelín.

'Fuentes was middle-aged with blood pressure and asthma. When he realised that everything had failed he sat down, and the boy said that when he went to him, he appeared to be alive because his mouth was open, and when a bull passed near him he moved his hand.'

'It takes eight days by horse from El Bravo,' Jaime Delgado continued.

'With cattle, a minimum of fifteen to twenty days if they are to arrive in good condition. The problem is Las Picotas. We have been asking all the time that this be sorted. It's no place to fall ill. If you can call a plane in time at 180,000 to 200,000 *pesos*, that's fine. If not, you simply die where you are. The first time I fell ill, I had appendicitis. I had to go to Argentina. The Argentines are very obliging in cases of illness. When the weather allows and the rivers are low, you can call an Argentine ambulance and they will come and look for you. They arranged a truck and took me to San Julián. As I was feeling a little better, I preferred to go to Chile Chico, but when I got to Ibañez, I was dying. They put me on the mining boat and got me to Chile Chico. I was pretty bad.

'Three winters ago I had an attack of the nerves—a month in bed—and the medical auxiliary from the *carabineros* and a lieutenant came to see me. This was in August. One of their horses fell over the precipice in the ice. They had to leave him and continue on foot, arriving at 11 o'clock at night. A lot of animals have died there—horses and cattle.'

Both men had tried persistently to persuade the authorities to provide a safer route through the pass.

For the early settlers expectations were minimal, with perhaps a hope that there might be a glimmer of real gold round the corner. They took their opportunities and occasionally created a humble and invariably isolated island for their families to inherit. Progress has followed slowly and may now offer some of those families new expectations and opportunities. However, in the upper reaches of the Rio del Salto and beyond, if there are prospects, they probably lie below rather than on the land. Had it not been for the advice given in the del Salto valley, we would have tried the left hand alternative first. Instead we knew our way lay up the right hand rock face, we had no cattle to drive and there was no ice that side. Sometimes Hector acted on impulse—usually he was right—but initially I was unwilling to follow the route he proposed, and I felt the horses would share my doubts. He linked all four horses and tried to lead them up the near vertical wall. There were footholds and small ledges but there had to be another way, and I set off down its base, looking for a promising slope. Hector, meanwhile, having failed to persuade the horses to follow their leader, then tried to lead them up individually. Piebald was willing and after much slipping, sliding and swearing he was left looking down rather forlornly from beside the white rock. Hector then scrambled down and selected Cuervo. It was not a good choice. Cuervo would not move and nor would the others.

By this time I had found an alternative which started much further back, and which seemed to go upwards far more gradually. Hector needed little persuading and soon all five were standing by the white rock, while I lumbered up behind. Any sense of achievement soon disappeared when I found that the cliff did not finish at the rock. Round the corner, we had another 200 yards to go but now at least the rock was mixed with earth and there was a track of sorts winding up to the top.

When eventually I reached the true top I was exhausted but amazed to be looking down on a beautiful green meadow, sheltered on the valley cliff side by thick bushes and sloping up the other side to further peaks. It was a perfect camp site, the meadow crossed with numerous narrow sunken streams and dotted with small yellow and white and yellow and red mini-bell flowers. The horses were already grazing their reward. There was plenty of wood for a fire, but the view simply had to be appreciated first.

At our level and across the valley opposite were two peaks covered with deep snow. My map of this tiny piece of frontier showed only 'Three Brothers-South' with a mysterious 'Mount W' behind, and the boundary line was marked *Limite Aproximado*. Assuming the other peak was the second of the trio, I searched in vain for the third. Glacial ice and water cascaded from them, some falling over the end wall, the rest descending vertically down the gulley tube described by Quelín and Delgado. I thought I could see a faint line leading in a curve to the base of the gulley. I shivered, imagining how a constant spray would have left the ledge in winter.

Turning to look back over the woods, I could follow much of our route past the Mellizos to San Lorenzo, now clear of cloud, and further on still, the León family with a vast white shimmer behind. All now stood against a spectacular blue sky streaked with yellow and interrupted by vertical pink spirals. Later, fed, rested, warm and with half a carton of red wine inside, we watched the light fade as a clear twinkling sky took over.

A seamless sleep ended as first one then the other eye opened to watch the last of the stars give way to the same blue canopy of yesterday. As that blue lightened, so skeins of pink gave way to greys and yellows as the new day awoke on us. The horses munched on foot without pause. Only Tía lay down. It was a good day to be alive and a perfect start to look down on the already misty memory of the toils of yesterday.

We climbed up through the meadows and flowers and as we paused at the top of the next long descent, a pair of condors appeared and circled soon to be joined by a third, then a fourth. We spent a breathtaking half hour sitting in the saddle as they swooped above, below and around us. The isolation seemed to give them a certain bravado and they came close enough to threaten with their sheer size. As they passed over us, the white ring round the neck drew attention to the head, which pivoted to return our stare—an ugly vulture head dominated by the dark red comb on the male. The two latecomers sported the grey-brown tones of the young.

As they dipped below us, we could see prominent white areas on the topside of those vast black wings. Change of direction was effortless and without any perceptible movement of tail wing or even the finger feathers at the end of each wing. The only movement was in that ugly head. We were all clearly alive, however, and interest in us waned as they circled off towards San Lorenzo and we clattered down a dizzy path over loose rock and shale on to Jacinto Delgado's 'lava beds'.

Our National Institute map gave no names, merely showing a white area of permanent snow into which was jabbed the tip of a small Argentine thumb. My backup Tactical Pilotage Chart preferred the anonymity of 'Relief Data Incomplete', a description normally reserved for the Ice Fields.

Glaciers continued to feature on the now modest slopes to either side, feeding innumerable nameless streams. There was no obvious route down the wide undulating valley, and it was a while before I picked out the small cairns of stones which Hector was following, and which Quelín, Delgado and friends renewed each year. Apart from defiant clumps of flowers, the area was lunar and inhospitable. White bones and skulls of horses and cattle lay clear against the grey, picked clean by the condors. At some stage we passed into Argentina and then back into Chile, but no one was interested.

A long descent through another arid valley eventually led us to a fork and a welcome return to friendly green grassy slopes. A massive rock seemed to block our exit, but as we came closer we noticed a narrow passage alongside, which led us past a cadence of glaciers and rushing waterfalls to yet another level and valley, dominated by the multi-channels of a young Rio Bravo. We were through the Cruzado.

A short diversion into a wood took us past the simple tomb of one José Rogel, who had died of exposure with his horse and dog. Nobody seems to know much about Rogel, other that he was in his mid-fifties. He was crossing in May or June and was caught in the snow. His grave was a tent of logs. Alongside was a tree to which a tin had been nailed, and in the rusty tin was a small bible and a bundle of candles. We both dismounted and lit a candle to his memory and placed some coins in the tin. I spent a few moments pondering how José Rogel had managed to cross the major horrors of the Cruzada in winter, only to become trapped in what was now the sheltered green around us.

We wound thoughtfully on down the valley, past a small group of skittish cattle, to a low grassy platform and rough wooden shelter—a site known variously as Veranada Diaz or Pampa Quelín, our next camp.

The shelter's roof and walls, sturdily built of thick half-trees, bore the graffiti of earlier visitors—Spanish names mixed with some East European. Since rats rustled in the nearby bushes, we strung our tarp over the grass nearby and hung our supplies from the roof of the shelter. We had reached a junction of valleys, one leg of which bent eastwards before being amputated at the thigh by the frontier line. Beyond the amputation lay an unseen Lago Magote, one of the eight lakes which form part of the Argentine Parque Nacional Perito Moreno. Apart from the route we had come down and the southern route we were about to take, these were the only ways into the Bravo valley. Pedro Calcamo was the first to settle the 'upper regions' in the 1920s, raising a significant herd of some 400 cattle before the loss of 100 head in the terrible winter of 1930 forced him to retreat to the Mayer, but whether he reached this far is uncertain.

Meanwhile, although our maps indicated a track following the Rio Bravo to the south-west, within the first hour Hector had led us out of the valley up a kidney bruising climb, which left Olympia and I breathless, and into thick wooded montaña. Thereafter, a relatively constant one-way slope gave us both a sense of direction and progress, despite the dips, rises and detours. The silence was broken only by our breathing and the soft sounds of our going. It was therefore a rude shock suddenly to hear the sound of voices and the lowing of cattle ahead. We arrived in a clearing to find a corral heaving with Herefords. Beside a huge fire a group of men were preparing their lunch.

The three were neighbours and in the Patagonian tradition neighbours helped each other when distances between them were measured in days. Quelín, at 88, was the oldest by 25 years. He owned the land and the cattle and now lived in Cochrane. Euricio Marin's grandfather owned the land beyond Lago Alegre. Heraldo Real looked after Quelín's land and an area stretching from the Rio Bravo to the Mellizos. We had been expecting to meet up with him at some stage, and had brought a supply of cigarettes and a letter from his daughter in Chile Chico.

Quelín was born on the island of Chiloë in 1916, leaving school at the age of thirteen to sweep and wash wool for the SIA at Puerto Aysén. He was never to return home. From Puerto Aysén, he travelled regularly to Coyhaique where he had a relationship with a young girl from which a son was born. He then crossed over to Chubut where he worked as shepherd and puestero on a number of large estancias—'until the job made me old'. Crossing to the Chacabuco he worked with Lucas Bridges, becoming one of his managers, and stayed in the Baker until 1944, when he decided to go off on his own. After seven months building a section of the Pan American to La Junta he joined a survey team as they marked out the town of Cochrane and remembered being paid in coloured discs. That same year, he was the first to bring cattle down from Cochrane to the Rio Bravo through the Paso de las Picotas. He purchased a plot in Cochrane in 1958 where he built his house, kept chickens and grew his fruit and vegetables, continuing with his cattle drives to the Bravo until 1964, when the Bravo was receiving its first *pobladores* and he decided to acquire his own land there. Over the years he acquired a collection of semi-precious stones, of which he was immensely proud and knowledgeable.

He had just returned from the day's roundup. Short and wiry but less sure on his feet than in the saddle, he bustled around collecting logs for the fire.

I asked him if he knew about José Rogel.

'Oh yes. I was the one who found him. In the spring. November 1973. No. It was 1974—the year of Allende. There wasn't much left, but the *carabineros* and I buried him and we built a shelter around the grave.'

'Who was he?' I asked.

'Don't know. I had never met him. They say he came from Cochrane.'

'Is it you who replaces the candles?'

'Yes. That was the least we could do for him. People leave money and I bring the candles.'

I thanked him for the hospitality of his hut at Pampa Quelín, but he did not seem to hear me and cupped his hand behind one ear.

'I don't hear too well,' he explained. 'It's all those cold winds. I haven't been out here for four years. This is the last time.'

It was time to call it a day—to collect up his cattle, brand the calves and then drive them all to Cochrane for sale. He noticed I was admiring the large gold turnip watch which he pulled out of his waistcoat pocket from time to time.

'Paid 5,000 pesos for it,' he said.

'Which is older? You or the watch?'

'Me, of course, but the watch keeps better time.' The watery old eyes smiled.

Over lunch there were no new takers for Hector's pasta, but we shared some delicious toasted bread which broke every rule in the cholesterol book, and some soup of unknown provenance which took warmth to the soles of the feet. Quelín and Marin sat quietly while Heraldo Real took over.

Heraldo was my picture of a gaucho back at home, save that in place of a battered straw hat he wore the *boina*—the black beret uniform of the Chilean gaucho, which use had turned to red. His face had both the texture and colour of dark wood and dark eyes twinkled out of slits—the result of years of cold wind, hot sun and smoky camp fires. While the others moved to avoid the smoke as it constantly changed direction, I noticed that Heraldo stayed put and seemed impervious to it. For a man so obviously fit and carrying nothing spare, his cigarette consumption was extraordinary. Those he rolled himself lasted longer, probably because he rolled them so tightly—a tradition he must surely have inherited from some Scottish settler. With the luxury of the packets we had brought, he smoked one after the other—on foot and on horseback.

The roundup had been successful. Only one cow was absent. Remembering Daisy, Buttercup, Lily, Rose and others from my childhood, I asked Heraldo if the cattle had names or numbers.

'No,' he said. 'No names. No numbers, but I know each one of them and where they prefer to be. That's why I know which one is missing and where she is. That's the advantage of going on foot in this country. The land is so steep and wooded that I prefer to walk.'

They had their sorting and branding to do and we were hoping to reach Heraldo's middle *puesto* before nightfall, so we took our leave and rode out past the rough corral. The endless milling and bellows of cattle and their calves reflected not only their anxiety at being contained, but at having others so close.

We continued our switchback way through the *montaña*. Olympia was in one of her vigorous moods, and her desire to trot, which I found uncomfortable, had to be constantly restrained to a fast walk, which she liked even less, particularly along the narrow cliff paths which provided glimpses of river far below. By degrees we worked down to river level and eventually to a collection of neat wooden corrals and huts. High above the entrance gate a large orange bag hung from a tree—Heraldo's meat larder.

Despite having met Heraldo, he had not formally invited us to use his facilities, and Hector decided to make camp away from the buildings in a nearby copse. We were fortunate to have our tarp erected and our fire established before the rains came. Constant clashes between tarp and trees, fences and other obstructions, however, had left us with a growing number of holes, which waterproof plasters only remedied short term, and although the rain ceased for a while the wind in the tree tops ensured a continuous drip which unerringly found holes with or without plasters. By early morning the rain returned with a vengeance, and when it became pointless to continue trying to sleep, I found that the dry-bag containing my clothing had assumed the shape of a basin with its drain hole running deep into the centre of the bag. There was one moderately dry shirt left inside.

Over the years, youth's scathing reaction to the sight of those seen as older, if not elderly, struggling to perform simple daily functions slowly gives way to a realisation that times and roles are subject to subtle change; that ingenuity is increasingly required to deal with an ever lengthening list of physical disabilities. Frustration, however, is an uncomfortable companion, and eventually has to give way to moments of resigned amusement. That morning in the soggy damp of that copse, suddenly everything seemed extremely funny. A flailing hand seeking a shirt armhole hit the tarp at the site of a plasterless hole, and the shirt, which had been merely damp, became soaked. The act of lassoing the left big toe with a bundled sock—honed to perfection by constant practice—caused excruciating cramps, and the boots which I was sure had been placed out of harm's way at the back of the tarp were as waterlogged as the supply of wood which we also thought we had protected. And our piebald replacement had lost two shoes.

Thus, when Heraldo appeared mid-morning out of nowhere, expecting us to be long gone, we were still having coffee under the tarp, it was still raining and somehow we were still amused. I doubt he was impressed or that he would have understood. Hector had been explaining that the most we could expect that day was to reach Heraldo's main camp, which lay just across the Rio Alegre, at a point when it curved away to join the Rio Bravo. Heraldo suggested we join him for the night and then continue via Lagos Alegre and Christie, a route which Hector knew.

Beyond the river lay first Lago Alegre, and then almost immediately, Lago Christie. Each was long—approximately twelve miles, slightly bent and thin but, according to my map, without any of the close set contours which might denote steep sides. However, I had learnt not to trust the map completely, and Hector warned me that once we reached Lago Alegre we were in for at least two days of the toughest riding we had met. Apart from the terrain, the number of suitable camp sites along either lake was very limited. We could not hope to reach the first such site from where we were, and would have to start the first of the two days from as close to Lago Alegre as possible—Heraldo's main camp. The rain looked set to stay and it was markedly colder.

For the next few hours we shadowed Heraldo as he and his horse followed a route they both knew well, weaving through the *montaña*, up steep slopes and down, at a constant unhurried and effortless pace. Hector, trailing Cuervo and Piebald, stayed close enough to maintain a steady conversation, and even Cuervo's usual theatrics ceased. Olympia and I took our place some way back, with Heraldo pausing patiently at the top of the steeper slopes to allow us to catch up.

Eventually we splashed across the Rio Alegre and climbing steadily again emerged on to a high open plateau. On past a small silent and anonymous lake, we finally slithered down a long wooded descent to meet an altogether different Alegre again. The rain which had dusted us with a gentle spray now cascaded down, slashing at exposed face and hands. The final crossing was wide and deep, but knowing that Heraldo had brought us to this point and that his camp lay beyond, there were no anxieties. Ten minutes later, we rode out of bamboo clusters onto a flat, wooden-railed paddock containing several wooden huts and protected at the back by a high ridge. The only signs of life were a number of chickens and a cockerel.

As Hector and I tethered and unsaddled the horses, Heraldo entered the smaller hut. He was gone some time, and since we had thought he was alone we were surprised to hear him talking. After a long conversation, first a black cat and then Heraldo emerged. The cat eyed us and disappeared into the long grass.

'He doesn't like visitors,' Heraldo explained. 'He'll come back when you have gone.'

The hut comprised one small room, one stable door and one shuttered window. The floor was earthen. In one corner were the ashes of a fire and a corresponding hole in the roof above. In another corner was a wooden platform bed covered with a jumble of clothes, sheepskins and bags. Round the walls hung odd bits of horse tack, ropes, a lasso and a number of large rat traps. There was no furniture, save for several logs stood on end—no decoration except for the illustration page of a calendar long out of date. At Heraldo's invitation, we stacked our baggage saddles and sheepskins on the veranda of the adjoining hut. This hut was an altogether superior design and construction, with sawn timber walls and floor and a wooden shingle roof. Inside were two large rooms: the kitchen with stove table and chairs, and the bed/bunk room with three wooden slatted bunk beds. There was even a relatively recent 'girlie' calendar. Outside and some distance from the two main huts was a smaller privy or 'thunder box', and further still a small stable and tack room.

Later and in answer to the inevitable question, Heraldo explained that he needed only one room, which in any event was much cosier, and clearly the cat agreed.

I wandered off the plateau to one of the many indicated streams to collect our drinking supplies, and as I crouched waiting for the containers to fill I noticed a cluster of round green berries and out of curiosity plucked one and put it in my mouth. To my astonishment, I recognised the unmistakeable taste of a gooseberry. In my travels around South America I had come to the conclusion that while prejudice might decide that some European fruits and produce were tastier than their South American equivalent, at least there were two items unique to Europe. Now I was left with only Marmite. The Patagonian gooseberry has the same mildly acidic sweetness but no thorns or spikes.

Despite the driving rain, the horses were delighted with their lush paddock, and by the time we had completed our tasks and joined him, Heraldo had built a roaring fire. As usual, resources were combined, Hector undertook the cooking and Heraldo produced a large piece of beef which he impaled on a metal spike—Chilean style—and stuck in the fringes of the flames. We each drew up a log, prepared our knives and settled down for a long evening. The rain was now a pleasant background to a softly steaming warmth.

There was little spare on Heraldo, and the mouth, masked by stubble on chin and upper lip, gave little away. A forehead, furrowed by time and weather, occasionally retreated sufficiently to reveal the eyes and a hint of his feelings. His movements and words were measured. His body still did what he asked of it, and when it told him to rest, he relaxed. He was at that crossroad when experience and physique peak, notwithstanding the health warning attached to his tobacco addiction. While he was the gaucho in my picture, Heraldos can be found throughout the world—north and south, and throughout Patagonia. His origins were a mix of Turk, Brazilian, Chilean and Argentine, but despite his preference for walking, Patagonia had branded him gaucho and he was clearly content to make that role his own.

He occupied the land in exchange for looking after it—the *puestos*, huts and fences. In return he was allowed to keep his own stock. No money changed hands. His visible possessions were minimal and clearly of no great personal significance. Most were the products of his own ingenuity and labour—one exception being the remains of a telescopic hiking pole, which doubled as a useful poker.

He explained that this had been given him by a group of East Europeans, who had arrived to climb an unnamed mountain. He had acted as their guide and, according to him, was the first to the summit of a peak still unnamed. The group had left the pole and a written appreciation in fractured Spanish, which he preserved in a battered school exercise book. Without revealing his level of literacy, Heraldo handed us the book to read, and when Hector gave him the letter he had brought from Heraldo's daughter in Chile Chico, he handed it back with the implied invitation for Hector to read that too. While he did so out loud, I found a reason for going outside. Coincidentally, I had heard a little of Heraldo's paternal role when I was in Cochrane. By that account he had been a stern father. His daughter was said to have been extremely intelligent and able, but Heraldo had insisted on her remaining in the kitchen. Only late in her twenties, had she escaped. It was a tale often told, but the Heraldo we were seeing was on his own, and our generous Patagonian host.

When I returned, Heraldo was fiddling with some old batteries, which he put in the hot ashes of the fire in the vague hope that they would recharge. Clearly it was something he had done before, and there was little expectation that this time the result would be any different. The batteries were the survivors of a dead collection which had once powered his radio.

He was hoping for some music. Apart from a momentary burst of sound, however, the radio would not respond.

'Don't you have any means of contact with O'Higgins or Cochrane?' I asked.

'No. I used to have a radio but the rats ate the cables. I asked the Municipality in O'Higgins to come and replace it, but when they came they wouldn't believe the rats had done the damage. They blamed me and took the antenna and radio away and refused to replace it.'

'But you must be one of the most isolated people in the region and the only one without a radio.'

'The Mayor is a communist,' explained Heraldo. 'And he knows I'm not. I don't believe in all that shit. They'll never give me another.'

It seemed that apart from that one visit—ostensibly to help, but which had resulted in his complete isolation—Heraldo had never been visited by any of the official social services. Remembering how much Hector and I had relied on him, the *monolitos* we had followed and the *puestos* we had occupied, I felt indignant.

'But what happens if you fall ill? If you find you have, say, appendicitis?' Heraldo's reply was 'spare'.

'If I can get in the saddle, I'll ride for help. Maybe to O'Higgins. Maybe to Argentina.'

'And if you can't?'

'Then I'll die here.'

There was no drama. No political speech. A simple acceptance of the reality in which he lived. His world he knew. He knew what favours it had granted him and he had not expected them. Yet he sought no reward for the hospitality he offered us or the help he gave his neighbours. *Quid pro quo* had no obvious place, yet somehow it was not difficult to imagine how the bureaucracy might view him.

There were many questions, but as I pondered them I realised most were irrelevant. Hector and I were also irrelevant, except that we had brought cigarettes and company.

'Is he always this quiet?' Heraldo asked Hector, who had been content to let the conversation take its Patagonian course.

'Not always, Heraldo,' I replied, and our eyes met briefly. There was perhaps a flicker of understanding.

Before Hector and I retired to our bunk beds, I wrote an appreciation in Heraldo's exercise book for others to read, and he listened impassively while I read it out. I assured him that I would do what little I could to get him a new radio. At first light the next morning he was gone, and as we rode past his hut I saw the black cat disappear inside. On a subsequent visit I was to learn that Heraldo had been visited by a foreign film crew, anxious to film something of his extraordinary life and environment. The crew included a number of young and attractive women, and apparently he much enjoyed the role of a film star. Fame had finally caught up with him, and maybe included a new radio.

A light drizzle was falling from a heavy grey sky, and for a while we were glad to be amongst the trees and soon caught a glimpse of the waters of Lago Alegre. I was half expecting a ride along the shores of the lake, but very soon we were forced upwards to a bare rock summit with the lake far below. Ahead lay roll after roll of unleavened rock, inclining steeply down to the water, each roll separated by fissures. Often these cuts were our route up or down when progress at one level was blocked. Invariably the cuts carried streams, which in turn formed bogs. These were another form of the *sarandas* described by Doña Dora many miles ago.

The horses, Cuervo in particular, sensed the danger, but the *sarandas* were not easy to spot, and there was rarely an obvious way through or across. Few cattle were driven in this area and there were few tracks. A routine quickly developed in which each flat section in the fissures was assumed to be a potential *saranda*. Occasionally we came across rough bridges of poles, just visible in the grass: *embarranados*. The obvious inclination was to use them, but the poles were rounded and slippery and often broke under the horses' weight. Each slip or broken pole caused a burst of energetic panic. Occasionally there were flat stretches, but otherwise no sooner had we reached the bottom than we were forced to turn and climb back up the next cut. For an exhausting eight hours we rode without stopping, until at last from the umpteenth summit we could see a small bay below with a flat green promontory out into the lake on which there was a hut. This was Caleuche, our camp objective, and the horses, sensing the end of the day's ride, quickened their pace as we clattered down a final rocky path and emerged on the gravel shore.

The hut, neatly constructed and sheltered by a circle of trees, was deserted. The area around was fenced, entry being through an unlocked gate, and within the fencing was a grass paddock and a corral. We put up our tarp under the trees, and since the available feed was limited the horses were left with trailing ropes to wander at will. After supper I walked across to the corral to check them and to watch the daylight disappear over the lake. The drizzle had stopped and a wind gusted down the lake, fluttering sections of its mirror surface. Nothing else moved, but I sensed the greyness pressing down on my shoulders, and the name 'Caleuche' made sense.

Hector had explained that the owners were a couple, but that it was the wife who was most involved. There was more than a hint of admiration in his description of how she and her horse negotiated the route to and from Caleuche, in comparison to which our progress had been not merely painful.

'She is the one who laid all the *embarranados*.'

There were no signs of recent occupation, and apart from one paddock planted out with what I suspected might be the *pasto ovillo* (literally 'egg grass', used as a textile), introduced by some of the earliest settlers, no sign of any recent activity or animal.

Many of the myths and legends of Patagonia involve water. *El Caleuche* is one such, and there are many versions. The word may come from the Mapuche language: *caleutun*, to change or transform, and *che*, people. The *Caleuche* is a ship which wanders the seas of Chiloë and the southern canals. It never sails in daylight. On overcast nights it is lit from bow to stern and emits an incessant music. The light and the sails are red. The ship produces its own thick cloud to hide it. The crew are all powerful witches, and if a non-witch approaches the ship transforms itself into a piece of floating wood or log. If an attempt is made to grab the log, it retreats and the crew change into seals or sea birds. It is said that each crew member uses only one leg for walking, the other being doubled up behind so that they jump or hop about. They are all idiots who have no memory, thus maintaining the secrecy of all that happens aboard. One must not look at the *Caleuche*. The punishment is either a twisted mouth, a head twisted round to face backwards or death.

I saw no ship, no floating log, no seals and no sea birds. While there had been many times when a head twisted backwards would have been useful, all in all I was grateful that the *Caleuche* was apparently sailing elsewhere. Atmospherically, the lake was *Caleuche* territory, but *Alegre* it most certainly was not.

Morning light came reluctantly, but eventually revealed that we were horseless again. It was a worrying moment. Any accident or loss of horses three or more days out from either Cochrane or Villa O'Higgins was serious. In the case of an accident we had agreed that the injured person would have to be made comfortable and left with enough of the supplies for a week. The other would then have to set out on foot with what remained of the food, and head for the nearest known radio transmitter. In our case this was either south, to the *carabineros* in Rio Mayer, or north back to Cochrane. If we lost our horses we would have to continue on foot to Rio Mayer, carrying as much as we could between us, and hoping either that we would catch up with them or find someone who had stopped them. Hector had explained that for approximately one year after any change of ownership horses find their way back to their place of origin, day and night, following the precise route by which they came.

Just as these gloomy prospects were starting to become relevant, there was a shout from Hector indicating that the truants had been found. They were feeding contentedly alongside a section of thick brushwood which formed an outer corral 'fence'. It looked to have been a weakness, but had defied any attempt to escape. Cuervo still tended to prefer his own company and Piebald either kept or was kept at a certain distance, but since none of them wanted to be left behind if one went walkabout the others followed. Food was their chief preoccupation, but I had been surprised at how little they drank.

Rodolfo Stange[1] tells of his admiration for horses' solidarity for each other, particularly when facing extreme weather conditions. He noticed how they formed a large triangle, each horse's head pointing towards the centre of the triangle, and each pressed tightly to the next for warmth. The weaker horses elect to form the outer edges of the triangle, taking the brunt of the wind, rain and snow, in effect sacrificing themselves for their stronger companions. Our band of four never had to face such conditions, but they showed us enough to make such reports entirely credible.

Our travelling routine continued with Hector leading the way, towing the day's pack horse on one rein and trailing by a second rein whichever team member had the day off. Olympia and I therefore had advance warning of any particular problem, while keeping an eye on the pack, and any sign of lameness or loose shoes. Except on open ground and when we found ourselves on horses with a similar pace, namely Piebald and Tía, we rarely rode alongside, and conversation was limited to our 'pit stops' (usually at my request), photo opportunities and at camp.

On our days alongside the two lakes there were no lunch stops. The previous day, we had ridden for over twelve hours and had been focused on Caleuche. That day we were faced with thirteen to fourteen hours and further uncertainty as to our next camp site. After an early start we spent the rest of the morning tacking up and down fissures and along the unleavened rock, much as we had done the day before. Since we provided the only colour in a landscape of greys, greens and browns, the occasional single scarlet flower of the wild *notro* came as something of a shock. We lost sight of Lago Alegre for several hours, and when the grey waters showed up again it was a while before I realised that we were now alongside its southern neighbour Lago Christie, and that the two were separated only by a narrow strip. Similar but smaller lakes with

---

[1] In 1958/59, Rodolfo Stange Oelckers, with nine *carabineros*, drove a herd of 550 horses from Tierra del Fuego to Puerto Aysén—a distance of some 1,100 miles—through extremes of weather. They took 120 days and lost 91 horses. This epic journey is described in the book *El arreo detrás de los glaciares* (*Roundup behind the Glaciers*). Stange, whose lifetime career with the *carabineros* started in Cochrane, subsequently rose to the rank of General and he was a member of the government Junta until 1990.

names alluding to their shape, Guitarra and later Riñon (Kidney), slipped by unseen to our east.

With an almost unbroken monotony of rock, it was difficult to spot any obvious route ahead, and Hector's policy seemed to be to keep moving whatever the direction. Time and again we descended almost to the shores of the lake, only to wind back up to cross an exposed promontory, at each of which a defiant blast threatened to blow us off the edge until we found relief in a narrow gulley beyond. Even though the scarlet *notro* dared to show itself in the most unlikely and inhospitable places, the total absence of life above or around us left a clear message. Although I later learned that the first settler arrived nearby in 1919 on some 40,000 acres and apparently prospered with a flock of 1,500 sheep, 100 cattle and 50 horses, this was a place where few could survive.

Eventually we came off the rock and on to flat, scrubby land, and for several hours we weaved round bushes, heading back towards the lake and a distant range of snow-laden peaks. Scrub gave way to areas of closely cropped grass, and before long we were amongst foraging sheep, who led us to a cleared area sloping gently down to a small bay. A single hut stood in the middle, its vegetable garden protected by a high wooden palisade. Despite a number of assorted chickens, who came to greet us, there was no smoke from the chimney and the hut was deserted.

There was no obvious site for our tarp and little grazing left for the horses, but there was no question of our continuing. We were exhausted. Light was fading, and the rain which had persisted all day had now reached the skin. Alongside the hut was a large stack of wood, and a search under it revealed that the ground was dry and level, and that there was a discarded oil drum stove which we were able to match to a piece of rusty pipe. We draped our battered tarp over the length of the logs and soon had a wind-free and watertight shelter with central heating, plus an unlimited supply of crystal clean water from the lake. The outstanding problem was the absence of feed. The horses had kept going all day and deserved better than the remnants left by the sheep, but there was no alternative to tethering each of them and moving the tethers every hour or so.

Soon clothes were dry, faces and hands pink with pleasure, eyes smarting and our rice on the boil. Escaping the smoke, I saw a rider in the distance.

'We have visitors, Hector.'

We were both out of our shelter when a man rode up, clad in yellow waterproofs and accompanied by a large pack of dogs. It was soon clear, however, that he was not the owner.

'I saw your smoke, and thought I would come and investigate.'

He confirmed that the owners were away, and we explained who we were and where we had come from. Since we appeared to be at least the hosts in terms of food and fire, we invited him to dismount and join us. The dogs, which had circled and inspected us, crouched at a respectful distance.

'I've got too many,' said our visitor, following my gaze. 'Six is all I need.'

There were eight, and while unintrusive and cowed they were all desperately thin.

Over supper we learned that our guest occupied a small farm about half an hour's ride away, and lived alone. Conversation was slow and the pauses long, but it seemed that grazing would be in short supply for at least another day, and strangely there were no fish in either Lago Alegre or Christie although our visitor could offer no explanation. He stayed until dark and left as quietly as he had come, minus two of the skinniest dogs which had gradually shuffled closer to the fire. We had only scraps of rice and stale bread to offer them, but these were accepted. There was no grabbing and no begging, and just a suspicion that we might have gained two new companions.

A warm and comfortable night ended with a clammy morning lakeside mist. The early morning sun made several attempts to break through, and for a while lit up the snow and ice slopes of Cerro Campanaria, which peaked to almost 6,500 feet on the far side of the lake. There were brief but magic moments as shafts of sunlight shone with searchlight intensity through holes in the mist, sharpening the outline of the mountain and raising a sparkle from its icy cover. The waters of the lake momentarily reflected the blue patches in the sky. Then, almost as suddenly, the clouds snuffed out the light and all turned a drab grey again as the rains built up behind.

We took rather more time and care than usual to restore the wood stack to its original state and in disposing of the ashes in the oil drum. Our two new canine companions waited patiently for breakfast scraps and finally we were on our way. The horses had not fed well, and we were anxious to allow extra pit stops as and when we came across any grazing.

Hector looked pleased. He had slept well, and we had made very good progress during the previous two days.

'We should reach the Rio Mayer by this afternoon.'

'What does that mean, Hector?'

'It means we will all eat well tonight.' He also thought we would reach Villa O'Higgins within two and an half days.

The bad news was that Olympia was developing serious saddle sores which defied our magic spray, and Cuervo was becoming more and more difficult. Neither of us was happy to ride him. It was a constant battle to keep him up to pace, and consequently he either carried the pack or had another day off. We both knew we would have to ring the changes very carefully between the remaining two. Piebald had proved strong, resourceful and good natured, but with a sensitive mouth. Tía had sustained a deep cut to a rear thigh when a pole broke on one of the many *embarranados* we had crossed, and she had developed a limp. Additionally, our food supplies and choices were reducing fast, and we had finished the last carton of wine.

Within half an hour we had passed our visitor of the previous night, busy putting up fences. The two dogs which had followed us, disappearing and then reappearing at regular intervals, then finally left us—to our great relief. Gradually the vegetation returned, and after a long pit stop for grazing the horses walked taller. Even the rain let up, and as the weather brightened a semblance of life returned to the shores of Lago Christie, and along its far bank a lush green *montaña* was broken by lighter green patches of cleared land and even an isolated hut. On our side, however, the rock returned and we slipped, clattered and slid our way down and then up, until finally the lake came to an end. We wound down long serpentine curves past several small hidden lakes to emerge at the base of a waterfall where the surplus waters of Lago Christie announced the birth of the Rio Pérez. Finally, we were through!

Pastures and woodland alternated as the wide valley of the Rio Mayer opened up to a high Argentine ridge far to the east. The horses seemed to sense that the worst was over, and their pace was relaxed. Tía appeared to have forgotten how to limp and even Cuervo developed an almost jaunty step. We swooped down a steep bank to splash across the Pérez and up on to the flat green plateau where Señor Pérez lived.

Husband and wife were now in their sixties. They had established their substantial farm and family, and recently one of the sons had taken control. Their house—luxurious and extensive by wooden Patagonian standards—was nonetheless simple and functional, and stood alongside a number of large paddocks on a high plateau. Along two sides thundered the Rio Pérez and the remainder looked out on the distant Rio Mayer.

'I was born Argentine, but Chile won me,' explained Papa Pérez.

We were sitting round a table in the kitchen which was the centre of daytime activities, warmed by the inevitable wood burning stove. I struggled with some lamb cutlets, but was unable to tease as much meat off them as the others, and had to resort to subterfuge.

The fences round the neatly squared paddocks were all new, and the sheep, cattle and horses in fine condition. Our camp site was in one corner just above the Rio Pérez and under a large tree. The rain had moved on and it was possible once again to sleep with one's head exposed to the stars. In the morning I woke to a twittering, and with one eye open watched a family of yellow treecreepers bustle just inches from my head.

The Pérez had a radio, and much time was spent in trying to establish contact with Villa O'Higgins to find out the latest information on the sailing. They were convinced that the boat sailed on the Monday, but they did not know the time. Despite all efforts, a persistent buzz and crackle was all that could be teased out of the radio, and it was suggested that since it would mean only a slight diversion we should call in at the nearby *carabineros* post the next morning.

Armed with instructions as to how to find the *carabineros*, we took our leave and within ten minutes we were lost. The rivers' influence was widespread during the wet season, and its withdrawal left a maze of marshes intersected by many streams. We followed many options marked out by tracks, but each led to a dense brush cul-de-sac. Ultimately, however, we emerged into the open and spotted an aerial in the distance. Splashing through a deep branch of an unknown river and over a sandy hill, we found ourselves looking down on a collection of huts crowned by a Chilean flag.

We were accompanied to a hut by one of the *carabineros* and I produced the 'Please help-us' letter from Coihaique. All was very friendly, helpful and relaxed, yet someone still remembered to ask me to produce my passport to establish that my visa had not expired—the first time this had happened in all my time in Chile. The personnel were much reduced, a patrol including the sergeant, who was also the paramedic, having gone out to visit an isolated farmer who had suffered a heart attack. Further unsuccessful attempts were made to establish radio contact with Villa O'Higgins, but there was general agreement that the sailing was indeed on the Monday, which left us with two days and some 25 miles to go.

The post was well sited. Apart from one promontory, the way across to Argentina lay open and cattle could be seen in the shallows on both sides of the frontier. Any movement on either side could be easily spotted and we imagined that the Argentines had a similar view from their side.

Turning our backs on Argentina, we rode along the Rio Mayer before rising through ancient woodland, and it was not long before we met the returning patrol. The initial exchange was unusually brief, and the Sergeant came straight to the point.

'What are you doing here? Where have you come from?'

Hector explained, adding that I was English.

I could see the next question coming, but was anxious to avoid any more interrogation, bureaucracy and, inevitably, delay.

'How is the patient?' I asked.

The Sergeant looked surprised.

'He's OK.'

'Then it wasn't a heart attack'.

'No. No. He's going to be fine.'

In this way a repeat of immigration procedures was avoided, and the rest of our exchange remained friendly, with the Sergeant adding his belief that Monday was indeed the sailing day.

Olympia was showing further signs of distress. The saddle sores had not healed and we were running out of both options and time. As we left the soft woodland floor the way ahead was steep and stony. I stopped, dismounted and, loosening Olympia's girth, I let her go down on her own. The descent was difficult even on foot, the pebbles giving way as soon as they felt the weight of boot or shoe, so that we each went down in a series of slides and slaloms. Finally at the bottom, rolling valleys cleared of trees opened up and led us once again to the Rio Mayer. This version was totally unlike the sleepy one we had left behind. It had worked itself up through a series of unseen curves and canyons, and as we looked down on its crashing surf far below it was clearly impassable. There had to be a bridge, and a very solid modern suspension bridge it proved to be.

On the other side we faced a climb over more bare grey rock, and as we rounded a corner we came across a group of men hacking out steps with picks and shovels. Unbeknownst to me, Hector knew their foreman, who was to provide grazing for our horses later before their transport back to Cochrane via the Austral. However, on this occasion Hector's conversation with him was short and we barely paused.

Once off the rock, narrow fertile valleys followed, each neatly and newly fenced. Fortunately, there seemed to be a wide swathe through the middle to accommodate both us and the Rio Mayer without our paths having to cross. The horses' morale improved with the abundance of rich pasture and the softness under foot. We stopped for lunch and *mate* at a group of huts, and once again Hector's wide circle of contacts and friends opened doors. The huts were occupied by an extended family: four generations were represented, the first by a silver haired grannie who reminded me of Doña Dora. They formed a new pioneer hamlet, pooling resources and labour.

We learned nothing new about the sailings, but that a new road was gradually extending up from Villa O'Higgins. For us, however, new roads were not always good news. They meant much heavy equipment, noisy camp sites and surfaces which neither horse nor rider enjoyed. We had a few hours of peace left. At least it was Sunday and activity should be limited.

At this point we and the now meandering Meyer had entered at the apex of a huge valley—an equilateral triangle dotted with lakes large and small.

The names of the larger lakes reflected either the environment—Claro, El Salto (Falls), Encandenados (Chains) Cisnes (Swan) and Ciervo (Deer)—or those who had been among the first to arrive: Briceño and Vargas. Others, too small and numerous to interest the mapmakers, remained nameless, save perhaps for those who came to know them best.

Without maps, the colonisation down the valley had followed the natural geography, but those who reached the far corner had the option either of settling on the large fertile plateau upon which Villa O'Higgins now stands, or to take the more westerly route, eventually across the Mayer and on to the La Florida Peninsula. This was the gateway to the Lake. Despite their proximity, however, the Mayer and its valley, the site of Villa O'Higgins and the Lake itself have each evolved distinctive histories, and even today a certain individuality is maintained.

Hector and I soon lost the Mayer altogether as it became distracted by the demands of the lakes and lagoons, and we found ourselves amongst dense woodland. Along the side of the triangle opposite, then out of our sight, the youngest section of the Austral had been blasted over the rocks that litter the base of the Cordón Gran Nevado, eventually to cross the Mayer at the south-west apex of the triangle and enter Villa O'Higgins.

It was not long before we met the vanguard of the new road from Villa O'Higgins to Entrada Mayer. Graders, diggers and bulldozers had gouged a wide scar, over which movement otherwise than on giant inflated tyres or tracks was extremely difficult. We took to the grass verges wherever possible, until we reached first the stones and then the gravel base of the advancing road. While not the surface of preference, at least we began to make good progress but it soon became clear not only that we were not going to reach Villa O'Higgins that evening, but that since fences go up with roadworks, we were going to have difficulties finding a break to a suitable camp site. Eventually we spotted one, opposite the entrance to a road camp, where judging from the sudden blast of relayed music most of the workforce were enjoying a Sunday evening in a way we had almost forgotten. A long path led down through woodland and to a perfect site, away from the unwelcome noise. The usual chores were completed quickly, and with our tarp erected and the horses feeding happily, Hector turned his expertise to conjuring up a vegetarian hotpot out of the remnants of our larder. Warmed inside and out, he sensed that I wished to be left alone with my thoughts and disappeared under his pile of sheepskins and was soon asleep.

I propped myself up against my saddle and watched the light fade on the darkening blue of Lago Claro, visible below us and through the trees. One by one and in pursuit of the best grass they had sampled for some days, the horses paraded their silhouettes against the lake backcloth, the

Two of the Jeinemeni Reserve's tricolour lakes, where nature draws a line in the waters. Cordon La Gloria behind.

The Paso La Leona therapeutic maté or the quicksands.

Exit from
La Leona
into the
Chacabuco
valley.

Lake Cochrane
from the Tamango
Reserve. Cochrane
town out of
sight to right
and Mount
San Lorenzo to
the left.

Cochrane
looking
south to our
subsequent
route.

The meeting of the Rivers Nef and the mighty Baker, west of Cochrane.

Impromptu rodeo and practice before the horse race in nearby Puerto Bertrand.

Cochrane central square looking south.

South of Cochrane,
looking west to Northern
Icefield, the peaks of
the Leon tribe, Lago
Esmeralda and Colonia,
the original centre of the
Compania Explotadora
del Baker (CEB).

Falls on the Rio del Salto
with Mount San Lorenzo
– one undisputed frontier
marker.

Glacier and lake source of the del Salto at
the base of the twin towers of
Cerro Los Mellizos.

the Paso de las Picotas/
Cruzada.

A view from 'the other side' –
Argentina – across Lago Belgrano.

Condor overflying the
glacier from Three
Brothers – South.

The lava
beds.

Heraldo Real.

Crossing the Rio Bravo to Heraldo's main camp.

The woods were so thick and the change of direction so frequent that one quickly became disoriented.

Unleavened rock side to Lago Alegre.

Through the falls from Lago Christie.

Villa O'Higgins. End of the road.

Sunset over Lago O'Higgins from the south (Chilean) side – Candelario Mansilla.

(Later) Departure south to Lago del Desierto.

Off the rocks for a change – a toast to the pioneers with ice from the Glacier O'Higgins.

darkest and largest being, unmistakably, Cuervo. As I poked the embers of our fire, a flare lit up his eyes and we looked at each other until the flare had died.

Few who have depended on animals to achieve their objectives will not have had moments when they are humanised. 'My horses'—since at that moment they were all part of me—had all the qualities that I had so long admired in pioneers. Indeed, since the pioneer and the horse are inseparable in Patagonia, the achievements of one are the achievements of both. Cuervo had been there at the start and would be there at the end. Not merely a willing 'servant' but a rebel at heart: a rebel who had been so against joining us both at Futaleufu and again at Coyhaique; who had supported the indignities of being hobbled and shod, who had been thrown on his side with his face in the dust and re-shod; who had been forced to cross suspension bridges against his will and rewarded by relegation to packhorse for the past eight days; and who, finally, had had to support a wire coat hanger contraption around his neck.

Olympia had carried me most of the way from Lago Verde, and despite early warnings had only tried to bite me once. Significantly smaller than Cuervo, she was nonetheless immensely strong. After that collapse on the first day out of Lago Verde we had worked out her limits together, and there had been many occasions when we had walked side by side. She had suffered badly during the last stage and would need time to recover. Tía had carried our baggage from Lago Verde, doubling as Hector's spare mount and even, on rare occasions, as mine. More reserved and uncomplaining than the others, she could now look forward to some peace and quiet, and, after her dalliance in the corral in Cochrane, to her first foal. Prudencia, Petaka and 'Piebald without name' each stepped out of the shadows to take their bow and receive their garland. In that twilight of emotional adjectives, my vocabulary failed me. How does one say thank you to such creatures?

I have no idea how long I sat gazing into the trees. As the lake disappeared into the darkening mist and the outline of the tree trunks lost their definition, so my thoughts lost their clarity as each rolled into the next. A shiver brought about by a sudden drop in the temperature snapped me back to full consciousness. The embers no longer glowed, and a glance at my sleeping bag reminded me how close my thoughts had already come to dreams.

The next day and without explanation Hector awarded me the 'Order of Piebald'. Some horses walk tall. Some have a long easy stride. While unlikely ever to win any beauty prizes, Piebald did both. Visibility was jacked up six inches and speed by at least 0.3 mph, and Hector and I fairly flew side by side down a wide and deserted gravel road, so that by midday we had reached the junction with the Austral. All concern over the boat had disappeared. If it had left that morning, I had missed it, and we decided to stop for a leisurely lunch of peanuts, raisins and black coffee beside the Rio Mayer.

What now remained was the eagerly awaited entrance into Villa O'Higgins, and once we were back in the saddle, that was my only thought. As always, the eagerly awaited takes its own time to arrive, and that last stretch went on forever. Each hill, each bend must surely be the last, until finally we topped the last rise, where by the side of the road, a simple wooden sign read 'Villa O'Higgins'. We stopped alongside and looked at each other and smiled a smile of a thousand stars. I leaned across and took Hector's hand in both of mine.

'*Gracias, amigo*'.

While so eagerly anticipated, that moment was never to be the stuff of theatre. There were no medals. No applause or cheering crowds. Not even a magic moment of exhilaration. Arrival had been too long in the making, and the even longer process of recollection had scarcely begun, but it was a moment to be treasured. I knew, too, that our journey had meant much to Hector. He had now ridden the length of Aysén, and while he might do so again in whole or in part, there could only ever be one first time.

So this—finally—was Villa O'Higgins. Not quite another frontier, but the end of a long road. Standing on a large plateau with its back to a high wooded wall of rock, the new town looked west across a distant glimmer of water to a backdrop of white dusted peaks. We rode down a wide gravel road alongside a fence which separated the town from its airstrip. There were sounds of hammers and saws as the inhabitants prepared with some urgency for the approaching winter. Later and from a *mirador* set into the rock wall, I enjoyed a panorama of the town. Laid out in neat squares, houses were simple, single-storied, built predominately of wood or cladding and painted in assorted colours and with the inevitable tin roofs. A number of larger cladded buildings stood out as library, school, police station, with blue being the favoured municipal colour: raised concrete pavements, green areas where horses wandered freely, few people and fewer vehicles. It was unusual to be able to view an entire town without moving one's head, and there was an atmosphere of 'a town in waiting'.

We turned down one street and stopped alongside a vacant plot of long grass and piles of building materials before dismounting. I felt a surge of emotion as I realised this was to be the last time. The horses were to be kept there until arrangements had been finalised for their transport back to Cochrane and Coyhaique. I had already given Tía and Olympia to Hector, and Cuervo would go back to Ian Farmer. Thus it was time to say farewell and I was unprepared. Final photographs of all four together, and it was as well that the rising mist in my eyes was distracted by the many tasks at hand: checking the boat had indeed departed (it had, early that morning); finding the local internet facility to check and send messages home and to Coyhaique; checking on bus movements (there was one leaving for Cochrane early the next day, but none afterwards for three days); collecting my rucksack, which had been sent down by air and which contained my clothing, maps and papers for the next stage, and to which an ever thoughtful Ian had added a bottle of champagne and a simple note headed 'Congratulations!'; and finding somewhere to stay out of many guesthouses, only some of which offered an evening meal fit for the champagne.

It was then time for decisions and there were two options: to stay on in Villa O'Higgins until the next boat sailed, occupying my time in tracking down local pioneers and historians, or to 'burn my boats' and head back to Cochrane and Coyhaique by bus. I was conscious, that if I chose the former I would step out of my comfort zone of a daily Hector/horse routine, that winter was approaching and that I was headed ever south via a stage about which I still had much to learn. I was also tired, physically and emotionally, and had probably been conditioning myself ever since doubts first arose that we would reach O'Higgins in time.

The border crossing between Villa O'Higgins and Mount Fitzroy had always been unusual and little known, even in Chile and Argentina. It had held a particular significance for me ever since I had first conceived of my journey down the frontier, and should have been a fitting climax. The lack of maps and official discouragement of the crossing were the consequence of a bitter boundary dispute over the ownership of Laguna (now Lago) del Desierto, which in turn had delayed the start of my journey for at least as long as the dispute lasted. I had heard that the first settlers in Villa O'Higgins and the Lake had been British, yet no one I had met and nothing I had read gave any clue as to who they were or why they had chosen such an isolated place, and it seemed unlikely that I would find the answers in Villa O'Higgins. There was much that would be at risk if I continued, hence I decided that I would bide my time. I would be back, unquestionably older but with a new energy and, hopefully, better informed.

CHAPTER TWELVE

Reminiscences

Although each country has had its national highs and lows, and sometimes these have coincided, the nineteenth-century frontier dispute fed
a latent animosity between the two capitals which continues to this day,
and the one element which continues to cause most friction is national sovereignty. It is therefore unsurprising that even after the bitterly contested
dispute, the settler-orphans, who had been pawns throughout should
remain anonymous, ignored and even despised by the sophisticates in the
capitals. Little by little, the settlers' complaints came to be heard, but the
principal concern and interpretation at 'head office' remained the potential loss of territory. Instead of a recognition that without the tenacious
pioneering and practical patriotism of the 'pawns' there would have been
no territory to lose, they continued to be regarded as 'immature' primi-
tives who needed first to be taught citizenship—double talk which José
Silva, an undoubted Chilean patriot, once described in 'gaucho speak' as
'a guitar sounding from both sides'.

Santiago, no doubt influenced by its 'rich *huasos*', believed that the
Aysén settlers had been so contaminated by their contact and interdependence with that symbol of Argentina—the gaucho—that they could not
be trusted. Pomar had reported that most consumer goods came from
Argentina or Brazil, that many children had been registered in Argentina
rather than Chile, that Argentine currency prevailed over Chilean. But
even he was clearly surprised by the extent to which the *pobladores* had
assumed the customs, culture, language and terminology of their neighbours—everyone called each other *Che*. He called it a *barniz gauchesco*,
gaucho varnish, and the expression stuck.[1] Since the settlers could not be
trusted, it followed that they needed instruction in how to be Chileans.
Much of that same prejudice survives, and even today Chile has yet to
allow any of her provinces the right to elect their own governors.

---

[1] Pomar also illustrated how the learning of gaucho customs was not always successful by
   relating the case of one *poblador*, whose facial scars were evidence of his failure to master
   the gaucho custom of holding one end of a piece of meat in one hand with the other end
   in his teeth, and cutting upwards with a sharp knife.

Although to most Argentines there was something particularly attractive about a national symbol which embodied elements of that Argentine persona, the *chanta*,[2] which many admired, Buenos Aires believed that its pioneers could not possibly be left on land adjoining its frontiers, even when that frontier was an Ice Field. Only the State had sufficient imagination to predict an invasion across 150 miles of ice, which no one had even attempted to cross. Consequently, large areas of frontier land were turned into national parks,[3] and those who had found, cleared, worked and defended that land were either evicted or their leases not renewed. Frontiers were policed by men dressed in the State's uniform, who were then left to make and enforce rules as they saw fit and to assume the prejudices of their masters towards those who were not Argentine. Inevitably tensions were raised by local abuses, and fresh disputes arose and festered until central government was forced to intervene and ultimately return to arbitration. The last occasion when the countries came to blows was as recently as the 1990s, yet issues continue unresolved, and the complexity of argument sometimes defies terrestrial comprehension.

Holdich, as a well-informed, independent, foreign arbitrator, had hoped that in time there would be no need for an international boundary and that Chilean or Argentine roads would be one and the same, but continued preoccupation with issues of sovereignty have ensured that the cost of road programmes alone—and not merely in terms of lives—has been astronomic and often duplicated, with only lip service being paid to cooperation. Meanwhile, the very settlers whom Holdich had been obliged by his terms of reference to call 'squatters', and whose occupation in the disputed areas 'each country had declared ... was of no relevance', have continued to give lessons in neighbourliness, cooperation and hospitality without regard for nationality.

Communications remain a nightmare problem, particularly for a long thin Chile. Accidents and administrative lapses have not helped, nor have they been exclusive to military or civil governments. In recent years there have been hopeful indications that the constant interventions of the military, which have virtually guaranteed the resurrection of frontier or sovereignty issues—some of which have been more deliberate than others—may have finally passed into history. Tourism within a unique natural environment carries the hopes of many in Patagonia, and there is a remarkable level of awareness of the ecological consequences of tourist

---

[2] *Chanta* is an Argentine word which defies exact translation, but which includes someone who has the qualities of a successful peddler or stall holder: shrewd, smooth-tongued, cunning and rascally.

[3] Chile was to follow a similar policy.

footprints. Today, however, that most desirable of natural assets—unlimited clean and renewable hydroelectric power—holds the greatest certainty of change. Projects for change can only succeed with the will of the pioneer *caballeros* of Patagonia, and if they are to have the say and share which they and their forebears have earned but which the indigenous Kogi and Mapuche have been denied, there will need to be a groundswell of change in the attitudes of those who seek to pull their strings, whether in Santiago, Buenos Aires or elsewhere.

I have since returned to Patagonia and Aysén on a number of occasions, and have crossed and re-crossed that frontier and visited both parts of that divided Lake O'Higgins/San Martín, and Laguna/Lago del Desierto and beyond. I was to recall the detail of that first entry into Villa O'Higgins when I was walking through Coyhaique, and someone called out my name in accented English. I knew it was Hector before I turned and saw a familiar figure. The same smile. The same youthful, reddened face and short powerful figure. Even the familiar checked shirt—although I suspect it was a new one. This time, there was no anticipation, no mere handshake, but a warm *Aysenino* embrace. Such moments have served to remind me that, as yet, the best of Aysén has changed little.

APPENDICES

1. THE ORIGINS OF 'PATAGONIA'

The most popular theory is that the name 'Patagonia' derived from observations made by Antonio Pigafetta, who kept a diary during Hernando de Magallanes' first voyage round the world in 1520. Passing through the Straits which have since borne Magellanes' name, a giant Indian was seen:' He was so big, that our heads scarcely reached his waist.'

Under orders to bring back 'samples', Magallanes' men tricked several of the Indians on board: 'The giants roared like bulls and cried upon their great devil Setebos to help them.'

They did not survive, but the remainder, whose legends foretold of foreigners who brought disaster, will have stored that experience. Magellan continued on into the Pacific, and his death there ensured that he would not touch Patagonia again.

It was the size of the footprints left by the Indians in the sand which is said to have been the origin of Patagonia. *Pata* is colloquial Spanish for foot, *grande* is big and *gigante* is giant: the combination became Patagonia.

Another theory, which brings together a series of 'tall stories', is that 'Patagones' is a corruption of 'Pentagones', five *codos*, or seven and an half feet high. When Francis Drake visited in 1578, he commented that 'Magellan was not altogether wrong in naming them giants, yet they were not taller than some Englishmen'. Sir John Narborough (1670) found them 'of common stature'. One hundred years later, Tomas Falkener reported that a Spanish captive of Chief Cangapol of the Tehuelhets (*sic*) described the Chief as '7 feet plus some inches'. Lord Byron, rested from his adventures with HMS *Wager* and who was just short of six feet himself, claimed that he could just reach the top of the head of one of the Indians he met in 1764, and then only on tiptoe. His fellow officer went further in estimating an average of eight feet, with some extending to nine and upwards. It has to be said that both claims were ridiculed.

The Indians wore leather moccasins, which would have made their prints bigger than their feet. They also wore skins, which may have made them seem taller. We now know that the Indians were probably from either the Tehuelche or their 'cousins'the Ona tribe, amongst the tallest in the Americas, but at five foot nine inches to six feet. To an average Spaniard of five feet, they would have seemed tall, but scarcely a giant—unless they were indeed seven feet.

Bruce Chatwin introduced another notion, that Magellanes had read a bestseller of that time, *Primaleon of Greece*, in which the hero meets and wounds a dog-faced beast called 'Patagon'. He would also have been aware of then current reports of Fuegian Indians wearing dog-head masks. Applying his abundant imagination, Chatwin supposes that Magellan would have put Primaleon and Indian together and made 'Ha! Patagon.'

Some 58 years after Magellan, Drake was to make the observation that the Indians 'would have none of our company, until such time as they warranted by their God Sattaboth [*sic*]', suggesting that while he and Magellan had different recollections for names, they had both read the same book, thereby perhaps adding substance to Chatwin's theory.

2. THE FOLK SAINT CULT

In the vast rural areas of northern Argentina although the Catholic Church and its saints are the predominant religion, a simple philosophy has combined with superstition and legend to produce a number of 'folk saints' around which shrines have been erected and which many thousands attend. The Widow Correa is one example and, apart from the main shrine erected at Vallecito in north-west Argentina, makeshift examples in her memory can be found in many places.

In the 1840s, during the Argentine civil wars between the *colorados* (red), supporters of unitarism, and the *celestes* (blue) supporters of Rosas' federalists, Deolinda Correa's sickly husband had been conscripted into the *colorados*, and Deolinda set off on foot with her infant son to try to save him. Carrying food and water she followed the tracks of the battalion across the desert until eventually, she was overcome by exhaustion and the elements and died. Her body was found by passing gauchos or muleteers but miraculously her baby survived by suckling his dead mother for several days. Deolinda is believed to have been buried at Vallecito, some 35 miles from the north-western provincial capital of San Juan, and over the years the simple hilltop cross has become a shrine, and a small village has grown up nearby. While neither state nor Catholic Church recognise her, she has become a folk saint, miracles have been claimed and intercessions answered—'She is one of us and understands our needs and requests.' Services are held at the shrine at Easter and on All Souls Day and attended by thousands of pilgrims.

The pile of bottles which Hector and I passed outside Chile Chico was a local shrine to Deolinda, although the particular local legend was that of a girl who had died of thirst trying to find help for her mother. I was also to come across a similar bottle shrine to 'the widow Correa' some four miles outside Puerto Natales in the far south. Both were in Chile and a long way from Vallecito. By custom, travellers and truckers leave bottles of water together with vehicle parts, number plates and model houses, and blow their horns out of respect. Failure to comply may bring misfortune on the defaulter.

A more celebrated example of a folk saint—at least in Argentina—is that of Gauchito Gil, about whom numerous versions of a legend apply. An honest gaucho, Antonio Gil from Pay Ubre (now Mercedes, in the northern Argentine province of Corrientes) had an affair with a local wealthy widow, with whom the local police *comisario* was also in love. The affair was discovered and Gil, falsely accused of robbery by the *comisario*, enlisted in the Argentine army and went off to fight in the War of the Triple Alliance. He returned home some years later, a hero, but was then caught up in Argentina's civil war. By inclination *colorado*, he was nonetheless ordered to enlist with the *celestes*. Tired of fighting and with no wish to be involved in fratricide, he refused and thus became a deserter, and when his possessions were seized he became an outlaw in the style of Robin Hood. In due course he was captured by the police, tortured and hung by his feet from a tree, prior to having his throat cut. In the meantime influential locals had organised a petition to the provincial governor for clemency, and somehow news of this development reached Gil, who pleaded with the Sergeant in command of his captors not to kill him as a pardon was on its way. The Sergeant, however, was determined to kill him regardless. Gil then told the Sergeant that when he returned to his village he would not only find the pardon order but that his own son was dying, and that since he was going to shed the blood of an innocent, he should pray that Gil would intercede before God to cure his son.

The Sergeant duly cut Gil's throat, but on arrival in his village and learning that what he had been told was indeed true, he prayed to Gauchito Gil for his son, and his son recovered. It was the Sergeant who buried Gil, building a small shrine for him and giving publicity to the miracle, although today no one recalls the Sergeant's name.

Similar shrines to Gauchito Gil can be found on roadsides through-out Argentina and are prominent through the abundance of red/*colorado* drapings. The date of Gil's death, 8 January 1878, is commemorated each year when as many as 100,000 pilgrims attend to remember him.

The folk saint cult even extends to those who are still living and memorable for more profane miracles. There is a church in Rosario com-memorating Diego Maradona, the Argentine footballer, and entitled DIOS (GOD)—D(iego) 10(the number on his shirt) plus S (which completes the word and justifies the cult's creation)—and where Christmas is brought forward to coincide with Diego's birthday on 29/30 October, and Easter to 22 June, the date when Argentina eliminated England from the 1986 World Cup. Perhaps unsurprisingly, no similar shrines are believed to exist in Chile, and in England it is the hand of this particular 'god' which is best remembered.

ACKNOWLEDGEMENTS

A personal preference for bends or curves rather than straights probably reflects a subconscious wish not to know too much about what lies ahead—a preference which undoubtedly helped the person who carried off my camera on the final bend of my journey at Heathrow, but one which also enabled me to survive the shock of losing the 350 photographs inside. I have written about some of those—human and animal—who made possible my journey of twists and turns, but the road on from Villa O'Higgins to a completed book has also been long and twisted and there have been as many deadends. Looking back at the various stages, I have marvelled at the number of people who have appeared when most needed to guide, encourage, advise and shelter, some of whom I can now publicly acknowledge and thank.

First and foremost come my wife Angela and our children Marie-Carmen, Marie Lisa and John Paul, who have been my constant supporters and valued critics. They have borne my absences and both my would-be rider and writer's tantrums as only a loving and forgiving family can. They have been joined by other members of the extended family and friends on both sides of the Atlantic—specifically in Peru, Pilar and Augusto Pancorvo, Jose Carlos and Wilma Salmon, Mariana Treguer, Cecilia Crosby and my ever-present mentor Carmen Salmon—in Chile, Christopher and Ruri Lyon—and in Argentina, Robin (Roberto) and Helen Welch.

In the preparation and execution of my journey, specific and invaluable inputs came from Ian Farmer and Jonathan Leidich and the family of Juan Carlos Campos and Eliana in Coyhaique, Eduardo Encalada and Julian in Bariloche. In Oxford, the surgical skills and positive encouragement of David Cranston, and the support and generosity of the Moxons, Richard and Marianne, and the Allports, Alan and Virginia.

The long and often solitary journey through libraries and records in Chile, Argentina and the UK have required the patient help of many guides, including Mario and Rosita Gonzalez Kappes in Coyhaique, Mateo Martinic in Punta Arenas, Danka Ivanoff and Hugo Wellman in Chile Chico, Rosa Gomez Miranda in Cochrane and Duncan and Gladys Campbell in Puerto Natales. Their lives have been dedicated to the collection and recording of historical detail without which no account of Patagonia can be complete.

On the seemingly endless labyrinth to actual publication, good fortune provided Tony Atkins who spent hours of his time in preparing maps and photos in return for regular thrashings on the squash court, Perry Gauci at Lincoln College, Oxford kindly read my original manuscript and encouraged me to write history and finally James Ferguson of Signal Books patiently edited and guided that manuscript to the form in which it is now presented.

Above all, to Hector Soto, my eternal thanks for his skills, patience, practical knowledge, good humour and friendship—in every sense a modern pioneer and one of the many of whom Aysen and Patagonia can be justly proud.

ABOUT THE AUTHOR

Jon Burrough traces his fascination for South America back to the time when a school friend, member of a group of Colombian folksingers, allowed him to play the maracas more or less in time to their guitars. They sang a wide range of colourful songs from every South American country with such success that, even without his involvement, they made a number of best-selling records. Such was the influence of that baptism, that when eventually he decided to make his first visit to the continent, he bought an expensive tape recorder, which was to prove one of the best purchases he has ever made. Given the £50 travel restriction imposed by Harold Wilson's government at that time, no amount of English teaching, counting of grain trucks or pretence at being a shepherd, could have sustained nearly two years of extensive travel throughout that vast continent. Music and the tape recorder were not only a focus to what was a long journey of exploration, but a connection to the heartbeat of South American culture. Together, they also provided an entry ticket to the music faculties of every university – with student accommodation and food at student prices – which in turn gave access to regional and national performers, amateur and professional, classical and folk, whose desire to share their rich musical culture knew no bounds. Many happy hours were spent hanging from rafters above stages, squatting on the edge of platforms or simply sitting in some musician's home, listening and recording. He returned home two stone lighter, but with six notebooks full of experiences, countless photographs and, most significant of all, over 24 hours of recordings to treasure of some of the best musicians in South America.

Some four years later, and with an accumulation of thoughts, ideas and advice and some modest funding, he returned to prospect the traditional technologies of Peru and Colombia for The Intermediate Technology Development Group (ITDG) – since re-named Practical Action. This initiative awakened an interest within the two countries for the development and improvement of their own appropriate technologies, and today Lima has –arguably – one of the most progressive and productive centres for appropriate technology in the world. This time, he travelled mainly on public transport, walked many more miles, rode once, shook a thousand pioneering hands and only lost a stone.

Jon Burrough then consummated his affair with the continent by marrying a Peruvian, and together they have raised a family of three bilingual, bicultural children. To support them, he returned to his profession as a solicitor. Inevitably there had been much to learn from that second spell in South America and his commitment to the principles of appropriate technology, and with the continued support of ITDG's Director George

McRobie and the guidance of one of Oxfordshire's unsung heroes, the late Stan Windass and his Foundation for Alternatives, Jon Burrough set up the Oxford Enterprise Trust (OET) – "to channel the resources of the community into the acquisition of buildings for small businesses and the support and promotion of employment products and services appropriate to the needs and environment of the Oxford District".

By 1983, when the OET was poised to bid for the purchase of a former goods yard in central Oxford, it became clear that the two roles of promotion of the OET and solicitor/partner in a large provincial law firm were on collision course. Something had to give, and with the priority of providing for his family, the casualty had to be the OET. By happy coincidence, Sir Martin Wood, founder of Oxford Instruments and one of the OET's Trustees, and his wife Audrey Lady Wood chose to take over the initiative and develop the highly successful Oxford Trust aimed at scientific start-ups, while the Oxford City Council created the Oxford Enterprise Centre. This allowed Jon Burrough to continue his profession of administering to the needs of troubled families, and to enjoy the privilege of being approached by people with real problems and the even greater challenge of trying to meet their expectation that he could actually play a part in trying to resolve them.

Over the years, there was also a dream waiting to be realised – to visit and travel the length of Chile and Argentina's Patagonian frontier and meet some of the pioneers who live there. Thus, when the opportunity for retirement came, suddenly there was no excuse for not going, save the reality that at 63, he was not as young as he had once been. Once the nettle had been grasped, there came the daunting prospect of having to ride 8, 10 or even 14 hours a day. Just as an ageing body was coming to terms with the new regime, there came a diagnosis of cancer. Three months planning and preparation and ten days into the journey, he had to abandon and return for surgery. Expectations were renewed after a favourable prognosis, and he returned to Chile one year later to resume where he had left off. After 43 more days in the saddle and half as many resting between stages, he was finally to enjoy a moment of supreme exhilaration as he rode past the sign reading 'Villa O'Higgins'. Mission all but accomplished, another two stone lost, but regrettably over 400 photographs later stolen at Heathrow airport.

The next task has been to take the thread of the journey and weave round it the tales of those present and past pioneers encountered, research the history (particularly of the frontier), and ultimately to write a book. Such has been the detail, however, that *Dark Horses at the Patagonian Frontier* is the first of two books: the second – *Patagonian Odyssey – A History of Frontiers Won and Lost* – is still in the process of being written.

The Map Drawn & Engraved by J. Rapkin.

Campana I.

Parallel Pk.

Dyneley.

C. Montague

Picton Opening

M. Corso I.

G. of Trinidad

Archipelago
of
Madre de Dios

C. Santiago
Concepcion Str.

HANOVER I.

St. Blas Ch.l

Cambridge I.

Nelson Str.

Diana Peak

C. Victory

Narborough I.

STR. OF MAGALHAEN'S

C. Pillar

C. Descado

Otway Bay

Rice Trevor I.s

C. Tate

Breaker B.

C. Gloucester

Grafton I.

Stokes Bay

Noir I.s

Kempe I.

C. Tamar

Land of Desolation

Otway Bay

Lion B.

Iceberg S.d

L. Capar

R. Chalia

Evre S.d

Falcon In.t

Castle Hill

R. S.ta Cruz

Canning I.s

San Andres S.d

M. Stokes

Pitt Chan.l

Chatham I.

Sarmiento Channel

Peel Inl.t

Last Hope Inlet

Disappoint
ment B.

Staines Plaza

Bernel I.

Smyth Chan.l

ADELAIDE I.

Obstruction S.d

M. Burney

Pinto M.

Shoal Har.

Gigdet S.d

Skyring Wr.

Buckle B.

Gulf of Xualtegua

Croker Pa.

Otway Wr.

Elizabeth I.

Brunswick Pa.

Famin

C. Froward

Clarence I.

Snow St.

Adventure Passage

Londonderry I.

Sandwich R.s

Darwin Sound

York Minster

Christmas

Cockburn Chan.

Camden I.

C. Desolation

Desolate Bay

Fury I.

St. Jago

C. Gregory

Oazy Hr. I.

Us

Dav

C. Valen

M. Sarmien

TIERRA

SCALE.

5   10   20   30 Miles

55